Elements of
Park and Recreation
Administration

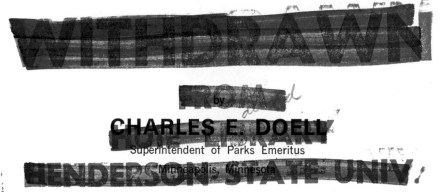

by

CHARLES E. DOELL
Superintendent of Parks Emeritus
Minneapolis, Minnesota

Burgess Publishing Company

426 South Sixth Street • Minneapolis, Minn. 55415

To my good friend
Harold S. Wagner
who first inspired me to
examine the roots of our
common calling
this book is fondly dedicated.

PREFACE TO SECOND EDITION

In the period of five years since the publication of the first edition, some notable developments have taken place in the field of park and recreation administration. Three developments illustrate how rapidly the evolutionary process continues.

First: The essence of a nation-wide recreation plan is now emerging in the Bureau of Outdoor Recreation of the Department of the Interior. As its name implies, it proposes to sketch the recreation needs of the entire nation and becomes a guide to all agencies supplying recreation to the people.

Second: A series of federal grants-in-aid programs have been provided by various federal agencies which have had the effect of focusing attention on state and local needs and of providing incentives for them to keep pace with population requirements.

Third: After many, many years of unilateral attempts at merger, five of the major professional organizations amalgamated into one great organization encompassing both lay and professional interests. Other lesser organizations continue to join hands in one general movement.

These developments have suggested broader audience for this edition. It also gave rise to a passing notion that the title might appropriately be changed to "Development of Recreation Resources." But in spite of significant strides in acquisition and development of land, in the extension of education to more universities, and in the greater intelligence on the part of administrators in utilizing the talents of university graduates, the over-riding and most difficult problem of recreation lies within the urban core of our great metropolitan complexes and their ever evolving internal form. To help emphasize this point, the name of this text book remains unchanged.

It is hoped that those colleges and universities which lately seem to emphasize outdoor recreation or forest recreation will not overlook the appropriateness of including in their curricula, a study of the principles which have evolved and are still evolving out of city park and recreation administration. With a nationwide plan of recreation, the old boundaries of specialization are becoming vague and indistinct.

Chas. E. Doell

January, 1968

PREFACE TO FIRST EDITION

As will become apparent from definitions appearing in this book, any consideration of parks must give rise to what takes place in parks or even on public property. The administration of recreation as a whole encompasses fields of endeavor outside the public domain and hence of a far greater scope than this book intends to cover. The intention here is to limit discussion to properties and services supported in whole or in part by government.

But most of the important recreation pursuits financed by government do take place in parks, and except where there appears in the governmental organization a separate recreation department, the park department (or park and recreation department) is the only agency specifically and exclusively charged with the responsibility of providing to the citizens opportunities for recreation. It has seemed appropriate, then, to use both terms, "parks" and "recreation" in the title of this work.

Also, since it is not intended to write an exhaustive treatise on the whole subject of public park and recreation administration, but only certain important elements of the total subject, the title is logically limited to "Elements of Park and Recreation Administration". Essentially, this book is for the student, the beginner, and a quick reference to the practitioner who wants only the essence.

Elemental as this work is, it is hoped that most of the fundamental principles of park and recreation are touched upon. Explanations are as brief as clarity will permit and discussions are quite limited. Inasmuch as thoughts expressed in many ways are often necessary to ignite the latent spark of enthusiasm, supplementary and more extensive reading from many authors is highly recommended.

The subject matter herein has been used for instruction at Michigan State University and for instructional and consultation work at Texas Technological College. To both institutions, I am indebted for the opportunities afforded for expanding notes into textbook form, for stenographic help, for research resources. I am especially indebted to Professors Louis F. Twardzik, and Leslie M. Reid, and Dr. Raleigh Barlow at Michigan State University and to Professor Elo J. Urbanovsky, Head, Department of Park Administration and Horticulture, Professor Mark Gosdin and others of Texas Technological

College — all for helpful discussion, criticism and encouragement.

The Park Commission of my home city of Minneapolis, Howard I. Moore, Superintendent, has been helpful in many ways and has provided me with records and pertinent material, all of which I acknowledge with thanks. I have also had the counsel of many colleagues too numerous to specifically mention.

It should be finally noted that the dearth of teaching material and elementary works of this kind is one of the impelling causes for writing this book in the first place. Lots more are needed, on both general and specialized subjects in the whole field of park and recreation administration. It is sincerely hoped that these needs will be adequately and more competently filled.

Charles E. Doell
January 1963

TABLE OF CONTENTS

Preface to Second Edition. i

Preface to First Edition iii

Chapter 1 - Preliminary Considerations 1

Nature of Park and Recreation Administration, 1 - Management — an Art, 2 - Clarification of Terms, 3 - Recreation, 3 - Limitation of Meaning of Recreation, 4 - Recreation and Leisure, 4 - Recreation in Today's Parlance, 5 - Tools of Recreation, 6 - What is a Park?, 7 - System of Park and Recreation Facilities, 8 - Correlation, 8 - History of Parks, 9

Chapter 2 - The Country's Physical Recreation Resources - The Cities and their Suburbs. 15

The Nation's Land Resources, 15 - The City and It's Suburbs, 17 - Parks and the City Plan, 18 - Classification and Standards, 19 - The Simple Application of Standards, 24 - Standards Applied in Theory, 30 - Standards Applied to Case, 32 - Value of Standards, 36 - The Suburbs, 37

Chapter 3 - The Country's Physical Recreation Resources - The Metropolitan and County. 46

Preliminary and Historical, 46 - Some Typical Systems, 47 - Comments on Typical Systems, 53 - Area Required, 54 - A System of Classification and Use Zoning, 55 - Parkways and Boulevards, 56

Chapter 4 - The Country's Physical Recreation Resources - State and Federal. 59

Preliminary Observations, 59 - Development and Purpose of State and Federal Parks, 61 - National Parks Before 1916, 62 - The National Park Service, 63 - Forest Service, Dept. of Agriculture, 70 - Corps of Army Engineers, 71 - Fish and Wildlife Service, 72 - BOR and HUD, 72 - Bureau of Outdoor Recreation, 73 - Department of Housing and Urban Development, 74 - Ratio of Acres to Population, 76 - Applicability, 76 - The Ratio Applied to States, 76 - The Ratio Applied to Federal Resources, 78

Chapter 5 - The Country's Physical Recreation Resources -
Summary 79

The Nationwide Plan, 79 - Zoning and Classification, 80 - Amount of Area
Required, 82 - Attention is Focused on the Urban Situation, 82 - A Case in
Point, 84 - A Stray Thought, 85

Chapter 6 - The Making of a Park Plan. 86

Preliminary to Chapters 6, 7 and 8, 86 - The Making of a Park Plan, 87 - Basic
Resource Material, 88 - Developing a Plan for a Park, 90 - Park Plans a Part
of Departmental Policy, 90 - Investigative Reports or Analyses, 92 - The
Drawing of the Plan, 99 - Development of the Preliminary Plan, 103 - Working
Drawings, 104 - Operation after Construction, 104 - Planning Procedure Sum-
marized, 105 - Chapter Summary, 105

Chapter 7 - Personnel Organization 106

Organization of Personnel, 107 - Types of Governmental Organization, 107 -
Essential Function of Whole Personnel, 108 - Assignment of Function to Person-
nel, 109 - Operation of Staff and Personnel, 120 - The Chief Executive, 120 –
The Board or Superior Authority, 122 - Staff Operations, 123 - The Executive
Staff, 124 - Preface to Departmental Operations, 126 - Maintenance Division,
126 - Recreation, 130 - Engineering Division, 133 - Public Relations, 134

Chapter 8 - Budgets 137

Chapter 9 - Policies – In General and on Relationships . 148

Policies in General, 143 - Policies in Relationships, 151

Chapter 10 - Acquisition and Development Policies . . . 163

Acquisition in General, 163 - Site Selection Notes, 163 - Financing Capital
Outlays, Acquisition and Development, 167 - Financing by Leases, Gifts, etc.,
173 - Processes of Acquisition, 179 - Land Records, 180 - Situations Particularly
Applicable to Development, 180 - As to Plans and Basic Data, 180 - Construction, 182 - Letting of Contracts, 183 - Conflict of Interest, 183 - Gifts, 184 -
Purchasing Agent, 186 - Supervision, 188 - Shifting From Construction to Maintenance, 190

Chapter 11 - Policies of Operation 191

Basic Ground Rules, 191 - Matters Requiring Board Action, 192 - Purpose of
Board Record, 193 - Administrator and Staff, 194 - Salaries and Wages, 194 -
Budget, 195 - New Projects, 195 - Matters not Covered, 195 - Operating Policies, 197 - Cooperation, 197 - Attendance at Professional Meetings, 197 - Fees
and Charges, 198 - Amount of Tax Support, 202 - Who Operates Revenue Producing Businesses, 204 - Permits and Leases, 207 - Circuses and Carnivals, 213

Chapter 12 - Educational Requirements. 221

Appendix. 229

Bibliography, 230 - Olmsted's Principles, 232 - Validity of Standards, 233 - Parkways, 237 - Charles Eliot, 248 - Lewis Mumford, 251 - Urban Planning of Highways, 253 - Philosophy of C. P. Keyser, 257 - Supplement to Chapter 7, 262 - Supplement to Chapter 8, 267 - Supplement to Chapter 9, 271 - Supplement to Chapter 10, 275 - Supplement to Chapter 11, 278 - Supplement to Chapter 12, 282 - Land Policy, Cook County, 284 - Hennepin County Park Reserve District Policy Statement, 294 - Park Board, Director, Relationship, 305 - Rules of the Board, 307 - Rules for Community Celebrations, Mpls., 317 - Miscellaneous Subjects, 320

Index. 329

CHAPTER 1　　　PRELIMINARY CONSIDERATIONS

"That in a well ordered state the citizens should have
leisure and not have to provide for their daily wants,
is generally stated."

Aristotle on Politics

Nature of Park and Recreation Administration

The discussion of park and recreation administration in
this book centers principally on tax supported services rather
than on those privately owned or supported.　This is not implying that privately owned services are not important, for they
do fulfill a very significant place in the total array of recreational opportunities available to the American people; but the
most comprehensive systems of recreation service are tax
supported, and tax support permits the development of a national policy on recreation.　The orderly development of recreation resources, as we shall later see, is of great significance to the nation's welfare.

Almost immediately the question arises as to the authority of the government in any of its levels to tax citizens for
providing recreation services or to prescribe its character.
Here it is in the preamble to the Constitution of the United
States:

"We, the people of the United States, in order to form a
more perfect Union ... establish Justice ... and promote the
general welfare" etc.　Then proceeding on to Section 8 of
Article 1, we find, "The Congress shall have power to lay and
collect taxes, duties, imports and excises to pay the debts and
provide for the common defense and the general welfare of the
United States" etc.

In the years since the adoption of the Constitution a multitude of public services has been adjudged "public welfare"
including the establishment of parks and recreation services
all of which prompted President Harding in 1921 to comment:
"Just government is merely the guarantee to the people of the
right and opportunity to support themselves.　The one outstanding danger of today is the tendency to turn to Washington for
the things which are the tasks or the duties of the forty-eight
commonwealths. "

President Harding notwithstanding, the U. S. Supreme
Court in sustaining the District of Columbia Redevelopment
Act of 1945 unanimously agreed: "The concept of the public

- 1 -

welfare is broad and inclusive. The values it represents are spiritual as well as physical, aesthetic as well as monetary. It is within the power of the legislature to determine that the community should be beautiful as well as healthy, spacious as well as clean, well-balanced as well as carefully patrolled. "

Management – an Art

To manage, (management), and to administer, (administration) are terms used interchangeably in this book. In some situations, by general local acceptance there may be a distinction between the words, i. e., one may mean the direction of a broader spectrum of functions than the other, but acceptance of such difference in meaning in all situations does not seem to exist. So the least confusing thing to do is to use the words interchangeably.

Park and recreation administration is not an exact science – at least not yet. The practice does not rest upon well established natural laws or on formulas derived therefrom, but upon policies emanating from tradition, experiences, popular demand, social evolution and similar more or less emotional manifestations of the body politic.

Scientists are certainly needed in the total park and recreation service – scientists in the biological field, the social field, the fields of humanities and the natural sciences. Professionals, technicians, skilled tradesmen are also needed. These include engineers, lawyers, foresters, some doctors, accountants, recreation specialists, mechanics, gardeners, clerical help, and common laborers. The task of coordinating all these varied talents into a single unified team operating with efficiency to manipulate the resources of land, structures, and money to the satisfaction of people and their elected politicians, may someday be reduced to formulas which, with the aid of computing machines may produce some administrative decisions. But, for the time being, such is not the case. The administrative process cannot yet be termed anything like a science. It can be termed a profession only because some in the business call themselves professionals and then only so far as the public accepts that terminology. But art it is, – art in the sense of creating beauty, and art in the sense of evolving a basis for action out of a nice evaluation of many social factors that relate to a recreation service. It is a most noble art because of its providing for wholesome recreation so essential to cultural and spiritual improvement.

Being an art rather than a science, management's decisions are to be accepted as being reached largely through the exercise of personal judgment and only sometimes through the application of national laws. Hence, the decisions reached are mostly opinions. The dogmatic statement, even when made by a widely accepted authority does not constitute an absolute and enduring verity. Minds must be kept open for new evidence; the attitude of practitioners and students alike must be one of constant inquiry even to the re-examination of previously accepted principles. Times change, environments change, cultures change, and conventions change. All of us need to keep abreast of these changes. In spite of this warning, the student will find in these pages principles of practice which have been widely accepted up to the present and the background reasoning that has won general acceptance. From this sort of springboard one may proceed into the future with reasonable confidence if one heeds the warning given.

Clarification of Terms Used in this Text

What is the Purpose of a Park and Recreation Service?

The purpose of a park and recreation service publicly administered is to provide opportunity for such recreation as warrants public support through taxation. Many public agencies in all levels of government – local, state, and federal – by whatever name, or whatever single or multi-function it is authorized to perform, find themselves now providing recreation functions either as a principle or a secondary function. Regardless of the degree of involvement, the elements of park and recreation administration are still present and the principles discussed herein apply.

What is Recreation?

In the many attempts to define recreation, a lot of hair-splitting has taken place and many words and paragraphs and pages have been written about it. Not all of that voluminous discussion can be brushed off as mere exercise in semantics for there can be delicate shades of interpretation important to those philosophically inclined. For the moment, and for us, it is sufficient to say that recreation is the <u>refreshment of mind or body or both through some means which is in itself</u>

pleasureful. If one thinks about this a little, it will be noted that almost any activity or mental process may be recreation depending largely upon the attitude assumed in the approach to the process itself, and perhaps, upon whether one is immersed in the process deeply enough to obtain re-creation.

In consequence, recreation may be a bodily exercise (which we may call active recreation) or a mental or contemplative exercise (which we might term passive recreation). A cultural flavor bordering on education is imparted when recreation is taken by employing cultural and handicraft arts such as music, drama, painting, sculpturing. Religious overtones are present when the spirit is moved by contemplation of inspiring environment. On the other extreme, if one is fiendishly inclined, recreation may be taken in any one of a number of degrading activities.

Limitations on the Meaning of Recreation in this Text

In this text, when we write about opportunities for recreation which are appropriate for the taxpayer to support, we reduce all recreation processes to those which are wholesome and socially acceptable by the general public. Anything that is degrading, off-color, or unconventional is left out. In addition, otherwise acceptable forms of recreation may also be left out because of financial limitations. These include high-cost processes and those forms of recreation which appeal only to minority sectors of the population unless it can be shown that providing recreation for minority groups actually promotes the general welfare and not the special welfare of a few enthusiasts. Theoretically, the taxpayer supports only such recreation as has wide acceptance and relatively low net unit cost to the taxpayer.

The kind of recreation, therefore, that is suitable for government sponsorship, changes with the changing times and may be different for different localities – a point which is well to keep in mind. Note, too, that there is no scientific or factually based formula that can be depended upon in the selection of appropriate kinds of recreation for government to foster other than as stated above.

Recreation and Leisure

In times past, recreation has been justified as being an aid to efficiency in work; it rejuvenated the mind and body for

renewed labor with a renewal of interest and vigor. Recreation was a surcease from work and was practiced at such times
as could be spared or made available after the hours spent in
survival activities – work, sleep, eating, and the personal
chores attendant to those necessities. These were the leisure
hours and hence there arose a close association of recreation
and leisure. While these have some attributes in common
(e. g. the absence of compulsion) they are not identical. Leisure in particular needs more explanation.

Leisure time is free, unoccupied time during which recreation takes place and, as we noted in the previous discussion
of recreation, the latter may be almost any activity or mental
process depending on the attitude one assumes in the approach
to the process. It may even be some activity that is usually
classified as work, but it is not work if it is done as recreation, that is, as a freely chosen project without any compulsion present. Some may call leisure a state of being free from
the necessity of doing anything that a person does not want to
do. An old American motto puts it in reverse but most succinctly: "Nothing is work unless you would rather be doing
something else. "

In our continually increasing affluence, leisure time is
growing in amount to the point where it may equal work time.
This observation causes some concern as to the ability of a
future society to wisely choose those uses of leisure time (recreation) which will promote the general welfare in contrast to
mere time consuming experiences – or worse. More and more
the philosophically minded are looking to the wise use of leisure as a manifestation of a culturally great people.

The Word, Recreation, in Today's "Professional" Parlance

Words are used to express ideas. If the same word is
used to convey different ideas in different situations, the message becomes confusing. Unfortunately, the word recreation
is such a word. When used by the general public it probably
has a more uniformly understood meaning than when used in
the "trade" – that is, the language used by the people in recreation work who come from a widely varied background.

Those who reached maturity when the ideological troubles
were taking place between so-called "recreation" people and
so-called "park" people (see history following this) refer to
each other just that way – "he is a recreation man, " or "he is
a park man. " This meant that one specialized in recreation

leadership and his thinking was colored by that sort of background, whereas the other was trained in facility construction
and maintenance and so he thought that way. These men were
usually engaged in municipal work, but that distinction carried
over into the state and federal services.

In the latter services (national and state parks, forests
and wild-life) the term recreation connotes a service on the
local or urban scene and seldom is associated with the state
and federal services.

"Outdoor" recreation, while not a new or recent expression, has carried a special meaning since 1961. It was then
used to distinguish the great unsupervised, unorganized recreation represented by hunting, fishing, traveling for pleasure,
camping, etc. as distinguished from the organized, promoted,
supervised and often scheduled recreation conducted by the
municipalities on the playgrounds and community playfields of
the cities. The former was supposed to be outdoor recreation
while the latter was simply recreation.

So, for the time being we have recreation as meaning, to
various people in the business, (1) what Webster and this text
says it is, (2) the restricted meaning of a municipal, supervised service, and (3) coupled with the prefix, "outdoor", all
unorganized, free time, non-urban recreation offered primarily by various state and federal agencies.

Let the student adhere to the meaning in Webster and the
text for we are in a transition period in which all government
sponsored recreation is finding a true kinship, and recreation
is the common denominator. Difference in meaning will dis-
appear.

The "Tools" of Recreation

Various things are required to provide recreation opportunities for the public, even on the restricted basis heretofore
outlined. We need land – land with many characteristics. We
need the native land in abundance where recreation can be taken
in solitude for the rediscovery of nature's processes and the
rejuvenation of the human spirit. We need land that has been
made suitable for games and outdoor exercise of various kinds.
We need land that has been made beautiful by the hand of man –
horticultural exhibits, beautiful lawns, gardens, buildings that
are architecturally attractive; land that provides pleasant ways
on which to travel leisurely (parkways); land that includes lakes
and streams, both native and man-made.

On this land we sometimes need to build structures to provide various facilities such as courts for games, fencing to enclose certain activities, ball diamonds of one kind or another, wading pools, swimming pools, children's play areas, and a host of other facilities necessary in carrying out a well-rounded program. We have mentioned buildings for various purposes, for so-called community center work, for workshops, for the housing of equipment.

The land and structures all require servicing through the maintenance of grounds and buildings, a police organization to guide and discipline, an organization to promote activities, organize leagues and supervise general use, and above all, an organization that finances and manages the whole recreation service.

There are, therefore, assets in land, assets in structures, assets in personnel; all have been assembled to produce a recreation service. The character and quality and quantity of that service is in harmony with policies evolved by the governing agencies. Those policies, in turn, are responsive to the will of the body politic in the same sense that laws reflect the attitude of people; in both policy and law determination both professional and lay guidance are required. The initial step in that guidance procedure is made by the administrator, if an orderly sequence and review is to result. The administrative function, then, is not only the management of the elemental assets that have been mentioned, but the proposal of broad policies as well.

What is a Park?

A park is a piece of land or water set aside for the recreation of the people. Improved land is that land which has been specially prepared for public use – ball diamonds, courts for games, playgrounds, picnic grounds, horticultural exhibits, etc. Unimproved land is native land. The latter should contain characteristics which in themselves induce and promote recreation such as hunting, fishing, hiking, winter sports. Native park land should also be of such a nature as to induce and promote recreation through contemplation, nature appreciation, history, geology, archeology, etc. Consequently, a park is both a tool for active supervised recreation and by itself, and standing alone, an instrument of recreation.

Land called parks are not the only land masses that are used for recreation. Others include forests, river and other water impoundments and adjacent lands, the public domain in general and specifically large mountain and desert regions, historic sites and battlefields, and others of lesser significance. These areas are used only partially for recreation purposes and hence cannot properly be called parks. Nevertheless, some forest areas are more than reminiscent of the forest parks of antiquity which were the progenitors of today's parks.

What is a "System" of Park and Recreation Facilities?

Without going into the details of how a park and recreation system is made up, it is enough for the moment to know that a complete system for a municipality, for a metropolis with satellite towns, for a region, state or nation, includes various sizes of land parcels. These may be improved as well as native, each performing a distinct function and so fitted into the complementary function of other parks making up the system of parks for that particular agency as to result in a service of the scope intended by that agency. Consequently, there are municipal systems; metropolitan, regional or county systems; state systems and national systems. Theoretically all such systems have a joint responsibility to adequately provide the complete spectrum of recreation opportunities.

That "joint responsibility" aspect has been long in evidencing tangible results, but great strides have been made in recent years. Through the Federal Bureau of Outdoor Recreation, federal aid for land acquisition is possible to the states on a matching basis. In turn many states make grants-in-aid to local governments. The Department of Housing and Urban Development makes grants-in-aid to local governments and, as a pre-requisite, the plans of the local government must be based upon the planned services of an agency of greater geographical scope. These measures, together with the expressed goal of BOR will ultimately result in a fully integrated and unified national recreation service.

Correlation

No park and recreation system, local, state or federal in scope, is a completely independent entity existing in isolation separate and apart from all other public and private services on which the public depends for existence. The recreation needs is only one of the myriad of services required for everyday living; any one of these needs may be paramount at some given time or situation. Such things as parks, highways, water reservoirs, sewer systems, transmission lines, power plants, businesses and housing are often at loggerheads over finances, land and the minds of men. All are vital in spite of competition. It is not a case of one or the other, but an adjustment or compromise which will result in a good service to the people. In a crowded society, it becomes the duty of the competing interests to work closely with each other in the early stages of planning to avoid ruinous confrontation and to work out compromised solutions.

Students and others are urged to keep this point in mind and to avoid taking too narrow a viewpoint in working out plans for recreation services.

Brief History of Parks

"What's past is prologue. A civilization knows where it is going only when it understands where it has been."
Alexander Winston, Harper's
March, 1965

Parks are as old as human history. They have always served as a locale for recreation pursuits and have always been a source of recreation in themselves. Ancient parks, for the most part, were the private pleasure grounds of the high and mighty. Not until the nineteenth century did public parks become the mode, although at one time, public parks were fairly prevalent in some of the Mediterranean countries.

The first parks were the hunting parks of the king, the prince, the noble – large native areas where wild animals were kept for the sport that hunting them provided. This has its parallel in today's private sportsmen's clubs. Sometimes tame animals indigenous to the locality as well as animals from other countries were kept for the enjoyment of visitors. These parks were the ancestors of today's zoological gardens.

A part of such a private domain in the vicinity of the castle became the garden and outdoor playground of the court family – the entertainment grounds for visitors to the court. Infrequently the commoners were permitted attendance. Here were conducted such entertainments as plays, song festivals, concerts, exhibitions by jugglers and gymnasts; if the area was suitable, races and athletic events took place.

There were other ancestors of today's parks – the market place, the town plaza, the agora, each was the site of social intercourse for the common people of the times. The British Commons of the villages constituted the playground (it served other purposes as well) of the common people of England. Commons were introduced into America by early European settlers; Boston Common established in 1634, is called our first park.

The prospective park administrator should not deny himself the pleasure of searching out the development of the public park idea as that history unfolds from time immemorial down to the present, and spreads itself over the entire face of the globe. Such an adventure in research will reveal the ever present longing of people everywhere for recreation in the many basic forms that it takes today – the longing for the native countryside, the woods and the streams, the high and the low areas; the desire to engage in sports and games and to enjoy good entertainment as well as to develop the more cultural aspects of life to the extent that available leisure time permits. The love of beauty has been always present. How over the centuries these desires have been attained in whole or in part under the various forms of social and political life is the fascinating story that breathes significance into park work and provides inspiration to the park administrator of today. One should not miss the opportunity of "traveling" through the parks of ancient Egypt, the Hanging Gardens of Babylon, the hunting parks of ancient Persia, the sacred groves of India and Greece, the parks, both public and private of Greece and Rome. Then, emerging from the dormant period of the Dark Ages, experience the particularly fascinating period of the Renaissance when some of the most elaborate and beautiful parks and gardens of Europe were created; the Versailles near Paris, San Souci at Potsdam and more pertinently to our purpose, the informal English parks as contrasted to the more formal gardens of the Continent. In this sort of exploration lies the seed for creating the real feeling for parks and their effect upon the lives of people in our day.

Our essentially professional interest in parks begins with the establishment of public parks in England and Europe in the first park of the nineteenth century. This inspired certain Americans, including such eminent people as William Cullen Bryant and Washington Irving, to say nothing of the indomitable A. J. Downing, to work for the establishment of parks in New York. Public squares, plazas and commons (all of small acreage) had been introduced into many of the American cities at the time of their original settlement; but no large park for suitable recreation grounds for the people had been established. (There was such a total lack of respectable places for wholesome recreation that a walk through a well maintained cemetary was a suitable recreation for genteel folks.) This whole history of the promotion for a large city park makes interesting and constructive reading for the student. It is enough to say here that Central Park in New York was ultimately established in the 1850's.

The design for Central Park was a subject of a competition which was won by Frederick Law Olmsted and Calvert Vaux. Vaux had had some architectural training in England before he came to the United States where he became associated with A. J. Downing, the publisher of the "Agriculturist Magazine" through the pages of which much of the promotion for Central Park was published. Olmsted was, it could be said, an agriculturist for he had done a little farming. His background training was a very informal one. It ranged over a large number of subjects at the hands of several tutors interrupted with great freedom to travel. His interests finally centered on a great love of the natural landscape; later he became the first to be known as a landscape architect. Olmsted and Vaux were in partnership for several years but Olmsted's longer professional career, nowadays centers attention on him rather than on the partnership.

Although there were rules and regulations laid down for the Central Park competition and according to these rules certain facilities had to be provided, nevertheless, there was enough freedom left to the designer's imagination so there could be produced a plan that would characterize the planner himself. Olmsted and Vaux presented a plan characteristic of the natural landscape as nearly as it could be reproduced in a large city park. They used native plant material as much as possible. The borders of the park were heavily planted to shut out all aspects of the city. They provided a more or less circumferential roadway along informally curved lines and separated the traffic on this roadway from the ordinary mixed city traffic which was to have a crossing through the park. Although the necessary small playgrounds, buildings, parade grounds, etc., were provided for, the over-all effect was one of pleasing native scenery wholly at variance with the nearby built up city. *

*See Olmsted's "Principles," in Appendix, p. 232.

The Olmsted plan characterized the large city park of the latter half of the nineteenth century. Indeed, Olmsted himself planned many such parks in a great many cities of this country and Canada. They always presented a pleasing landscape of broad lawns, background of trees and heavy plantings, winding walks and driveways, all to be used by people seeking recreation in the quiet, leisurely, sedate, and sometimes cultural uses of the outdoors. No emphasis was placed on sports grounds or playgrounds except as brief diversions, certainly not as day-by-day activities. Indeed, in those days government had not accepted its responsibilities of providing for the daily play of children or of neighborhood recreation of an active nature. These came later.

Public responsibility for the active play of people and later for a whole range of recreation pursuits came gradually over a period of the first 30 to 40 years of the twentieth century. First came sand lots and small playgrounds in the congested areas of large cities; then outdoor gymnasiums appeared in the first decade of the current century. These were followed by summer playgrounds and later, by all year around programs for both sexes and all ages. It was during this 30 to 40 year period that the words "parks" and "recreation" began to mean different things to different people and sometimes created unfortunate conflicts in public administration. Here is how that happened.

As the recreation movement grew, public demand for recreation service grew with it. Recreation space was required; space for ball diamonds, tennis courts, playground apparatus, and many other things all to the consternation of park directors who were creating and maintaining grounds heavily if not wholly, based upon horticulture and the beautiful landscape. The invasion by some of these recreation facilities into a well-designed park took place regardless of their interference with the original plan. The fact that parks had always been used for recreation was often lost sight of by park purists. So too, was the fact that provisions for active recreation on the expanded scale it was now assuming required additional space commensurate with its new place in the family of public services. The proper place for such addition was within the park system, but not all park administrators were ready to assume that responsibility. In many instances this situation resulted in the establishment of a new public agency known as the Recreation Department. In spite of the many important amalgamations of park and recreation departments that have taken place in the last decade or so, the 1961 Year Book of the National Recreation Association still listed 949 separate recreation departments out of a total of 2,762 public agencies dealing with both parks and recreation. However, the 1966 Year Book lists only 818 separate recreation departments and 428 separate park departments as against 1304 combined departments.

Up to this point the historical discussion has dealt principally with city parks. There is good reason for giving special attention to it.

In the first place, city park systems have a longer history in American recreation service than any of the other state and national recreation services; so, in a real sense the cities have pioneered the way. Although the first national park in this country, or in the world for that matter, namely, Yellowstone, was established in 1872, a true national park service was not instituted until 1916. Individual state parks (e. g. Mackinac Island and Mariposa), existed long, long before the significant state park movement took hold in the early nineteen-twenties. A division of Forestry was set up in the U. S. Agriculture Department in 1881, but recreation in connection with forests was not given much thought before 1918 when Prof. Waugh suggested the now famous slogan, "the greatest good for the greatest number," which could scarcely omit recreation as a "good," for the forests had been used by campers and others before that. Any interest in a consciously conceived recreation approach in wildlife management before 1930, was pretty well hidden in its conservation aspects of wildlife management which, of course, aided hunting and fishing, but without relationship to a general recreation movement. (The barrier of semantics in recreation understanding was operating.) Until very recent years, the recreational assets of large reservoir impoundments were wholly disregarded. The experiments of the Reclamation Bureau and the National Park Service in Recreation Areas at such places as Lake Mead in the depression years of the thirties must be excepted.

Secondly, because of its longer history and closer association with greater numbers of people, city parks have undergone a longer period of evolutionary development as social

*Much valuable history covering the foregoing aspects are contained in a paper prepared in 1964 by Al La Gasse (of American Institute of Park Executives and later of National Recreation and Park Association) and others for the National Conference on Professional Education for Outdoor Recreation at Syracuse University that year.

amenities and have reached a more advanced stage. One can get arguments on this point, but much more can be gained by accepting this as fact, rather than by arguing about it. In a number of important aspects of both policy and administrative technique, the city development is a microcosm of the development of recreation in the state and federal situations. What has been in the city, one can expect to ultimately experience in the higher levels of government operation. This comes about because of the relative shrinking of distances, the growing population and its need for more space, and the expanding opportunity in time and money for a greater variety of recreation experiences.

Perhaps one general example of a number of other possible examples may help clarify. Forest recreation started the whole thing in ancient times. Adaptation of the natural environment as an antidote to city living inspired the public park and particularly the Olmstedian theory of American parks and park systems. Recreation was obtained from the environment as a major objective even as it was in our great state and national parks and forests. Under public pressure in our cities the Olmsted type parks and systems became modified by the introduction of parks dedicated to a more intense and active use – playgrounds and community playfields. In recent years the states and the federal government have found it expedient to satisfy public demand for a park providing facilities for more active use – Recreation Areas. Going a step farther up the evolutionary scale, the city – especially the larger ones – must now provide for a system of recreation grounds covering the whole spectrum of recreation wants from the smallest play-lot to the mammoth and all-encompassing recreation grounds in Griffith Park in Los Angeles. Even Central Park has succumbed and is now fighting a rear guard action to preserve its essential identity. What portends in the state and national scene might be signalled by what is happening to some county systems such as Milwaukee's, where the county is now almost completely urbanized and the original county system has become in fact a city system; or one might examine the Los Angeles County system.

This one example can be duplicated in several aspects of both physical development and administrative techniques of policy and operation to justify examining the history of city parks for precedent in the operation of county, state, and federal operation.

CHAPTER 2

THE COUNTRY'S PHYSICAL RECREATION RESOURCES— THE CITIES AND THEIR SUBURBS

"Great national parks and great national seashores located in far-away, distant places do not satisfy the needs of the people who are a part of our urban civilization. The serenity of nature must be more than a once-a-year experience ..... This experience should touch our daily and weekly lives."

President Lyndon B. Johnson
Signing Cape Lookout National
Seashore Bill, 1966

A General View of the Nation's Recreation Land Resources

As noted under the sub-heading, "The Tools of Recreation" on page 6, publicly owned land is the essential resource base for a recreation service. What, then is the land situation in the United States? How much is available now for recreation? How much is actually used now? How much is needed? Where are the shortages, if any?

Of the total land area of the United States, estimated at 3,648 million* acres, 234 million acres are devoted to outdoor recreation according to the Outdoor Recreation Resources Review Commission report. Add another million acres for urban parks not included in the ORRRC report bringing the total to 235 million acres. Major items in the total are as follows in millions of acres: National Park Service, 26; National Forests, 186; Sport Fisheries and Wild Life, 10; the balance in the Corps of Engineers, other federal agencies, and in the states. All told about 6% or 7% of the land area of the United States is government owned land that can be considered to be a recreation resource. There may be additional reserves that have not as yet been "discovered" to be of recreational potential.

The amount of land now actually used for recreation is considerably less than the above stated 235 million acres, pro-

---

*One million acres = 1560 square miles or a rectangle forty miles by 39 miles, roughly, a little less than a forty mile square.

bably much less than 50%. Because of various ways of interpretation, classification and compilation, figures available are
no more than estimates, but they are indicative nontheless.
With that in mind, we may estimate land used for recreation
by cities and counties to be 1.5 million acres; states at various
estimates from 10 to over 30 million, so let's say 20 million;
national parks, 26 million; and that part of national forests
which is actually devoted to recreation, (aside from the very
sparse use of all of it), 20 to 30 million; a total of about 80
million acres. Add to this, parts of state forests, wild life
refuges, Corps of Engineers holdings and the total will be well
over 100 million acres, 40% to 50% of available recreation land.

Against the amount of land available and the 50% of that
total which is now used for recreation, how much land is needed?
To get some idea of this we must resort to some rule-of-thumb
standards, widely used, but known to be little more than general guides. Nevertheless we will use them for general approximation of needs.

For cities, counties, and regional parks in general, twenty
acres per thousand population are required. About 150 million
people live in metropolitan areas, so the total requirement for
recreation land is 3 million acres. This is twice as much land
as is now used, hence there is a distinct shortage in this cata-
gory.

States require 65 acres per thousand population or a total
of 13 million acres for a 200 million population. More than
twice this amount is available.

The federal requirements, at 150 acres per thousand population, are only 30 million acres whereas many times that
amount is now being used to some extent and more is available.

It would appear that while acute shortages seem apparent
in the cities and counties, the states and federal government
are amply provided for. But the latter assumption is not true
for a number of reasons that are not disclosed by a general
over-view. The large land masses of scenic parks, forests,
wild life refuges, and river impoundments are not and cannot
be located with reference to large concentrations of population.
Even with the great mobility of people, these resources cannot
be intensively used; indeed their real recreational usefulness
prohibits intensified use. Much like the introduction of neighborhood parks and community playfields in the Olmstedian
scheme of municipal park systems of the late nineteenth and
early twentieth century, so in recent years it has become desirable to introduce high and medium density recreation areas

into the state and federal systems.   This trend toward more
recreation areas will continue for years to come.   These active
recreation areas must be located with reference to where people live, an altogether different requirement than existed for
the large scenic parks and forests.   A maldistribution of areas
and perhaps some inefficient use of present areas alters the
picture reflected by general statistics alone.

Partly to indicate the density of use above mentioned and
partly to complete the national picture of recreation lands,
some statistics on use are appropriate.   Here again, figures
are not at all precise, but are indicative enough to permit a
general observation.   City parks are used by the equivalent of
the population they serve about once a week; state facilities
about once in two months and federal resources about once in
ten months.   This is a descending ratio of attendance of one,
to one-eighth, to one-fortieth.

The City and Its Suburbs

Of the several park systems mentioned in Chapter 1, page
8, the city or municipal system is the first one that will be
considered in this text.   Incidentally, it is the oldest of the
nation's park and recreation systems and, as previously mentioned, the one that is in the most advanced evolutionary stage
of park and recreation systems.   Particular attention is, therefore, drawn to its discussion which will probably be in more
detailed treatment than the federal and state systems which
follow.

A city of 50,000 population and upwards, is composed of
many features which become more numerous and more varied
and more complicated with the increased size of the city.   Some
of the major items of the city's composition include business
and commercial areas, industrial areas, and areas for living
such as, single family dwellings, duplexes, apartment buildings.   Zoning laws, based upon land use plans, usually designate these various areas in compact groups in an attempt to
make the composition of the city more orderly.   Residential
areas are sometimes shown as being subdivided into neighborhoods, each bounded by such "barriers" as arterial streets,
railroads, commercial and industrial districts.   The purpose
is to facilitate the placement of neighborhood services including
neighborhood parks and elementary schools.

Woven into and among the areas set aside for the above
purposes are parks to perform various kinds and degrees of

service for the recreation of the people. The principle characteristics of the city system that should be kept in mind are
these:

A. Parks are a part of the city plan and the total system
cannot be agreed upon independently from the city plan itself.
Conversely, a city plan cannot be devised independently from
the plan of the park system. Parks and the city plan are inter-
dependent. A system of park classification with corresponding
standards of size and ratios of area to population facilitates the
making of the plan for the park system as a whole, at least in
its preliminary phase.

B. From the point of view of the park and recreation administrator, a system of park classifications, accompanied by
standards of ratios of areas of each class to units of municipal
population, a standard of size for each park within a class, the
function that each class performs, and suggestions as to physical content of each class help to formulate administrative judgment in these ways:

1. Provides convenient identification.
2. Makes possible an analysis of the system of parks for
     comparison with accepted patterns elsewhere.
3. Facilitates the planning of the system as a whole as
     well as of individual parks.
4. Facilitates the formulation of methods of maintenance,
     operation, use patterns and policing.

C. There are factors which complicate precise application of standards.

D. Trends, now discernible, may influence future accepted standards.

Parks and the City Plan

The more or less concurrent planning of a city and its park
system (or any of the components of the city plan) usually starts
with informal discussions between the city planner and the park
administrator. The purposes are to exchange philosophical
attitudes toward the mutual problem, to discuss goals and to
agree upon possible standards. Professional planners in private practice have so often encountered wide variations from
nationally publicized standards, have so often experienced complications in applying those standards and have seen various
ways of expressing standards among American cities, that some
are inclined to throw up their hands in frustration and say "Why
attempt standards? Why not just custom tailor each project
according to our good planning sense. "

We should custom tailor each park to fit the characteristics of the population it serves, but to do so without regard to a city-wide scheme of park classification would, indeed, be a step backward. That is about the way park systems were planned in the past; and that is one important reason why so many are now deficient in one or more categories. It is also a possible reason why our cities are now having so much difficult planning situations to cope with. In spite of the variations in both standards and classifications, and in spite of the frustrations in applications it remains that an analysis or planning or administering a system of parks without reference to some rather definite goals and limiting guidelines is a process of shifting objectives. A system of classification and standards is a must for the orderly administration of a park and recreation system.

Classification and Standards

A. As a Means of Identification.

When parks have been classified in any given situation, the expression "neighborhood park", for example, brings to the mind's eye a picture of a definite thing to all people familiar with that system of classification. Communication has been firmly established. There is small chance of misunderstanding. How cumbersome it would be to have to describe in detail what is meant by "neighborhood park". How easy it is then for intelligent communication to break down.

B. As a Means of Analysis and Comparison.

Comparing one's park system with those of other cities is a constant practice of park administrators as well as of citizen's groups of taxpayers. Where do we stand? Are we above or below the average? If nationally accepted standards are available, comparison of our city with these standards are most significant; hence the desirability of having a set of classifications and standards that is as close to nationally accepted standards as possible.

C. As an Essential to Planning.

The planning of individual parks and of a whole system of parks could not be done in any sort of orderly way without assigning to each park a function, size limitation, radius of service or influence, and a general listing of facilities. There are still other matters which have to be considered in the planning process but without knowing the class which a given park is in, and hence what its purpose and general character is, the utility of the finished product is bound to be of low efficiency. Without due consideration for class, a system could be planned in a wholly unbalanced manner, e.g. all community playfields or none at all. Recreation service would be entirely at "sixes and sevens". A good system of classification and standards enables a whole system of parks to be planned in a balanced way for uniform and all inclusive recreation service. All sections of the city can be properly served and all age groups and classes of citizens are impartially provided for.

D. In the Formulation of Administrative Policies.

When parks are classified, the function of each is determined. It is planned accordingly and a feature of the plan is that its use in that particular instance is fixed and noted taking into account the character of recreation service, (highly organized or entirely unorganized), intended for it. Noted, too, is the kind of maintenance that each of the various areas is to receive and what variations may be permitted in the future.

Maintenance, function, public use – these having been analyzed and noted on the plans or in text accompanying plans, a policy statement on these matters is now before the administrator. Reference to this statement will forestall impulsive decisions "off the cuff" or "off the top of the head" in the case of public use, policing, and the introduction of incompatible or inconsistent structures, devices, or uses. This information contained in a classification and standards system is an important feature for the adoption of such a system.

A case in point might be one in which persistent over-use has made satisfactory maintenance impossible. Such a situation often develops before the eyes of the administrator when he has made no reference to classification of the park and the policy statement that may accompany his plan. That policy statement could have named a maximum attendance per acre, as well as a notation as to the character of use, made as a result of previous careful analysis.

The resultant over-use and misuse, which takes place gradually over a period of time, occurs because both classification and the application of standards have not been periodically reviewed. If they had been reviewed, uses inconsistant with the park class and over use would not have happened, because additional and suitable additions to park property would have been made elsewhere. At least the administrator would have had the firm basis for a concerted appeal for relief if he had used his classification and standards as a basis for his appeal.

It can be argued that in cases such as the foregoing, other suitable park lands are not obtainable. More often, the administrator permits the unfortunate situation to develop without recognition of what the consequences may be.

That situation would not happen to a successful Texas rancher. He knows that over-grazing results in poor cattle and worn out land which takes precious time and loss of production to recoup. His simple remedies are (1) to reduce the herd, or (2) get more pasture land. Why can't park administrators advocate similar courses?

E. Factors that Complicate Application:

1. The shape and size of neighborhoods as bounded by such "barriers" as freeways and arterial streets, industrial districts, railroads, etc. are not of uniform size or of uniform shape; any neighborhood may be a half mile wide and a mile long instead of a nice 3/4 mile or mile square; it may be irregular in outline; it may contain the standard one square mile or only a small fraction of that. These situations must be studied for a suitable facility to serve the day-to-day needs of that particular neighborhood.

This search for substitutes requires a close examination of the existence of available school grounds, Y. M. C. A. and other buildings and open spaces for recreation use. Many churches now contain considerable indoor recreation facilities. Makeshift areas of the play lot size or small one or two acre playgrounds may have to be resorted to. Other possibilities will occur to an imaginative person.

2. School districts made up of several individual pockets, some quite remote from the school, can solve their peculiar resident problems by busses. Parks not so equipped – hence school-park developments are not always possible which often complicates recreation service to small neighborhoods.

3. Topographic features such as lakes, streams, steep hills, ravines, etc. break up the normal neighborhood pattern.

4. Abnormal age group patterns (predominately old or predominately young) affect the selection of appropriate rec-

reation service. So, too, may ethnic, racial, and social groupings in concentrated patterns.

Population characteristics are not permanent neighborhood attributes; they change as often as every decade. The suitability of the neighborhood for certain classes of people is a similar factor but not quite the same. An eye to suitability is a more stable factor.

5. Density of population has an overwhelming effect on the application of standards. The standards given in the text, page 27, will fit neighborhoods and communities having from five to as much as ten thousand people per square mile. They will not fit where the population density is much less or much more than that.

A great deal of observation, study, and experimentation still needs to be done on the total effect of this factor. In whatever direction such studies may take us, it would appear that the mind must be kept on the requirements of neighborhood, the day-to-day, hour-to-hour, the short period, use by the neighborhood people of whatever characteristics they may have – old or young, rich or poor, black or white. That "close to home" service is paramount, and if it takes facilities other than our standardized neighborhood park, suitable modifications must be made. The same goes for the study of a community (3 to 5) of neighborhoods.

6. The political organization of large metropolitan complexes consisting of a central city and numerous suburban satellites often precludes the application of the standards. The text has pointed out, that two or more contiguous villages may jointly have sufficient population to justify large city parks, to name one example, but acting independently their populations do not justify it.

These similar difficulties encountered by jealous and chauvinistic attitudes preclude sensible park and recreation development in the suburbs. The same is true for many other services necessary to an urban population, the whole problem of metropolitan political organization has assumed primary importance in those regions of the United States and Canada where suburban entities are a part of the metropolitan urban complex – and that includes most of the continent.

Experiments are being tried. In some large city complexes, the county is emerging as the metropolitan authority. Toronto, Canada, has created a metropolitan authority, to assume those functions which are metropolitan in nature: water supply, sewage disposal, etc. In that case, those classes of parks which are above the neighborhood and community playfield classes are governed by the Metro. (A couple of exceptions still exist.) What patterns of Metropolitan government in this country are ultimately adopted are questions still to be answered.

F. Future Trends:

In addition to the previously mentioned factors that affect the precise application of classifications and standards there are some future developments whose trends are now discernable that may have an effect on the classification and standards of the future. Some of these are:

1. The redevelopment of the central parts of our cities. In this process more open space is bound to result. Some open space will be in public parks. What kind? So-called "rest parks", "ornamental parks", parks for occasional exhibition or attraction (skating act, visiting choir, a famed "personality", etc.)? We may even spawn a new class of park.

2. Redevelopment of all or a large part of a city. This possibility seems remote at this writing and yet there are small towns (10,000 to 25,000 population) which are old, obsolete, and yet healthy and apparently permanently important to a degree that could qualify under an expanded program of redevelopment. Such a situation might warrant a re-examination of present classification and standards.

3. A solution to metropolitan political organization. This has been discussed previously.

4. "Surrounded by parks". Some progressive planners have envisaged a locale for living set in the midst of parks – parks surrounding the home, parks as ways to and from school, shopping, and church, parkways to and from work. Surely such a profusion of parkland could take place only in a few special places and would be in accordance with new standards.

5. New ideas in subdivision plan. This is a modification of the foregoing and occurs when open space and building space are each planned as more concentrated areas but not necessarily changing the proportion of each. Often this permits a more useful park space instead of such space being cut up into smaller yards. Also more park area may be made available at the expense of streets and alleys.

6. Move from suburbs to city. This trend is significant but not large so far. When it happens it usually means that older age groups have moved to apartments (usually the better class) thereby creating a denser population. When whole neigh-

borhoods are thus reconstructed, the possibility of a new class and a new standard of parks may be in the offing.

7. County and state zoning. It appears logical that with a continued expansion of urban centers more attention will be given county and state zoning. The requirements for recreation areas in less dense population requires revision of standards.

8. Five to ten acre tracts for the ex-urbanite. This is akin to point 7.

9. "Green Belts in future planning." Presently we are not sure how economically feasible green belts about our urban areas are. If they become prevalent they will affect both standards and classification.

10. The effect of private enterprise. As the people become more affluent and are willing to spend more for recreation, the private entrepreneur is encouraged to provide such facilities as bowling alley complexes that simulate the community center; deluxe motels cater to more than the traveler; whole cities are built about a large industrial or commercial undertaking; family resorts, ski areas, and similar recreation areas, even county and state park facilities may in the future affect neighborhood and community recreation standards.

The Simple Application of Standards

The application of a set of standards to present cities that change their physical structure as rapidly as they do in this era, and of applying them to the great variety of satellite towns that spring up, sometimes even as a whole new, planned and developed city by a single organization, may seem at first to be an exercise in futility. But it need not be so. One should keep in mind that all new attempts at town planning are attempts to produce something that is more adaptable than what was previously available in the way of happy living – and at a less expense. Innovation itself is a pretty good sales pitch. Considering that many cities in the past have done less than an adequate job of providing an efficient park and recreation system, there is ample room for innovation – both good and of questionable merit.

The simple fact remains that there is always a need for parks within a short walk from where people live (neighborhood parks) and near where they leisurely stroll (the rest park, a variation of the neighborhood park). Older teenagers, young adults, and hobbyists will always need facilities within easy "biking" distance or within a short driving distance – the community park or playfield with its pool and community center building. There will be a need for a place to get a feel of open space, different than the crowded home environment. Needed will be picnic facilities and some attractions and entertainment – the large city park and the special use parks with floral displays, pretty landscapes, a zoo, a museum, golf course, even large sports centers and outdoor theaters, perhaps parkways to drive over to get to these attractions. Such facilities are fundamental needs; it is only a matter of providing for them in a variety of ingenious ways, or even under the guise of alluring names that tends to make the simple pattern of a park system seem obsolete. The wants are unchanged from those shown on the table on page 27. Imagination in application is the challenge and indeed many administrators of the recent past have had their ideas about modifying the standards first published many years ago by the National Recreation Association.

There appears to be no one standard of classification adopted by all national organizations and accepted and adhered to by all authorities throughout the continent. About the time the professionals have adhered pretty much to one classification, others are proposed in other directions so that finally there is no unanimity at all. In spite of this, there is great similarity in all of these classifications, the difference being mostly in nomenclature and in the degree to which the list of all possible characteristics of parks is broken down into finer subdivisions. For our purpose nothing is gained by reviewing a lengthy and minutely detailed classification if a shorter one will serve our purpose. The one reproduced here is one which was used in a study several years ago involving the Dallas, Texas, park and recreation system. It is representative of the average of all such classifications and standards expressed in a reasonably brief way.

The major categories of the Dallas schedule mention play-lots, but suggests that, in the main, they should be operated by private persons and organizations, and ordinarily should not be included in the parks operated by the municipal government. Although this is generally true, there is scarcely a city in the country that has not found it necessary to become involved in that sort of operation. Even in a new situation, instances may arise in small and congested areas in which this type of park is the best solution available to provide some degree of recreation service. This does not alter the conclusion of the Dallas schedule that these situations should be minimized and, if possible, eliminated. No definite acreage per

thousand population is consequently attributed to this classification.

Otherwise then, the smallest and most elemental classification, is the neighborhood park of one to two acres per
thousand population. Playfields are expected to service two
or more neighborhoods, usually three or four with a radius of
influence of a mile and a half to two miles. Again one to two
acres per thousand population are required. Large park areas
constitute the next category to which has been attributed five
acres per thousand population, and the character of which is
noted in general terms on the schedule. Special use parks
follow, with two acres per thousand population attributed to
them. This makes a total of ten acres per thousand population
for the entire park and recreation system of the municipality.
The table does go beyond that by suggesting that any metropolitan or regional park system ought to contain an additional ten
acres per thousand population, but for the moment we will con-
fine our consideration to that of the municipality proper.

The widely publicized standards published by the National
Recreation Association are substantially the same as those of
the Dallas survey, but expressed as one acre of neighborhood
park space for a population of 800 and one acre of community
playfield for a population of 800. The Dallas classification and
set of standards has been chosen here because of its brevity
and simplicity as compared to the more extended and detailed
N. R. A. compilation. There is no appreciable difference in
values. (See expanded list, p. 39, etc.)

As a matter of clarification of the material which follows,
it is well to pause here and make some observation as to the
predominant character of the various classifications. The
first two – neighborhood parks and playfields – are predominantly characterized and influenced by active recreation for
the age groups from about eight to the early twenties not ignor-
ing, however, both younger and older age groups. The neighborhood parks are the parks which can be reached by walking
to them; the playfield type requires the use of bicycles and cars
although a fair number can walk to the location. The younger
children and the adults use these facilities but not to the extent
that other age groups use them. Areas for athletics, games,
amusement, club gatherings, and the like become the controlling feature of the design. Pleasing patterns, beauty of landscape and peaceful environment are part of the designs, but
are not the controlling factors. The influence of the recreation
directors and the recreation program not only influence but
actually dictate the character of the parks in these two classifications.

PARK AREA & SERVICE STANDARDS

RECOMMENDED

Type of Park Area	Size	Area per 1000 Persons	Service Area	Location	Usual Facilities & Remarks
Playlot	Less than 1 acre	Special Facility	Usually limited to single block or project	High density neighborhood where usual private yards do not exist	Paved areas, sitting area and play equipment for small children. Usually private responsibility
Playground (Neighborhood Park)	6 acre minimum additional for parking & natural scenic areas desirable	1 to 2 acres per 1000 persons depending upon shape & intensity of development	Approximately 1/2 mi. or a 1 sq. mi. neighborhood same as elementary school	Preferably adjoining the elementary school near center of neighborhood unit	Softball & other games, play equipment, multiple use paved areas, turf areas & planting, some rustic & passive areas desirable, minimum of automobile parking
Playfield (Includes Athletic Field)	15 to 25 acres may be part of larger scenic area if location provides convenient service	1 to 2 acres per 1000 persons with at least 1 acre active play area per 1000 people	Approximately 1 mi. or 4 or 5 neighborhood units. Similar service area to high school	At or near the intersection of major or secondary thoroughfares near center of 4 or 5 square mile service area	Baseball, football, softball, tennis and other active athletic areas, possible field house community center & swimming pool. Some facilities may be lighted for night use substantial automobile parking required. May include playground type area
Large Park	Minimum of 100 acres, preferably several hundred acres	Approximately 5 acres per 1000 persons	3 miles or more with good accessibility by auto	Where appropriate sites can be obtained incorporating natural features, one area for each 50,000 to 100,000 persons desirable within urbanized area or on the periphery	Active athletic areas similar to playfield but at least 1/2 area should be rustic & provide picnicking, hiking, archery, etc., golf courses, fishing, boating, & water sports may be included. Much of street parking required. Shelters, swimming pools & quiet, passive areas desirable
Parkways Ornamental Areas Special Parks	Size varies depending on conditions & nature of area	Approximately 2 ac. per 1000 persons	No specific service areas as most facilities serve entire urban area	Along waterways, as esthetic treatment for civic buildings, subdivision, etc., zoos. Botanical museums & gardens. Exhibitions should be near center of urban area	Largely scenic areas but may include picnicking & play facilities. Special parks may include golf courses, hobby centers, zoo, monuments, fair grounds, & a variety of special functions
Reservations & Preserves	Several hundred to a thousand or more acres	10 acres per 1000 persons. May include some close-in regional recreation areas	Entire urban area	Usually on fringe of urban development at appropriate sites	Rustic & wild areas, camping, nature & hiking trails, bridle paths, bird sanctuary, boating, fishing, and similar uses not requiring intensive development
Regional Recreation areas	Several thousand acres	No specific standard. May be partially included in area of reservations & preserves	Entire region	Within 1 to 3 hours driving time of urban center	Lake, river or reservoir providing fishing, boating, water sports picnicking, hunting, camping & similar facilities

It is noted that neighborhood parks and playfields are relatively new introductions into the pattern of municipal park
systems.   Prior to 1900 or even 1910, park systems were
constructed in the best tradition of the "founding fathers".
They consisted of several large parks (100 acres or more) in
the several radial portions of the city, connected by a parkway
system. Parks not on the parkway system were still relatively
large, widely spaced and like all other parks, were designed
for rest, contemplation, appreciation of scenery, and sedate
use rather than for active play.   Indeed the responsibility for
either sports or complete recreation programs had not generally been assumed by government, and hence, there was no
need for an extensive system of playgrounds and sports fields.
Since the city pattern was by that time pretty well fixed and the
city largely developed, the introduction of the neighborhood
parks and playfields posed a difficult problem and an expensive
one to solve.   In the older cities such is still the case.   It is
not too surprising that the use of numerous playlots has been
resorted to in some cases, and in others the absence of neighborhood parks allowed to continue.

The functions and features which distinguish large city
parks from special use parks are often vague.   In most situations special use functions have been separated from the formerly large city parks and given a home of their own – conservatories and flower gardens, zoos, arboretums, outdoor
theaters, museum sites, golf courses, large municipal stadiums
and sport centers.   That is because so often the space required
for such functions under present standards is too great to be
put "in a corner" of a large city park.   But many large city
parks are still extensive enough to encompass land required
for one or more of these functions and for the most part such
functions are not incompatible with the original idea of a large
city park.

Olmsted and Vaux set the pattern for the large city park
when they designed Central Park in New York City over a century ago.   As Olmsted himself once put it, "The kind of recreation that these large parks supply, and nothing but these large
parks supply, near a city, is that which a man insensibly obtains
when he puts the city behind him and out of his sight and goes
where he will be under the undisturbed influence of pleasing
natural scenery".

"Pleasing natural scenery" not being available at the site
of the proposed Central Park, it had to be reproduced by the
landscape artists' ingenuity.   The surface of the earth was

molded, trees and shrubs were planted, carriageways and paths constructed, service buildings placed in unobtrusive places, broad meadows and "parade grounds" provided to permit the feeling of countryside distances. The rules for the Central Park competition had provided that there should be a parade ground of from 20 to 40 acres, 3 playgrounds of from 3 to 10 acres each, and sites provided for a hall for exhibitions and concerts, a principal fountain, a Prospect tower, and a flower garden of from 2 to 3 acres.

One can understand from such descriptions that the mood of the large city park was one of sedate leisure, quiet contemplation, and when activities were provided for, they were not of the sports or competitive, noisy activities that might mar the landscape. Later, evolution in design brought to the large city park picnic areas, day camps, water activities, and such other innovations as would not disturb the relative tranquillity of the environment or mar the beauty and scope of the landscape. Such is still the theoretical nature of the large city park; unfortunately, competition for open space in large cities has reduced many former large city parks from spacious, landscaped parks to mammoth outdoor playgrounds.

With that sort of historical background in mind one can readily understand the difficulty of drawing a hard and fast line between the large city park and the park of special uses. Except for special purposes and for matters of verification, the two classifications might well be considered as one, using 7 acres per 1000 population as a standard for the combined classification.

The above classification includes parkways and boulevards which have a different background and in some respects, a different function. Parkways are roadways through parks or through such an environment as to constitute an elongated park. Boulevards have less horticultural embellishment, a more restricted right of way, and are like a grand tree-lined avenue. The function of boulevards is simply to provide an attractive way from one place to another. To some extent the same may be said for parkways, except that in the case of parkways there is a much greater degree of scenic and horticultural effectiveness about them.

As has been noted, the important function of parkways in the early plans for park systems of municipalities, was that of connecting one large park with another, providing a continuous, pleasant tour through and between parks. Not a few of the fine parkways of the country have since been debased by permitting on them commercial truck traffic as well as passenger traffic, and using them as general traffic ways rather than as a leisurely and pleasant way of getting from one place to another. * This has tended to restrict the introduction of parkways into new city plans. While parkways also were an important feature of some of the early and more famous county and metropolitan park systems, the use of parkways and boulevards in present day design for county park systems seems questionable, except bordering lakes and streams where they are effective in several ways. Rapid transit from home to regional or state parks along a system of adequate highways tends to be more significant than providing for slower and more leisurely ways of getting from home to the scene of our outdoor recreation desires except as noted.

However, on a much larger scale there has been built, and still being planned, national parkways traversing more or less continuous open country of pleasing scenery. These parkways have ample rights of way, do not follow a straight line, but tend to fit the landscape in pleasing curves both vertical and horizontal. They are built for leisurely driving and not for speed. Sometimes easement rights have been acquired beyond the right of way in order to preserve the adjacent territory in status quo.

With these general observations in mind, an attempt to apply these characteristics and classifications and standards to specific cases will prove interesting and revealing.

Standards Applied in Theory

In the accompanying diagram (Fig. 1), there is shown an 80,000 population city, three miles wide by five miles long, containing 15 square miles or 9,600 acres. The 80,000 population is assumed to be the potential maximum which the city will reach in approximately 25 years. If the standards for various types of recreation areas are applied to this city, the following would be the result:

Applying the standards to the foregoing yields these requirements:

Neighborhoods .... 1-2 acres per 1,000 = 80 x $1\frac{1}{2}$ = 120 acres
Playfields .... 1-2 acres per 1,000 = 80 x $1\frac{1}{2}$ = 120 acres
Large City Parks.... 5 acres per 1,000 = 80 x 5   = 400 acres
Special Use Areas... 2 acres per 1,000 = 80 x 2   = 160 acres
                                            Total.... 800 acres

*See "Future of Minneapolis Parkways and Boulevards" in Appendix.

Michigan State University
Dept. of Resource Development
Park Management
Winter Term 1961

A SYSTEM OF PARKS

LAID OUT ACCORDING TO STANDARDS

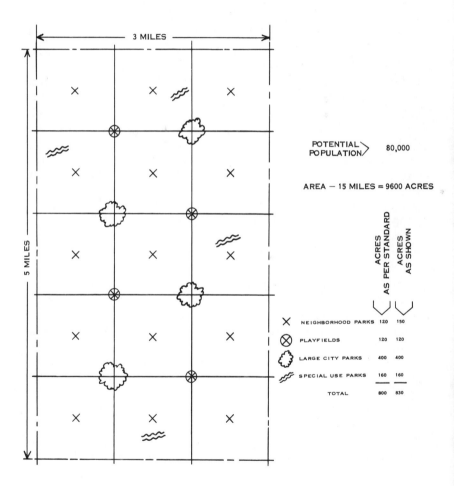

Figure 1

The total acreage arrived at in this manner is sometimes compared with 10 percent of the area of the city, which in this case is 960 acres. We, therefore, come to the conclusion that a park and recreation system properly distributed for this city of 80,000 ought to be somewhere between 800 and 960 acres in total.

Now, mark off our city of three miles wide by five miles in length into 15 equal areas each one mile square (Fig. 1). Since a neighborhood is to be presumed to be three quarters of a mile to a mile across, we can in this case assume 15 neighborhood parks at about 10 acres each or a total of 150 acres. Playfields are to serve two or more neighborhoods or an area from a mile and a half to two miles across. With 15 neighborhoods to accommodate, we can nicely assume that four playfields will satisfy the requirements yielding four times about 30 acres, or 120 acres. In the category of large city parks we require 400 acres and, since our diagram does not reveal any topographic or other features, we can assume about four such parks at 100 acres each or a total of 400 acres. In a similar manner, the special use parks we might assume to number about four at 40 acres each or a total of 160 acres. All this totals up to 830 acres which is within the requirements of 800 to 960 acres previously calculated.

Standards Applied to Actual Case

This assumed diagrammatic city very probably does not exist. To indicate the necessity of adjusting our ideals and compromising with the schedule of requirements, let us assume an actual city three miles wide and five miles long. The kind of map or maps which will be needed for our study of a park and recreation system include the following: a map showing the streets, the highways, the arterial streets as distinguished from ordinary residential streets; a map showing the topographical features, including vacant areas and wooded areas; a city master plan if it is available showing the future development of the city; maps indicating the locations of schools and a possible allocation of future school sites. All of the foregoing are basic and essential. If the study which we are about to undertake gets down to details, other factors become important. These include land values, characteristics of the population, local history, extent of ownership of facilities which may be used by a recreation service, the extent of museum and library services, and similar factors.

Michigan State University
Dept. of Resource Development
Park Management
Winter Term 1961

APPLICATION OF PARK STANDARDS

TO

SIMPLIFIED TOWNSITE

3 Miles By 5 Miles = 15 Sq. Mi. Potential Population = 80,000

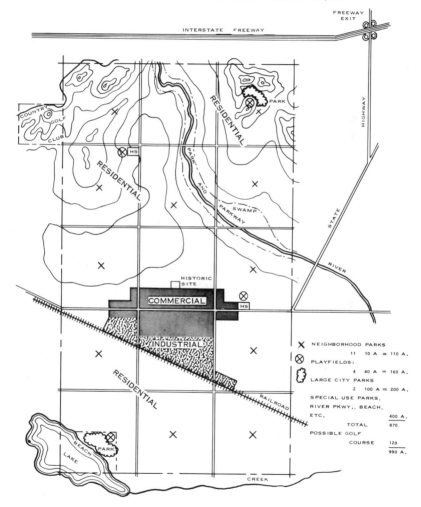

Figure 2

The fact that so much related material is necessary to intelligently explore the possibilities of a park and recreation system highlights the desirability of friendly and amicable relations with all the foregoing agencies that have to do with the matters in hand. It also points up the fact that the park administrator must be equipped with some general knowledge of the operation of the related functions which we have enumerated.

Figure No. 2 of our 15 square mile 80,000 population city has been drawn with some of the important features in it. For example, the state highway coming through the town, has been shown as well as the interstate freeway which by-passes the town. The assumption is made that each of the section lines will have rather important arterial streets on them. A central business section has been shown. A possible industrial area along side a railroad track has been shown; topographic features such as rivers, streams, lakes, a couple of hills, some wooded areas, country club, have also been indicated. But as a whole, the city has been drawn rather simply, leaving out a number of the more complicated and frustrating situations.

In selecting our park sites in this situation, we look first for those features which are of special scenic, topographical or historic interest or are otherwise unique; and secondly, those areas which may prove most beneficial for some special uses.

In the example shown in the diagram, the logical first step is to establish control of the river which flows through the town together with sufficient area in some locations to provide for a large city park. Secondly, we are assuming that the lake in the southwest corner of the city has some swimming beach possibilities and consequently, we set aside some area for that. Next, we find that at least two of the high schools have been located, and assuming that areas adjacent to them are available, we pick those out as being suitable for playfields. Inasmuch as we probably will need more than two playfields for the population, served by the two schools, we will tentatively locate one in the northeast section of the city. We have discovered the possibility of an additional playfield in the southwest part of the town primarily because of the intervening railroad which seems to separate approximately four square miles from the rest of the town.

In locating neighborhood parks, we encounter the usual situation that the neighborhoods are of neither uniform nor of standardized size, but still the situation is not complicated enough to prevent us from placing neighborhood parks in most of the square-mile neighborhoods of the town. It is assumed that these will be where elementary schools are located, but this is not always so.

Now, if a tentative summary is made, we find that we have eleven neighborhood parks at 10 acres each for about 110 acres; four playfields at about 30 acres each for 120 acres; we can assume that our park along the river is mostly parkway, and that there is a possibility of enlarging the area along the swimming beach to considerably more than is required for a beach alone, probably even enough to combine this with our playfield area so that the total of special use areas might be 400 acres or more. The northeast corner of the city, because of its interesting topography, provides the basis of a very interesting community study. This might disclose the possibility of a fairly large park together with a playfield with a portion set aside for a neighborhood park – all in one general territory, or all in one piece of land. Such a large park, in addition to the one in the southwest part of the city, could easily amount to a couple of hundred acres.

The matter of a golf course for the city is open to question. A country club has been located just outside of the city on the northwest section, and while this is privately owned and operated, it goes a long way towards satisfying the golfing demands for the city. If this course should be a privately owned public fee course, it would satisfy the wants of the city entirely. However, there is the bare possibility that a golf course may be desirable, and the people might be willing to pay for the cost of operation over and above the income from fees, the acquisition of which would add to the acreage set aside for special use parks. Incidentally, the northwest section of the city, adjacent to the country club, apparently has topographic features of enough interest to provide the basis of another very interesting study as to the development of the entire two or three square miles.

There is a small historic site adjacent to the central business district which needs to be preserved. While no neighborhood parks have been shown near the central business district, it is barely possible that there are enough living quarters of one kind or another – be they over commercial buildings or in apartment houses – to justify the location or the establishment of one or two playlots.

A breakdown of our total acreage now looks something like this:

Neighborhood parks....... 11 at 10 acres = 110 acres
Playfields .... 4 at 30 acres = 120 acres
Large parks .... 2 at 100 acres = 200 acres
Special use areas –
river parkway, pos-
sible golf course,
and others.............................. 520 acres
                          TOTAL...... 970 acres

If we compare this 970 acres and its breakdown to the 830-acre total of the idealized city of Diagram 1, it will be noted that we actually have exceeded our 10 percent of our gross area of the city; if the golf course, (which is a questionable item) is eliminated, we reduce the figure to approximately 850 acres which is not too far from the 830 acres of our idealized situation. However, comparing the two tabulations more in detail, we find that we have set aside less playground area, more playfield type area, and more large parks and special use area in our Diagram 2 than in Diagram 1. Were it not for the river parkway and the desirability of controlling the banks of the river and the existence of unusual topographic features in the northeast section of the city, and the bathing facilities at the lake southwest of the city, our condition would have been entirely changed and we probably would have less than 800 acres set aside for park purposes.

Value of Standards

The foregoing discussion shows that precise application of accepted standards is impractical; deviations are necessary to secure and preserve natural topographic features and to adjust for odd shaped neighborhoods and interfering but essential elements of the city plan. The deviations are not great enough to destroy the essential validity of the standards and yet their application should be flexible enough to allow for differences in population density, (more about this later), unusual amount of scenic topography, and unusual extent of commercial and industrial development and other similar peculiarities of a given city. In the final appraisal of its worth, a park and recreation system must be adequate enough to serve the recreation needs of the people and extensive and attractive enough to enhance the aesthetic, social and economic values of the city.

In summary, let it be said concerning park classifications and corresponding standards that however inexact they may be, how general the need is for modifications in applying them, how subject they may be to criticism because of the unscientific way in which they have been compiled and the empirical experiences on which most reliance is placed, there is enough inherent merit to them to justify a high place in the list of tools which are used in evaluating and planning a park and recreation system. Classifications and schedules of standards are essential to the park administrator.

The Suburbs

As was previously stated, the 80,000 population city just studied (with all its urban area within the city's corporate limits) has not included "a number of the more complicated and frustrating situations". Let us now explore some of these complications while we examine the situation in the suburbs, keeping in mind that suburbs have much the same physical characteristics as the city except that any one suburb may not contain all the characteristics of the city. The population of a suburb is smaller. The area may or may not be less, the density of population differs, some suburbs are almost exclusively residential, others almost wholly industrial. Collectively, the suburbs may be much like the city or conversely the city much like the collection of suburbs if the city were broken up into a number of separate governmental units, each with its own independent municipal services.

Many metropolitan areas of the country which have taken their names from the central city are actually aggregations of a number of municipalities, composed of the central city and a number of satellite towns and villages usually known as suburbs. Even these suburban communities have attached onto themselves other towns and villages of like characteristics. Annexations of suburbs by the central city is reasonably simple in some parts of the country where the demand for adequate water supply and other situations invoke the necessity of amalgamation, but there are other areas of the country in which there is no such inducement and where the feeling of local autonomy is very strong and where the destiny of each of the satellite towns and villages rests upon its own resources. The application of park standards to some of these individual localities and to a number of them taken collectively reveals a situation much more complex than that of cities. We are dealing

Michigan State University
Dept. of Resource Development
Park Management
Winter Term 1961

ARRANGEMENT OF SUBURBS
ABOUT THE CENTRAL CITY

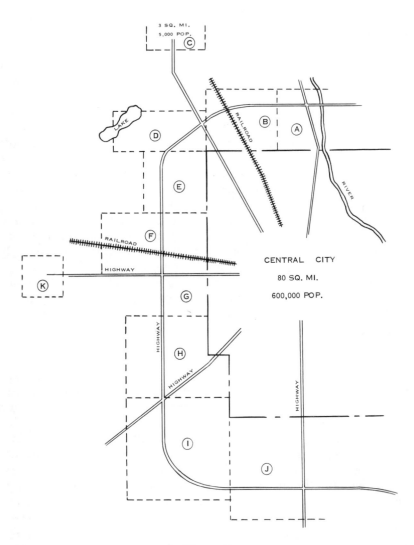

Figure 3

with a much more complicated jurisdictional structure than the central city.

There has been prepared, and included herein, a diagram of a portion of the outlying district adjoining a central city. (Figure 3). It is assumed that the central city has a population of one-half million or more. Towns and villages have been shown on the outskirts of the central city; these towns and villages are of various sizes and characteristics. A table has been prepared showing the probable area of parks in the various classifications which would reasonable take care of the park and recreation service required of each of those towns and villages. (Table No. I, p. 43 and No. II, p. 43.) Some of the figures contained therein prove to be interesting.

It will be observed that the table shows there is not the same number of neighborhoods in towns of equal population. This comes about by reason of the character of the town itself. Some of the communities are heavily industrialized and commercialized while others are predominantly or wholly of the residential character. Some of the towns have distinctive features brought about by other circumstances. Consequently, variations of figures attributed to towns of comparable population size must be taken for granted by the student. It can be authoritatively stated that the circumstances resulting in the tabulation are not farfetched but are quite realistic. In other words, the situation revealed here is quite usual.

Now in judging the adequacy of some of these park and recreation systems, it is well to give some thought to a few additional generalized standards in order to illustrate the points to be made. The *National Recreation Association has suggested for neighborhood parks and community playfields 1 acre of each for each 800 population. This differs slightly but not materially from the Dallas table heretofore reproduced. In addition to the foregoing, NRA suggests the following standards:

1 baseball diamond for each 6000 population
1 softball diamond for each 3000 population
1 tennis court for each 2000 population
1 hole of golf for each 3000 population
15 square feet of swimming pool or beach wading area for each 1 to 3 per cent of the total population (a 50 by 165 foot pool having an area of 8000 to 9000 square feet would accommodate a population of about 20,000.)

* National Recreation Association has now been absorbed by the National Recreation and Park Association, 1700 Pennsylvania Ave. N. W., Washington, D. C. 20006.

A selection from the following group of facilities should be provided at the rate of 1 for each 1500 population:

Archery range	Hard surfaced, multiple
Boccie court	use areas
Bowling greens	Roque courts
Fields for soccer, foot-	Shuffleboard courts
ball, field hockey, etc.	Shooting ranges
Handball courts	Golf driving ranges

A selection from the following group of facilities should be provided at the rate of 1 for each 2500 population:

Bicycle trails	Recreation piers
Bridle paths	Ski jumps
Boating facilities	Toboggan slides
Casting pools	Tracks, running, skating
Ice skating areas	or bicycles
Model yacht basins	Wading pools
Picnic centers	Yacht harbors

A selection from the following special recreation features should be provided at the rate of 1 for each 10,000 population:

Band shell	Nature trail
Botanical garden	Outdoor theater
Camp	Arboretum
Community garden	Stadium seating 1000 or
	more

A neighborhood in a central city with single family dwellings on 50 fool lots will contain 6000 to 8000 people. According to the standards previously enumerated, it should have a neighborhood park of about 8 to 10 acres. This is sufficient to justify, too, a baseball diamond, two softball diamonds, three tennis courts, and a number of other things. Suppose now we have a 1 square mile neighborhood in the suburbs with only 3000 population, requiring theoretically only 4 acres of ground for a neighborhood park. We are now limited to 1 softball field, 1 tennis court, and no baseball fields. Such a limitation of acreage has several disadvantages:

√ The size itself is too small to permit sufficient embellishment to raise the play area from a neighborhood nuisance to one which enhances property values.

√ The elimination of a baseball diamond is open to question. Its elimination tends to limit the use of the neighborhood park to a lower age group, probably under thirteen or fourteen years of age. While it is true that the older children can go some distance for full-sized regulation ballfields, it is also true that for full neighborhood use the athletic fields are used for more than just athletics. Most of the other essential facilities can probably be provided in the more commodious private yards.

√ The construction of a single tennis court is more expensive than the construction of tennis courts in batteries of two or more.

Altogether, it would seem that 4 acres is really too small an area for a neighborhood, even though the neighborhood is of low density population. Although there are lots and lots of neighborhood parks that are of no more than 4 acres in extent, this is hardly a goal to shoot at. Our minimum ought to be closer to twice that figure. Failing that, the variety of uses provided for should be so limited as to permit enough lawn and plantings to make it pleasing in appearance.

A neighborhood in a section of the city which is wholly built up in multiple dwellings, particularly large apartment buildings, might have a square mile population of 30,000 or 40,000 people. This would call for a neighborhood park of over 30 acres. Theoretically there should be six baseball fields, 10 or more softball fields, 16 or more tennis courts, and other items in proportion. In addition thereto, we now have a population to contend with which is sufficient to support a full-size community center building with probably two gymnasiums. Applying our theoretical standards to a situation of this kind will produce design problems of great complexity and the cost of acquisition of the land in places that would in all probability be prohibitive. This is an example of the other extreme of the effect of population density.

The foregoing two examples are sufficient to indicate that both density of population and area requirements for facilities present problems of necessary deviation from the application of general standards that apply to the average.

It takes a population of approximately 20,000 to justify adequate expenditure for major swimming facilities. In the case of isolated towns in the plains states of the country, or in arid regions, lesser populations can frequently support a swimming pool. But normally, in satellite towns and villages, as well as in built-up areas of any urban community, it usually requires 20,000 to justify a 50' x 165' swimming pool. Consequently, in suburban communities of 10,000 to 15,000, there is little justification in setting aside areas for swimming pools which normally are included in the playfield type of park.

Playfields themselves are justified when two or more neighborhoods are involved, preferably, three or four neighborhoods. Residential neighborhoods vary in population from 3,000 to 10,000; consequently, in a 15,000 to even 20,000 population town the establishment of playfields can be doubtful. Generally speaking, playfields with community center buildings in them can be justified only with population extending from 30,000 to 50,000.

Eighteen-hole golf courses are not justifiable except for populations ranging from 60,000 to 100,000.

Large city parks of a size justifying the name can extend for a mile and a half to three miles away from the center of population. Therefore, in towns smaller in area than three to five miles across, the desirability and the necessity of establishing large park areas is doubtful. On the other hand, some towns of the above size may have unusual amounts of natural recreation possibilities – lake and river shores which ought to be publicly owned but cannot be locally justified.

Summarizing the factors that cause deviations from the general standards, the following may be considered some of the more usual causes:

√ Density of population.

√ Facility area requirements, the shape of neighborhoods, neighborhood physical characteristics such as possible changes in zoning, the effect of rehabilitation and redevelopment programs, topography, land values.

√ Neighborhood population characteristics such as age groups and the trend of change, traditional and ethnic background, racial characteristics.

√ Climatic conditions. This has a close relationship to geographic location which in turn affects some of the factors in neighborhood population characteristics.

√ Permanence of other community recreation assets such as churches, schools, volunteer agencies, such as YMCA's, Scouts, and so forth.

√ Private and commercial recreation — their relative permanence and community effectiveness.

The foregoing should suffice to indicate why there is an absence of some of the park classes listed in the accompanying tabulations. When we consider that no mention has been made of such occasional and distinctive features of large cities that are usually absent in the suburbs such as municipal stadiums,

TABLE I

PROBABLE STATISTICS OF SUBURBS SHOWN IN FIGURE 3

(Arranged alphabetically)

Suburbs	Area Sq. Miles	Potential Population	Neighborhood Parks Number /Acreage	Playfields	Large City Parks	Sp.Use Parks	Total Acres Theory	Total Acres Actual
A	7	24,000	5/50	2/40	1/120	1/48	240	258
B	10-1/2	38,000	4/40	2/60	x	1/30	380	130
C	3	8,000	1/15	x	x	x	80	15
D	6	20,000	4/40	1/30	100	100	200	170
E	7	24,000	4/40	1/40	x	1/50	240	130
F	13	44,000	10/100	2/60	200	200	440	360
G	4	10,000	2/30	x	x	x	100	30
H	14	48,000	10/100	3/100	2/200	1/80	480	480
I	20	65,000	15/120	4/120	2/200	2/150	650	590
J	48	100,000	25/250	7/210	2/400	2/200	1000	1060
K	3	7,000	2/30	x	x	x	70	30
Actual		388,000	805 acres	660 acres	1070 a.	708 a.		3253
Theory			582 acres	582 acres	1940 a.	776 a.	3880	

ACTUAL EXCESS ACTUAL SHORTAGE

Standards
Neighborhood Parks	1 to 2 acres per 1000 population
Playfields	1 to 2 " " " "
Large City Parks	5 " " " "
Special Use Parks	2 " " " "
TOTAL	10 " " " "

TABLE II

PROBABLE STATISTICS OF SUBURBS SHOWN IN FIGURE 3

(Arranged according to population size)

Suburbs	Area Sq. Miles	Potential Population	Neighborhood Parks Number Acreage	Playfields	Large City Parks	Sp.Use Parks	Total Acres Theory	Total Acres Actual
K	3	7,000	2/30	x	x	x	70	30
C	3	8,000	1/15	x	x	x	80	15
G	4	10,000	2/30	x	x	x	100	30
D	6	20,000	4/40	1/30	100	100	200	170
A	7	24,000	5/50	2/40	1/120	1/48	240	258
E	7	24,000	4/40	1/40	50	50	240	130
B	10-1/2	38,000	4/40	2/60	x	1/30	380	130
F	13	44,000	10/100	2/60	200	200	440	360
H	14	48,000	10/100	3/100	2/200	1/80	480	480
I	20	65,000	15/120	4/120	2/200	2/150	650	590
J	48	100,000	25/250	7/210	2/400	2/200	1000	1060

large outdoor amphitheaters, museums of various kinds, zoos, planetariums, aquariums, arboretums, horticultural conservatories, marinas, we can understand why small cities have fewer purposes for the establishment of park and recreation areas than do large cities. It is an anomaly, but a fact, that the larger the city, the larger per capita area that should be devoted to parks and recreation, and that the larger the city, the larger amount of money that should be spent per capita.

The accompanying tabulation according to size of suburb (Table II) leads us to conclude that cities under 25,000 can do little more than provide neighborhood parks. Yet, if we total the entire population of the surrounding towns and villages, we find that the total is more than half that of the city. In fact, if we totaled the population of all of the towns and villages completely surrounding the city, we might find that the population was more than that of the central city. Collectively, these suburban towns require the same sort of service that is encountered in the city; however, if there are a number of towns under 25,000 population, we are bound to be deficient in all categories of park areas above the neighborhood level. In less than 50,000 population, there is going to be a deficiency of everything above the playfield type of area. In the total suburban complex, there is bound to be a deficiency of areas set aside for park and recreation purposes, and yet, every citizen in every part of the urban area of this metropolis ought to have access to the same sort of park and recreation service.

Something akin to this situation sometimes prevails between the central city and any one or all of the suburbs. In the initial stages of development, the central city is often disposed to act as a tolerant parent to the suburbs in helping them plan their development in many ways, but as time goes on, the "children" become numerous and tend to "grow up" taking advantage of the facilities in the central city which they cannot provide for themselves. "Parents" get tired of being imposed upon and retaliation sets in. Shall the central city shoulder the entire cost of such metropolitan facilities as zoos and other of the big city park facilities enumerated above?

Will schools help? School districts usually are not coterminous with suburban areas. This comes about because of the early establishment of school districts encompassing enough area of sparse population to justify the construction of a school. Children are probably transported to the school in the first instance and the school buildings are built upon land which is oriented and intended, exclusively, for educational purposes.

Because school boundaries do overlap into more than one suburb, there does exist a possible vehicle for community coordination between villages. Sometimes this happens in the early
stages of a recreation program where a school district employs
a part-time or even full-time recreation leader and conducts
the recreation program for the entire school district. The
long-range effectiveness of such an operation, however, is
quite limited, for it does not satisfy the situation of park area
or of proximity to the individual neighborhoods. A large school
might go a little way towards satisfying some of the requirements of the community center building, but the total athletic
requirements of the community exceed that required by the
educational process both in quantity and in extent. Even indoor
swimming pools established for the physical education program
of the schools are generally far too inadequate in size to care
for the requirement of 20,000 people. The fact is too, that the
actual pool is only part of the recreational value of pool sites.
Utilization of school districts to accomplish any degree of cooperation between the suburbs is without much long range hope.

It would appear that political organization on a metropolitan or urban basis, encompassing the central city and all of
its suburbs, might solve our difficulty. A few experimentations
along that line are proceeding, but the results, so far, are in-
conclusive.

Our hope, then, may have to rest upon the possibility that
a regional park system could take up the slack and supplement
for the suburban towns those services which the individual cities
and villages cannot seem to provide. Unquestionably, this is
going to produce some complications in finance and some pretty
neat maneuvering on the part of pressure groups within these
communities. There is liable to be considerable heeing and
hawing in spite of the fact that the vehicle seems to be present.
It is barely possible that this function is one which might be
assigned to the regional or metropolitan park systems, a subject which we are now about to embark upon.

CHAPTER 3 THE COUNTRY'S PHYSICAL RECREATION RESOURCES— THE METROPOLITAN AND COUNTY

"The great towns are rapidly overgrowing and destroying the scenes of natural beauty adjacent to them. People escaping from the towns are as rapidly occupying for private purposes the remoter spots of special beauty."

Charles Eliot
Boston, 1891

Preliminary and Historical

Three-fourths of this country's population will soon be concentrated in metropolitan complexes ranging in size from 50,000 people to many millions of people. For quite a long time people have been migrating to the metropolitan centers in quest of the benefits which mass markets and mass opportunities offer. At the same time there has been a mass movement away from the core of the metropolis to the suburban periphery in an attempt to gain more of what was insufficient or lacking in the central city: space, quiet, peace, and privacy. Slowly at first, the urban area merely expanded to the open country side, except for the expensive country villas and estates of the wealthy which used the more carefully chosen scenic and probably more remote locations. Recently a much more accelerated movement of a different pattern (or patterns) has characterized the expansion — something like a seething couldron of viscous and boiling fluid that spatters large globs of stuff outside and away from the kettle's edge. Each glob forms a separate self-contained community of homes and businesses, and each glob, in turn, overflows to fill up surrounding vacant space. Sometimes the pattern is that of a fissured container releasing rivers of stuff to flow along the paths of arterial highways, at intervals forming nodules that are the centers for homes and business; these, too, expand to urbanize adjacent vacant space.

Accompanying this massive population adjustment has been the development of non-urban park systems, each arising in its time and place to fulfill a current local need. Because the precise needs were evident at different places and in different decades it should be apparent that there was no standardized form or even a common motivation for the formation of each. These park systems are caught up in an evolutionary process that now commands our attention in this chapter. A quick look at some of the more significant of these systems is a good starting point.

Some Typical Systems

First note that a county, metropolitan, or regional park system is known by any one of a number of names; for example, regional park systems, metropolitan park systems, county forest preserves, park districts, park reserve districts, regional park and planning commissions, and metropolitan authorities. Each name is an attempt to distinguish each from a city park system and, at the same time, to provide a name that will characterize the objective of the service to be offered. Regardless of variations in primary purposes, each does attempt to provide a recreation service somewhere between that offered by the city and that offered by the state.

The earliest such system was the metropolitan park system of Boston, which was established as a sort of made work project in the early 1890's. For several years, the noted landscape architect, Charles Eliot, had been badgering public authorities on the subject of preserving for public use some of the fine areas about Boston (and in New England generally), which were very rapidly being purchased by individuals for the establishment of private mansions and estates. The many arguments he advanced in support of his views can be profitably reviewed by present day conservationists, so appropriate do they seem. The primary purpose of a system of metropolitan parks (the system included parkways for pleasing access) was to preserve some of the best naturally scenic and topographic features of the Boston environment. It should be kept in mind that in Eliot's day and from his personal viewpoint only undisturbed nature was the antidote for the damaged health and spiritual well being of city inhabitants. The contaminations of foul air, polluted streams, and unsavory city slums are still with us.

Within a year or so of the establishment of the Boston Metropolitan Park System, the first county park system was established in Essex County, New Jersey. The purpose here was somewhat different than the Boston system. The Essex system was to provide for all the park needs of the entire county including its cities and towns. This purpose should be kept in mind for as matters developed in later years, it might have been well for all counties having metropolitan potential to adopt the same type of managerial authority, thus obviating to some extent the difficulties encountered by the systems of peripheral suburbs which became attached to growing cities. However, it was not until a half century had passed that this virtue was generally realized, and by that time some of the shortcomings of the first type of county systems had developed, as noted later herein.

Adjacent to Essex County is Union County; its county park system was established thirty years after the Essex system but it had the same general authority and purpose. Active recreation services by this time had become an accepted responsibility of cities so Union County supplies such services as horseback riding, bridle trails and horse stables, skeet and trap shooting, day camping, skating ponds and winter sports centers, nature trails and small nature museums. Like the Essex system, Union County supplies the park and recreation needs of the whole county including its cities, but cursory examination leads one to believe that much more attention has been given to non-urban service leaving its principle city of Elizabeth sparsely supplied with urban facilities. Likewise, Essex County has left its principle city of Newark in a similar situation. In 1965, Essex County had 5151 acres of parks for one million people; Union County had 5031 acres for 530,000 people; statistics in both cases include cities.

Following the establishment of a few other such systems prior to 1900, little was done toward the establishment of regional park systems until approximately 1920, to use a convenient date.

In some states, permissive legislation had been passed by means of which the organization of park districts was encouraged. The park district law of Illinois was an old one and there, park districts were organized about almost any individual park – actually any district of less than 500,000 population. At one time, Chicago had in excess of 20 such districts which later were combined into one Chicago Park District. However, other districts involved not only municipal parks but large parks and sometimes systems of parks along the streams and throughout the countryside. The law permits (1) Park Districts, (2) Pleasure Parkway and Park Districts, and (3) Township Parks.

Ohio has a park district law permitting the establishment of regional park districts. Perhaps the most important of such

Ohio Districts are those of Cleveland Metropolitan Park District and the Akron Metropolitan Park District, but there are others of similar importance.

Being on the south shore of Lake Erie, Cleveland services a population which is spread out in a semicircle to the south. Following a definite plan for the metropolitan park district, a number of rather large-sized parks were established in a rough semicircular route about the city. It was intended that these large parks would be connected by parkways and several important stretches of the parkways were actually constructed. It will be noted that this sort of pattern was not unlike the pattern of the large city parks of the previous generations. The individual parks were chosen for their scenic and topographic interest and were intended to supply a demand for native reservations and native landscapes, together with the ordinary means by which such features could be enjoyed, that is, roadways, hiking trails, particularly hiking trails with nature study evidence throughout the entire route, nature museums, and similar facilities. Provision was made for a certain amount of camping; certain volunteer agencies such as Boy Scouts, Kiwanis Clubs, and so forth, were permitted to build their own structures on various sites in some of the parks, a practice later regretted and discontinued. The 1965 acreage is 17,000 and population is 1.7 million.

The park system of Westchester County, New York, drew nation-wide attention when it was developed in the early twenties. (It was created in 1922.) Some of the distinguishing features of it included the elimination of dumps and neglected and polluted areas along the streams leading through Westchester County down to Long Island Sound. The establishment of parkways along these river banks, the establishment of large parks in which were developed recreation areas similar to that of large city parks, as well as the purchase of large native tracts in the more remote sections of the county established the Westchester system as having the characteristics of a model city system on a county scale. The purchase and rehabilitation of an old amusement park at Rye, New York, its redesign and operation, set a model for such amusement areas, both public and private. At the time of its establishment, it was the first and only such area in the park systems of the country. Some of its features have since been incorporated in other parks, but so far none has equaled the operation at Rye.

Certainly the system at Westchester went much farther in some respects than any similar metropolitan system had previously attempted. The man-made parks of a large city park character, including swimming pools, athletic fields, children's playgrounds, and similar recreational facilities, was more a transplant of city facilities into the county than any regional park system had previously attempted. The parkways along the Hutchinson River, Sawmill River, and Bronx River were models of its kind, and the transformation of poor property into attractive park areas created considerable additional private property values and highlighted the effect of creating such valued by the establishment of parks and parkways.

In more recent years, Westchester has been squeezed in at least two directions which has altered the picture considerably. The parkways, being such convenient facilities for traffic into and out of New York City, have, to a large degree, become passenger trafficways rather than parkways, and in 1961, the Hutchinson River, Sawmill River, and Cross County Parkways were turned over to a state agency. The tug of war between the county and the municipalities within the county as to who is to support what in the way of recreation has caused a downgrading of the recreational features in some of the large parks. In some cases playgrounds have actually been removed because of the unwillingness of the county to maintain facilities for the benefit of nearby cities. The use of some of the golf courses in the county parks is now restricted to residents of the county in order to reduce or eliminate the influx of New Yorkers. Fees have been established for the use of picnic areas with some discrimination in the amount of the fee in favor of Westchester County residents. These and similar factors have tended to downgrade what originally seemed a fine example of applying to the county the principles of city park requirements in vogue during and immediately following the Olmsted era. In 1965 Westchester County had 11,658 acres of parks for 950,000 people.

The Cook County Forest Preserve about the city of Chicago has adopted and pretty well adhered to a definite land policy. This is not called a park system, but a system of preserves – forest preserves to be more exact. In 1965 it encompassed 54,089 acres for $5\frac{1}{2}$ million people. It almost encircles the city of Chicago. It has followed a consistent course of acquiring forests wherever they were, preserving those areas and rehabilitating many with additional forest plantings. They have kept facilities for active use to a minimum, largely to picnicking, nature trails, bridle paths, some wayside developments, and a very few athletic fields. Sometimes the latter have been close to adjacent villages and towns, but officially the department insists that these areas have been located not with reference to the town locations but to the use of all of Cook County.

Perhaps no system has been as diligent and probably none quite so successful as Cook County in adhering to its original policies of forest preserves. While this has appeared to the officials and residents of Cook County as being the major purpose and justification for the establishment of this system, the officials and students of urban development are inclined to think that a by-product which was originally unforeseen, may now equal in importance the original purpose. Reference is made to the Green Belt area, for it so happens that the location of the forest preserves are in such geographical shape as to form almost a continuous belt of forest preserve properties about Chicago. Its function in interrupting the continuous urbanization of land outside of the city of Chicago is looked upon as something of great merit. Incidentally, one can almost compare this with the situation in Cleveland where their system is often given the name of the "Green Necklace of Cleveland". Cleveland's is not nearly as extensive in width as that of Cook County nor does it cover such a long stretch as Chicago's.

The city of Milwaukee for a long time has concentrated many people in a relatively small area. Quite early in its history, a large number of suburban towns were attached to the rim of Milwaukee so that the urban metropolis was far greater than the city proper. At one time the city of Milwaukee had about a thousand or eleven hundred acres of park land for a six hundred thousand population. Milwaukee County established a county park system in 1907, but its major developments took place in earnest in the 1920's.

The original planners planned well in acquiring a number of large park areas and developed a fine system of parkways. The developments within these large park areas were not dissimilar from the old type large city parks with their well-designed, horticulturally improved scenes and garden-like devices. Swimming pools were frequent. Today, the Milwaukee County park system which in recent years absorbed the park system of the city of Milwaukee (and all other incorporated towns in the county) has more of the characteristics of an urban system than of a regional system. All of Milwaukee County is now incorporated into towns and not much is not urbanized. The whole county is now virtually one metropolis served by one park department. It contained 12,836 acres for 1,109,460 people in 1965.

Geographically, Los Angeles is a mess. On occasion, its frontiers reach out in long tentacles between well built-up adjacent towns and villages; in some cases the city completely surrounds other towns and in still other cases patches of the county still remain completely surrounded by the city. In such a situation, a division of jurisdictions and jurisdictional functions is complicated. It is not surprising, therefore, that the ownership of the individual parks anywhere in the urban area of Los Angeles is a continual source of curiosity to the visitor. Many of the county parks are no different than city parks and perform the same functions. Generally speaking, the systems of the county and the city tend to complement each other in providing recreational service. The county is attempting to acquire the larger park areas to supplement the systems of the smaller cities of the county in cases where the local governments "can't afford it".

The Maryland National Capital Park and Planning Commission has planning and zoning functions as well as the responsibility of providing parks for two counties adjacent to the District of Columbia. Certain acts of Congress have facilitated the acquisition of stream beds leading into the District. Otherwise, the Commission properties have characteristics similar to the large parks and local playgrounds of a city system.

Detroit is a city typical of a number of American cities that did not keep pace with its growing population with enough parks after the Olmsted-Eliot era. By 1965 it had only 5848 acres for its 1,671,062 inhabitants, less than four acres per thousand. Some years ago, Wayne County in which Detroit is located formed a park system under a Michigan law that permits county boards of supervisors to establish park systems. By 1965 it had 4330 acres to help offset the inadequacy of Detroit's system, but that still was not enough. Under a special legislative act five counties (including Wayne) banded together to set up the Huron-Clinton Metropolitan Authority. It has 13,532 acres, but in the meantime population in the five counties has grown to 4,200,000. Even though the many suburbs have added their own systems to the total, making an estimated 27,000 acres, the ratio of parks still is only about six acres per thousand population. This is an example of rapid expansion of park acreage in a metropolitan complex barely keeping pace with the population – running fast to stand still. And the Huron-Clinton system has some fine properties containing swimming, fishing, boating, golf, picnicking and a number of large city park facilities in a more native environment than Detroit can possibly provide, even at the nationally famous Bell Isle Park.

A few more regional park systems are of significance. San Francisco-Oakland area has its East Bay Regional Park District that has added enough acreage in recent years to bring its total to 25,000 acres, serving a population of 2,500,000. This system is largely of a native character but by no means exclusively so. Phoenix, Arizona, has its Maricopa County system of mostly mountain parks with the impressive acreage of 91,538 acres. The Muskingum Conservancy District of Ohio, as its name implies, is a native area of 52,000 acres featuring the ecology of animals and birdlife. There are a number of other rather large and locally important park systems of the regional category, but the foregoing sufficiently illustrate the scope of purpose and cause of development of these systems.

Comments on Typical Systems

Perhaps the characteristic most common to all of these systems is that they were conceived and established for a recreation purpose that the founders believed answered a current or potential need in each of the local situations. They were opportunistic in conception, individual in purpose, and individual in design. They were needed, each in its own way, and built and operated to fulfill a current vacancy in recreation service. That vacancy represented services which the incorporated cities and villages either could not or would not provide. The demand led to a vehicle outside the cities and the urbanized periphery.

In almost all cases, the underlying service that county and regional parks attempt to supply, is a sense of spaciousness which is difficult to provide in a completely urban environment. The functions are akin to those of large city parks such as Olmsted saw them to be plus a more recent development of the large city parks as the setting for a wide variety of special uses and attractions such as museum sites, sports stadiums, cultural complexes, arboretums and floral conservatories, and so on.

Olmsted conceived the large city park "in and near" a city (Central Park was then on the outskirts of New York) as a piece of native landscape in which peace and quiet could be experienced in distinct relief from city conditions. As large and as well designed as was Central Park, it could not fully retain its original purpose in spite of the many heroic measures taken by its past administrators to "save" it. The dense population of its environs were inadequately supplied with recreation

grounds and of necessity overflowed ˙ɪɪto the park, upsetting
its previous restricted purpose and design. To a more or less
extent this typifies the large city parks laid out in the Olmstedian era extending into the first decade of the twentieth century.
Extensive native areas, never extensive enough for present day
mobility of person, are fast dwindling in our growing cities to
make room for more sophisticated uses and a more "polished"
type of maintenance. Most of them are not extensive enough
to harbor modern zoological gardens or any of the wide variety
of special uses previously mentioned without complete usur-
pation of native scenery. Moreover, many of these special
facilities require a broader base of financial support than can
be supplied by only one of a large number of municipalities
comprising the entire metropolis. These trends call for a
county or regional park authority.

The great future population increase is predicted to take
place in metropolitan centers, which means that present centers will expand to encompass present regional park systems.
Therefore the county and regional park systems must be viewed
as parts of potential city systems. Presumably, but not always
the case, neighborhood parks and community playfields will be
provided by the local suburban towns and cities, so that the
regional systems would be supplying only the large city parks.
It is only logical that regional parks be endowed with those facilities, which were inadequately provided for in our present
cities; enough land in each park to provide large native areas
that can be "preserved" and enough land that can be developed
for active and special uses without disturbing extensive native
scenery.

Area Required

In the discussion of rule of thumb requirements for a city
park system a ratio of acres of land to population was set at
ten acres per thousand population.   The present discussion
seems to say that this ratio is not enough expecially for large
city parks, and in some respects it is not.   The ratio is adequate only if the city system is supplemented by a regional park
system that has a ratio high enough to compensate for the inevitable future "squeeze" of the city parks and at the same
time provide a future metropolitan population expansion with
an adequacy to satisfy a future generation.   This means not
only ten acres per thousand population for regional parks (as
is the case for cities) but somewhat more, in order to have the

extensiveness for native environment and other special developments. The required ratio is more like fifteen to twenty acres per thousand population in addition to whatever is required for neighborhood and community facilities that local suburbs do not provide for themselves.

The size of these parks ought to be in hundreds or thousands of acres rather than in tens of acres.

The area to be served should be a metropolitan area regardless of political subdivisions, if at all possible. Under present circumstances of traffic a distance of 25 to 30 miles from the center of the metropolitan area should be a sufficient distance outward.

The land acquired should have the characteristics of uniqueness in scenery, history, archaeology, geology, and the scientific values as much as possible. But if the native areas are not conveniently located, other areas must be acquired and the native characteristics which are missing must be supplied by human hands.

Stream valleys and other topographic or scenic features should determine parkway locations, if they are provided at all.

A System of Classification and Use Zoning

Like city parks, regional parks serve several purposes and are subject to classification as are city parks. In the city systems described in Chapter 2 it will be observed that functional classification has the earmarks of a system of use zoning. Neighborhood parks and community playfields are planned to fit certain compatible situations – those found in specific neighborhoods and communities of neighborhoods. With reasonable attention to administration, the uses will automatically be consistent with the design. The uses of the large city parks will also be consistent with its planned purposes so long as the administration does not misinterpret demand for additional functions and space as a demand for substitute uses that need a home of their own. This principle of design by zoning is applicable to other park systems – regional, state, and federal.

A logical classification of county or regional properties may be as follows:

1. The large reservation of native land containing 1000 or more acres. These may be zoned according to intensity of use, e. g. (a) Native sanctuaries which are rarely invaded and in which native ecology is to be maintained as much as possible, (b) Native areas for light intensity use – trails for hiking,

horseback riding, for nature centers, very light picnicking and camping, (c) Intense day time use for swimming and boating, intense picnicking and similar active recreation. Only about one-fifth of the total area would be subject to development for intense use.

    2. Recreation areas or parks. These are in the hundreds of acres in size – They may be largely developed for active day time use but with a native environment predominant. These may be closer to the urban areas than the reservations.

    3. Special use parks include any of the numerous facilities mentioned previously such as zoos, stadiums, museums, cultural complexes, all of which are located after special study of the factors involved in such undertakings.

    4. Parkways or scenic highways are really part of No. 3 but with special park-like characteristics. These will be discussed more explicitly in the following chapters.

    5. Historical parks of no particular size except large enough to encompass the items of historical significance without crowding; of course, they occur where history was made.

Parkways and Boulevards *

Boulevard – Originally the flat top of a rampart, hence a broad avenue or thoroughfare.

Parkway – A broad thoroughfare beautified with trees and turf.

    These brief definitions found in a College Dictionary need a little more clarification according to professional park people:

    A parkway is a roadway through a park or a roadway with a generous enough right of way to permit park-like embellishment so that it looks like a park.

    A boulevard has a much more limited right-of-way but it too is beautified by turf and trees but is more like a grand avenue than an elongated park.

    To be part of a park system, both parkway and boulevard must carry only non-commercial vehicles.

    A third form of park-like thoroughfare that has recently come into prominence is the scenic highway. It passes through attractive native scenery and differs from a parkway in that

* See Minneapolis Parkway, p. 237 of Appendix
  Also Eliot, p. 248 and Mumford, p. 251.

mixed traffic – commercial and non-commercial – are permitted because it is a part of the highway system. As discussed later, closer study has emphasized some of the weaknesses of the boulevards of the Olmsted era.

Parkways and boulevards were the sinews that bound together the Olmstedian parks to form a unified park system. After seventy-five years or more, the sinews have become frayed, broken, and their binding power too often is only in name. Those that remain vigorous are along streams and lake shores, yet the idea of a system of park-like ways strongly persists in the minds of planners. A new factor that adds spark to the parkway embers is a realization that automobile driving for pleasure is the most frequently used form of recreation. Since this was noted in the ORRC report of 1962, every state highway department has been instructed to map out a system of state scenic highways. The National Park Service has planned both state and national scenic highways – some have been constructed. The idea is a carry-over from the old parkway systems of the cities, but with important differences.

The differences come about because of changed design factors and high cost of lengthened right-of-way. Travel on the old parkways and boulevards was at a horse's pace of 5 to spurts of 15 miles an hour. Sharp curves, short forward as well as side vision meant meager rights-of-way. Even in the early twenties, when parkways were often used in county and regional systems, speeds of 25 to 35 miles per hour were common. Today the speeds are twice that; both horizontal and vertical curves must be lengthened accordingly. This is all very admirably explained in the excellent chapter on highways in the book, Man-Made America, by Tunnard of Yale and Pushkarev of Regional Plan Association of New York.

Some of the old boulevards were no more than 100 feet wide. Their apparent "grandeur" induced the construction of fine residences, mansions and first class apartment buildings fronting on them. Time depreciated the environment and mixed traffic did the rest to reduce the boulevard to an ordinary city street. Parkways fared better where their scenic corridors were wide enough to provide a park scene at relatively high vehicular speed; hence the advantage of an extensive body of water on at least one side. In the design of scenic highways, these factors are all important and have been instrumental in halting many proposals. Corridors of a half mile to a mile or more are often necessary and distances in length are likewise formidable. Resulting large right-of-way costs could not be

legally financed out of taxes that were levied for exclusively
transportation purposes.   Significantly the newer county and
regional park systems are without connecting parkways –
Huron-Clinton Metropolitan, East Bay Regional, Cook County
and a host of lesser ones.

In summary, what failure there has been in the connecting
boulevards and parkways of the past, is due to their inadequate
size of scale; failure to own or otherwise control a wide enough
scenic corridor to preserve the park-like aspect in the face of
increasing speeds of travel on the roadway, and the length of
forward vision to accomplish the same purpose.   Contributing
to the hesitancy in incorporating the encircling parkway scheme
into present day county, state and national park system plans
is the cost of acquiring and difficulty of otherwise controlling
the necessary scenic corridor.   But the attractiveness of the
encircling parkway plan has great appeal and where the inhibi-
tions above referred to are not present, parkways and scenic
highways will be used – even though the "encircling" feature
has to be sacrificed for only "stretches" of parkways.

CHAPTER 4

THE COUNTRY'S PHYSICAL RECREATION RESOURCES— STATE AND FEDERAL

"There is certainly something in the amiable simplicity of unadorned Nature that spreads over the mind a more noble sort of tranquility, and a loftier sensation of pleasure, than can be raised from the nicer scenes of art."

"On Verdant Sculpture in the Garden"
Alexander Pope, 1713

"The Himalayas must be beautiful. I should like to see them before they become fashionable."

Prof. Frank Waugh
Circa, 1928

Preliminary Observations

Similarity of State and Federal Services

The recreation resources of the state and federal governments have so much in common by way of origin, purpose, physical characteristics, and variety of administrative agencies, and both are so distinctive from the local aspects of recreation service that treating them in a single chapter makes for overall clarity. To be sure there are differences in administrative responsibilities between state and federal agencies, particularly in the overriding responsibility for national policy of the Federal Bureau of Outdoor Recreation; but these differences do not outweigh the great similarities of the service rendered by these two levels of government. Besides, these two services share a latent appreciation of the full scope of recreation as now embodied in a national recreation plan which, at long last, recognizes the singleness of purpose of the recreation of children in the neighborhood parks of the city and the fisherman, hunter, and camper in our great national forests.

Transition Factors of Recreation Service, Local to Federal

As the horizon of the study of parks extends from the local neighborhood park through the other parks of the city and the

county and then into state and national parks, there is a continual increasing or decreasing emphasis placed on certain
factors and functions which are common to all classes of parks.
These factors are: the degree and variety of organized and
supervised recreation programs, the proportional amount of
native environment to active recreation areas, the distance
from home, the length of stay, the expense per visit, the frequency of visit, and other factors of lesser importance.

Although there is much free play and unsupervised use of
local neighborhood parks and community playfields, even by
children, the facilities provided in these parks, and frequently
their arrangement into the park design, is dominated by the
kind and content of the supervised recreation program offered
by the city, and to some degree, as to how it is administered.
We have previously spoken of the fact that active recreation
dominates the design of these local parks, leaving such things
as aesthetics to be expressed by arrangement and the subtle
use of materials and colors and a minimum amount of land-
scaping.

Organized and supervised recreation becomes less dominant and less influencial in the park design as our study progresses through the large city parks, most of the special-use
parks, the county parks, the state parks, until on the national
level, supervised recreation has almost disappeared, unless
one includes in supervised recreation the interpretive programs of the state and federal park services. Heretofore,
however, interpretive programs, have been considered to have
as much kinship with education as it has with recreation.

More space, space per occupant, space for native environment, for longer views, for inspection and appreciation of
individual plants and animals and the ecology of the environment — all these increase in an ever-increasing degree as attention is drawn from the local scene to the national scene.
The form of recreation, therefore, changes from something
which needs direction to something which comes from within,
is more contemplative, more peaceful, more inspiring, and
more edifying. Space for tranquility and a relief from a busy-
ness caused by urban living is the great appeal. This is an
even greater escape from urban life than Olmsted expressed,
but in his day the countryside was much more accessible.

The experiences of state and federal park visitation are
not daily ones, as is the case in city parks. The visits are
much less frequent, but the length of visits are much greater.
A visit to a city park may be just a "passing through", or a

half-hour or an hour's time with children, or a couple of hours by the children alone. A visit to a state park may last for half a day or, on occasion, an overnight stay, possibly even several days for a camping trip. Visits to federal resources are often longer.

For such an experience the visitor will travel much farther from home – a matter of a half-day or more, to state parks, maybe a week or more to federal parks. This, in itself, costs more than a local visit to a city park; but especially is the expense greater when camping equipment, boats, winter sports equipment, special clothing, etc. are required.

When Congress established national parks, it imposed upon them a function which is not imposed upon city and county parks. National parks, being made up of nationally unique features, were to be <u>preserved</u> because of those very features. Access to these parks was to be permitted and provided for so that people could see and enjoy them, but these unique features were to be preserved at all costs. Use, (active recreation) and preservation are not always compatible. Consequently, as demand for more use became evident (a situation which would endanger the superlative qualities of the national and state parks), it was apparent that more land was needed and that this land could be less than superlative in quality, although far better than the average, and that it could be devoted more extensively to such activities as picnicking, camping, water sports, nature lore, and others. Also, it was apparent that these new recreation areas ought to be located with reference to centers of population. Hence, these areas could then satisfy the popular demand for national and state parks closer to home than the traditional state and national parks had been.

The Development and Purpose of State and Federal Parks

State parks are a more recent invention than national parks as was noted in Chapter 1. Consequently, the function of state parks at first was conceived to be substantially that of the National Park Service transferred to a state level. The policy of the National Park Service had been to set aside and to preserve, while at the same time making accessible for public enjoyment large areas of the superlative in scenery, geology, archaeology, history, uniqueness in flora and fauna. States followed suit by doing likewise for the unique areas of each state. Such areas were wherever they were found and were

not located with reference to centers of population. In the ensuing years, the National Park Service was perhaps more successful in adhering to high standards of quality in their selec-
tions than the states which were often importuned to acquire
state parks closer to their principle cities.

Following some early and significant federal and state
recreation holdings, actual consolidation of these must be characterized by the birth of the National Park Service in 1916 and
the organization of the National Conference on State Parks five
years later. Let us now trace some of this history with a view
to following the development of policy in which we are more
concerned than in areas and budgets. Bear in mind that as the
federal park service leads, the states generally follow.

National Parks Before 1916

There was very little professional theorizing behind the
Congressional Act which established Yellowstone as the first
national park in 1872. Very simply, Yellowstone was thought
of as a large area containing the most wonderful, the most in-
credible, and the most fantastic and spectacular geological and
scientific features of this wonderful country of ours, and "we
ought to protect it within government ownership for all posterity". It is improbable that appreciation of these wonders was
considered to be a part of recreation, as we view recreation
today. Yellowstone was something too wonderful to permit it
to be destroyed. It was precious and it should be preserved.

Over the years a number of other historical, scenic, and
scientific sites were thought to be important enough to maintain
intact, and some even enough to acquire. A number of archaeological and some historical treasures, some even in the public domain, were being plundered, ravaged, and destroyed.
In 1906 the so-called Antiquities Act was passed by Congress
which authorized the levying of a fine or imprisonment penalty
on anyone mutilating or destroying any object of antiquity in
the public domain. It also authorized the President to set aside
by proclamation, historic spots, landmarks, and other sites
and objects of the nature of an antiquity, and to receive gifts
of such sites. This was an important step forward from a
preservation standpoint, but still in all likelihood there was
little conscious connection between preservation and recreation. At any rate the government continued to acquire properties of national significance, and in 1916 it created the National
Park Service to administer all these holdings and to do a lot
more.

The National Park Service

As noted above the National Park Service Act and subsequent supplementary acts brought together under one administration not only the then existing national parks, but a number of other miscellaneous holdings. These included monuments, military parks, memorial parks, battlefield parks, battlefield sites and others. By 1966 the total number of administrative units had been extended to 214, and the total acreage involved was 26. 5 million acres. Included in the above were 32 national parks with 13. 6 million acres, 77 national monuments of about 9 million acres, 3 national parkways of over 106 thousand acres, the park system of the national capital at Washington, D. C. totaling between 39 and 40 thousand acres, six national seashore areas of 198 thousand acres, and 11 national recreation areas totaling 3. 5 million acres. The attendance at all these areas exceeded 133 million in 1966. Total budget for 1967 was $147. 6 million. The federal government has spent so little money for the acquisition of land that appropriation of some federal funds for the recently established Cape Cod Seashore Recreation Area marked a new trend.

As to congressional instructions to the administration regarding purpose and general administrative objectives, the National Parks Act gives this often quoted statement:

"The service thus established shall promote and regulate the use of federal areas known as national parks, monuments, reservations hereinafter specified by such means and measures as conform to the fundamental purpose of said parks, monuments, and reservations, which purpose is to conserve the scenery and the natural and historic objects and the wildlife therein, and to provide for the enjoyment of the same in such manner and by such means as will leave them unimpaired for the enjoyment of future generations. "

Park administrators often place emphasis on the apparent inconsistency of the two stated objectives of conservation and enjoyable use. The point is that if uncontrolled access and unlimited enjoyment of the natural recreation resource is permitted, preservation to the point of unimpairment of the natural asset becomes an impossibility. In actual practice and with some few exceptions, the National Park Service has done a creditable job of preservation while at the same time providing access for public enjoyment. Part of this is due to the large areas involved as well as the careful administration of the Service. Today's excessive use in localized spots together with estimates of future public demand now seem to be so impressively large as to demand a second look at the administrative policies.

For our present purpose it is interesting that in 1916 Congress was thinking not only in terms of preservation with a sort of nebulous objective, but was also concerned with the preservation of these unique things for the purpose of providing pleasure to the people, and it charged that these objects and their environment which give pleasure (recreation) to the people shall be preserved for all times so that the pleasure they give can always be present for the people of future generations. In other words we have something here which by itself and standing alone provides recreation to the individual, and Congress said that "that something" must be retained forever so that the pleasure and inspiration which it exudes shall be there for all times.

How has this policy been interpreted by the various administrations since the enactment of the Act in 1916?

Stephen Mather was the first of a succession of able administrators. Professor John Ise in his "Our National Park Policy" published by the Johns Hopkins Press in 1961 for Resources for the Future, reports a letter dated May 13, 1918 from the then Secretary of the Interior, Franklin K. Lane, to Mr. Mather in which an administrative policy is outlined:

"First, that the national parks must be maintained in absolutely unimpaired form for the use of future generations as well as those of our own time; second, that they are set aside for the use, observation, health, and pleasure of the people; and third, that the national interests must dictate all decisions affecting public or private enterprise in the parks."

Then he goes on to make note of several other policies:

The grazing by cattle, but not sheep might be permitted.

There should be no leasing for summer homes.

No cutting of trees except for buildings and where it would not impair the landscape.

Roads must harmonize with the landscape.

Private holdings and exclusive jurisdictions ought to be eliminated.

All outdoor sports including winter sports should be encouraged.

Low priced camps should be maintained and high class hotels.

Concessioners should be protected against competition if they were giving good service, and they should yield a revenue to the government, but the development of revenue should not impose a burden on visitors.

Auto fees should be reduced as motor travel increases. Advice was given as to the publicizing of the national parks.

The Service should keep informed as to municipal, county and state parks and cooperate with them as well as with the Canadian Park Service.

In setting up new projects, the Service should seek to find "scenery of supreme and distinctive quality or some natural features so extraordinary or unique as to be of national interest and importance". The national parks system as now constituted "should not be lowered in standard, dignity, and prestige by the inclusion of areas which express in less than the highest terms, the particular class or kind of exhibit which they represent".

The first paragraph in Secretary Lane's letter simply repeats what was placed in the law together with a rather obvious statement that the national interests must dictate all decisions. Other important points suggest the elimination of private holdings or vested interests in public areas; encouragement of educational and recreational use of the parks, and the establishment of services which would aid in that direction. The cooperation with other levels of government was stressed and admonition given toward maintaining the high standard to a superlative degree in all future additions to the system. It is a noble statement, and by and large, it was lived up to except in those few instances where inferior parks were acquired because the people, through their congressional representatives, said they were entitled to some of these national benefits which for the most part were concentrated in the western part of the country. The establishment of National Recreation Areas, State Parks and State Recreation Areas, indeed the beginning of a unified National Recreation Plan by the Bureau of Outdoor Recreation have now obviated much of this difficulty.

Times and conditions change and in retrospect now we can see that even such an able man as Mather could not clearly anticipate the situation fifty years in the future from his time. Congressional support for adequate appropriations were hard to come by so considerable attention was given to informing the public, important people, and especially the Congress about

the wonders in the national park system. Mather and his successors continued on that theme and in 1967 their efforts, supplemented by other startling developments made us think of
ways of relieving the pressure of excess attendance at the more
famous of our national parks. *

Early emphasis placed upon the desirability of using national parks for sports and other active recreation purposes
is not exactly what is being advocated today. That is the kind
of activity that we now wish could be diverted to other less
precious of the nation's fine scenery, so that the best areas
may remain unimpaired and preserved for the one kind of recreational use for which they are best fitted.

Mather's great interest in promoting the establishment of
state parks (he was the principle promoter) was probably less
motivated by the idea of providing state parks as a relief from
the pressure of attendance at national parks as it was to induce
states to acquire inspiring areas in their own states because
of their value to the people of the respective states. There
might have been a feeling, too, that if the states acquired the
areas of secondary importance, there was less chance of those
areas being foisted upon the federal government. Today both
objectives are valid and in this respect Mather operated probably better than he knew or could foretell.

The National Parks Service Act of 1916 did not give to the
National Park Service administrative control over a number of
miscellaneous properties. A number of military parks, battlefield sites, military and historical national monuments, miscellaneous memorials in the cemeteries were turned over to
the National Park Service by presidential executive order which
was authorized by Congress in 1933. It was during this reorganization process that the parks of the District of Columbia,
(the National Capitol Parks) were placed under the jurisdiction
of the National Park Service. Between 1916 and 1933, several
important national parks were added to the list of properties
and some thoughts on administration policies as well as purposes involved in the acquisition of the new properties were
expressed. Let us examine some, using as our principal authority the aforementioned Professor John Ise and his book on
"Our National Park Policy."

Ise reports that in November 1916, Mather wrote, referring to Yellowstone, "Golf links, tennis courts, swimming
pools, and other equipment for outdoor pastime and exercise

* Note Prof. Waugh's observation at the beginning of this chapter.

should be provided by concessions, and the park should be extensively advertised as a place to spend the summer instead of five or six days of hurried sightseeing under constant pressure to keep moving...there are no national parks better suited by nature for spending leisurely vacations." Ise further comments in his own words as follows: "At the time, this was not bad, perhaps, but it involved a confusion of two functions of parks which should have been and later were distinguished — the function of preserving the natural wonders and making them accessible to the public, and the function of mere recreation, which is appropriate not to national parks, but to state, municipal, and county parks and private recreational agencies. A criticism often aimed at Yosemite was that it was devoted too largely to recreational activities, mere amusements, while the scenic wonders were too little considered. *

Nearly all park administrators today would agree that if Mather's idea had been pursued to the present time, the functioning of our national parks for its fundamental purposes would be greatly impaired. The guidance that can be given by a park administrator toward the appropriate uses of our national parks must be buttressed by the establishment of other public recreation grounds in such amounts and in such locations to make compliance with the restrictions in our national parks an automatic thing. Even so, let us not be too surprised if on rare occasions public pressure has caused the introduction in national parks of some of the features mentioned by Mather.

It is interesting to note that entrance fees to national parks in the early days were high — made high partly because of the needed revenue. Over a period of time the entrance fees have been reduced suggesting that the importance of the revenue angle was diminishing.

The history of the National Park Service is replete with administrative difficulties such as vandalism, various aspects of the concessioner problem, the fending off inroads by power, timber, and grazing interests all of which can be treated more appropriately elsewhere. For our present purpose here, one of the more interesting difficulties encountered was to fend off the establishment of so-called inferior national parks — those that did not live up to the standard of excellence that park enthusiasts thought proper.

The preservation responsibility of the National Park Service received quite an impetus when there was passed in 1935

---

* This lack of suitable classification and segregation of purposes now has been taken care of in the National Recreation plan of the BOR.

an act calling for the preservation of historical sites, buildings, objects, and antiquities of national importance, known
generally as the Historic Sites and Buildings Act. The Antiquities Act of 1906 had been applied largely to the preservation
of archaeological sites and structures, although its authorization was somewhat broader than that. The act of 1935 supplemented this authorization by being more specific concerning
historic sites, particularly buildings. Under this authority it
was possible to expend money to learn all about these historic
structures, to reconstruct them, restore them, to preserve
them, and maintain them and charge fees for the admission to
them. It was also possible to contract and make cooperative
agreements with states and their political subdivisions and with
associations and individuals.

    This museum type responsibility of discovering, restor-
ing, and maintaining the visual parts of American history as
it does, has a combination of purposes: the fostering of national pride, education, and recreation if one approaches this
study with recreation as the major motive. The element of
recreation is there but certainly not predominant, but it has
its parallel in the functioning of almost all park departments,
local and state. Almost all park departments have found it expedient to respond to the public's desire to have historic sites
and objects suitably preserved or commemorated. Accepting
such responsibility, the park departments are not acting illog-
ically because historically and traditionally they have generally accepted this responsibility and it is not unrelated to their
major responsibility of providing recreation service to the
public.

    More important to the purely recreational aspects of the
National Park Service's responsibility was the passage in 1936
of the Park, Parkway and Recreation Area Study Act which
directed the Park Service to cooperate with practically all other governmental agencies in the various levels of government
to prepare a study of the whole problem of recreation in the
national, state, municipal, and county parks of the Nation. The
authority for actual study was of no greater impetus to the park
movement than was the inspiration it gave to the general ideal
of park planning everywhere, and particularly to the state systems. (This function has been transferred to the Bureau of
Outdoor Recreation of the Department of the Interior established in April 1962.)

    It was during this depression period, too, that a great
deal of help in park development was given particularly to the

states and to county and metropolitan park systems. Then probably for the first time in the history of the country there was provided through Federal aid a sufficient amount of recreation leadership in all levels of government to demonstrate to the public that recreation included many things other than summer playgrounds and sports – e.g. music, drama, art, and cultural pursuits in general.

In 1936 a number of the so-called Recreation Demonstration Projects were turned over to the National Park Service as a part of its responsibility. These areas had been established on lands which were submarginal from an agricultural standpoint, but had recreational possibilities. Through the Civilian Conservation Corps under the direction of the National Park Service, a number of these areas were developed for recreation purposes on a regional scale – actually, a new type of development for that period. For the most part, they were not far away from large concentrations of population and those population centers were not always in a single state. The service that these areas rendered often extended beyond metropolitan or county lines and yet were not typical of state park service. These were true demonstration areas suggesting a more varied development for active recreation than was then prevalent in other Metropolitan or State Parks. However, the National Park Service did not retain them as a part of its system, as they were later transferred to the lesser levels of government.

National recreation areas, however, emerged, probably as a result of the experience of the National Park Service in their demonstration areas as well as the gradually unfolding of an enlarged recreation responsibility felt by the National Park Service. Perhaps it was their responsibility to provide areas of national significance more suited to more active recreation than the superlatively unique areas of National Parks. At any rate NPS accepted responsibility for the Demonstration Area around Lake Mead created on the Colorado River when the Reclamation Bureau built Hoover Dam. Others followed in the wake of the construction of other large reservoir lakes.

In the thirties the National Park Service became interested in the acquisition of wilderness areas (the Everglades in Florida); began surveys of the shore lines of the country, the Great Lakes as well as the ocean shore lines.

The NPS was being criticized from both extremes – those who believed that there was a gradual deterioration of the high standards for national parks and those who believed the Service was not providing enough in the way of recreation. According to Professor Ise, the National Parks Association criticized the confusion in the classification of park areas. "State parks, recreation areas, national parks, and primeval national parks have been shuffled and jumbled until today a confused American public scarcely knows which is which. " Later administrations have been similarly criticized by the same association and others on the ground that recreation and general development have been stressed too much to the neglect of "fundamental national park principles and of rigorous protection of scenic values. " Professor Ise continues, "It is easy to see how a director might do this, for most of the forces operating push him in this direction, particularly if he is ambitious and anxious to see his department grow. Albright and Cammerer were accused of the same sin – if it is a sin. There may be honest differences of opinion of this point. "

These differences in opinion soon developed into a mounting realization that somehow there must be established a much more realistic approach to what the federal government and the states should do about the great increase in recreation demand that became apparent after World War II and the alarming forecasts that were made of demands to come. Other federal and state agencies had already begun to respond to public demand for recreation use of their properties for camping, fishing and water sports, hunting, picnicking and some forms of recreation to which such properties had not been previously subjected. These agencies included federal and state forests, wildlife refuges, huge reservoir lakes impounded by Army Engineers and state water conservancy districts and many others. The 1966 Recreation and Park Yearbook of the National Recreation and Park Association mentions 72 federal agencies that have some interest in recreation service. Only a few need special attention here. The reader is referred to the above publication for more detailed information.

*Forest Service — Department of Agriculture

"The management of forest and grasslands administered by the Forest Service is governed by the Multiple-Use, Sustained Yield Act of 1960 under which resources are appraised, evaluated and then administered to yield the greatest public benefit. " Public benefit includes recreation.

* Quotations are from the 1966 Recreation and Park Yearbook of NRPA.

The Forest Service had actually been in the business of providing facilities for camping and other recreation purpose long before 1960, but only in recent years had recreation commanded important attention. By 1966 there were 154 national forest and 19 national grasslands located in 41 states and totaling 186.3 million acres and having over 160 million visitor days of use. Facilities can accommodate 800,000 people at one time. The 1967 budget for out-door recreation was $74 million.

"Virtually all National Forest lands and waters are available for public use and activities are typically unrestricted. – Only those types of recreation appropriate to the forest environment are encouraged. " This indicates the complete absence of recreation "supervision" or "guidance" so prevalent at urban city parks and even of the interpretive programs of the National Park Service – literally the "end of the line" in the retrogression of recreation guidance previously referred to. Another note of the prevalence of principles in all recreation administrative and physical design factors is the "zoning" factor suggested in the following quotation.

"The most pristine type of recreational experience is to be found in the wilderness and primitive areas of our National Forests. The status of the National Wilderness Preservation System, established by the Wilderness Act of September 2, 1964 is noted in the following table.

National Forest Wilderness and Primitive Areas, Dec. 31, 1965

Types of Area	No. of Areas	Acres	Visitor Days
National Forest Wilderness Area	54	9,108,082	3,129,100
Primitive Areas	34	5,474,987	1,393,000
Scenic Type Areas	92	726,000	--

Corps of Army Engineers

Recreation has not been one of the essential functions of the Army Engineers. In fact only in the last ten years have values of recreation use been recognized in the economic justification for the many projects of water supply, navigation, or power development which are the primary purposes of the Corps. But once great river impoundments were created and water surfaces used, the available shorelands became useful for picnic grounds and many other recreation uses. The value of these resources for recreation became apparent, so the Corps found itself in the recreation business and began to capitalize on its virtues. Facilities and annual use are now impressive.

The Corps administers over 8 million acres of federal land. Besides its 28,000 miles of improved inland and coastal waterways, it operates 350 reservoirs in 44 states. Principle uses are fishing, hunting, boating, camping, and picnicking. Many of its land facilities are leased to other governmental agencies and some to commercial concessionaires, while some are operated by the Corps. Annual visitation is about 130 million. The budget for construction and development of recreation facilities was $31 million for 1967.

Fish and Wildlife Service

This department's role in recreation is to protect, conserve, and restore our fish and wildlife resources. They report that in 1965 there were over 33 million anglers and hunters who spent 700 million recreation days (or some part of a day) at their favorite recreation.

The functions of the department are varied and many, and they manage many acres of land and marsh for game production; also 312 game refuges in all but five of the states covering 28.5 million acres. Compared to attendance figures of other recreation agencies its annual attendance of about 13 million seems small but this has more than doubled in the last 10 years.

BOR and HUD

From the standpoint of the park and recreation administrator in all levels of government and in all phases of work, the two most important and influential federal agencies are the Bureau of Outdoor Recreation, (BOR), of the Department of the Interior, and the Department of Housing and Urban Development (HUD). Among the many functions of the former is the responsibility of preparing a national recreation plan (formerly a function of the National Park Service) and the allocation of federal recreation funds to other federal agencies and of grants-in-aid to the states and through them to political sub-divisions of the states. HUD, having responsibility for urban affairs allocates grants-in-aid to urban communities from funds raised for urban development. These two agencies, together with all other federal agencies that have an interest in recreation are brought together at Cabinet level by the President's Council on Recreation and Natural Beauty.

Neither BOR nor HUD have any responsibility in land management for recreation because they are not operating agencies. Their immense influence stems from two main sources: (1) the formulation and promulgation of national policy, and (2), the allocation of grants-in-aid to recreation, mainly for land acquisition and development. BOR aids non-urban projects as well as urban projects, while HUD is restricted to aiding only urban projects.

Bureau of Outdoor Recreation

The Bureau was created as a result of recommendations which the Outdoor Recreation Resources Review Commission, (ORRRC), submitted to the President and Congress on January 31, 1962, after a 3-year study of the nation's outdoor recreation resources and needs. The 27 volume report available from the Supt. of Documents either in single volumes or in a total at $2.00 a volume. The summary is titled "Outdoor Recreation for America". This report has had a profound effect on recreation planning and administration due to a documentation of evidence pertaining to recreation preference, degree of use, and an inventory of resources.

By virtue of several public laws enacted since the BOR was established April 1, 1962, the Bureau is authorized to –

√ Prepare and maintain a continuing inventory and evaluation of the Nation's outdoor recreation needs and resources.

√ Formulate and maintain a comprehensive nationwide outdoor recreation plan.

√ Provide technical assistance to and cooperate with states, their political subdivisions, and private outdoor recreation interests.

√ Sponsor, engage in, and assist in outdoor recreation research.

√ Promote coordination of federal outdoor recreation plans and activities.

√ Administer a program of financial assistance to the states, and through the states to local public agencies, for planning, acquiring, and developing public outdoor recreation resources.

√ Coordinate a program of recreation and acquisition by the National Park Service, Forest Service and Bureau of Sport Fisheries and Wildlife.

√ Provide outdoor planning assistance to federal water projects.

√ Provide the Executive Director to the President's Council on Recreation and Natural Beauty.

The BOR has requested state recreation plans from all of the states and has provided a method by which these plans shall be made. It is directed to submit its Nationwide Recreation Plan to Congress by 1968.

Since its inception and including 1967 BOR has provided funds for the acquisition of 9393 acres of land totaling almost $15 million, and 101,878 acres for over $15 million for the Forest Service. States have been allocated $152 million for the fiscal years 1965, 1966, and 1967. This latter allocation of funds is predicated upon the approval of a comprehensive state outdoor recreation plan.

As a point of interest in our underlying premise that area zoning in recreation resource planning is a key factor, this classification by BOR is presented: Class I, High Density Recreation Areas; Class II, General Outdoor Recreation; Class III, Natural Environment; Class IV, Outstanding Natural Feature; Class V, Primitive Area; Class VI, Historic and Cultural Sites. A single property, if it is large and varied enough, might contain several or even all of the classes. Since classification affects both plan and administration, a zoning process has taken place in which use and physical characteristics are harmonized. This process was seen in the classification of the Wilderness areas of the Forest Service; it appears in the more recent state plans of state systems as well as in individual parks and it is in evidence in plans of local systems and local parks.

Department of Housing and Urban Development

This department, created in 1965 by combining several other agencies with new and additional functions, administers federal programs for urban renewal, public housing, urban planning, open space land, mass transit, and community facilities. Open space grants-in-aid to urban agencies are available up to 50% total cost. Planning assistance up to two-thirds of cost is also available for comprehensive planning of urban needs including parks and recreation. Estimated grants for fiscal 1968 are $90 million for the acquisition of 72,000 acres of land.

Inasmuch as all requests for grants-in-aid are predicated upon plans validated by planning agencies having larger jurisdiction than that of the applicant, it becomes apparent that approved plans must be integrated with plans of greater area scope.

In the discussion of BOR and HUD the full scope of available aid programs, or of authority and influence of the agencies themselves have not been enumerated. New programs have appeared with fascinating frequency; the federal government is deeply concerned and reasonably responsive to park and recreation problems, once the case is made clear and urgent. This discussion of other federal agencies has not exposed all of their responsibilities and all agencies having an interest in recreation have not been mentioned. Enough has been presented to reveal the major resources and to indicate the general pattern of administrative policy prevalent in the federal government.

The states have administrative departments paralleling the major federal services, often combining several services under one administrative head, called for examples, State Resources Department or Conservation Department. Within such a department one usually finds divisions of State Parks, State Forests, State Minerals, Waters and Drainage; and also a BOR and State Planning. Each of the divisions may or may not have divisional planning sections, but if so, these are coordinated in the State Planning Division. In recent years, some states have recognized the recreation function by including it as part of the State Parks division. The state division or Bureau of Outdoor Recreation with liaison functions attuned to the federal BOR usually coordinates the federal and state recreation programs and oversees the allocation of state funds to its political subdivisions.

Federal grants-in-aid are not expected to wholly finance recreation facility projects, but to act as an incentive for the states and local communities to wake up and do something for themselves. As of early 1967 over $100 million in qualified projects had been received by the BOR from the states which means that the states (or subdivisions) were prepared to spend an equal amount. A number of states had authorized bonds ranging from $1.5 million to $200 million. In addition an untold amount of financing took place by cities and counties through HUD aid.

To keep abreast of these fast moving programs, states and urban communities have had to add administrative personnel.

Ratio of Acres to Population

Its Applicability

In Chapter 2 it was mentioned that ratios of park acreage to units of population are but rules-of-thumb guides in assessing the adequacy of park lands in a given stiuation. It has been noted that certain factors involved in park statistics show either progression or retrogression as one considers the transition from city parks to national resources. The ratio we now discuss is one of those factors. The ratio is more meaningful when applied to the local scene, less so to the state resources, and most difficult when applied to federal resources.

The reasons for this seem obvious:

1. A major part of non-urban recreation resource area is made up of outstanding natural features which are not uniformly distributed over the nation or uniformly over the individual states. The great national parks and forests are predominantly in the West where some states are "overrun" with them. Some states also have large areas of state significant resources while others have very little. Hence, a ratio of acres to thousand population applied to states like Idaho or Nevada with large National holdings would not be anything like the results as applied to Kansas or Nebraska where there are few such National assets.

2. Federal resources occurring as they do in much larger units than do state resources, tends to increase the disparity noted in paragraph 1.

However, in some instances, e.g., State and National Recreation Areas, the ratio analysis does have some merit.

The Ratio Applied to States

Several sources suggest that the states should have about 65 acres of parks per thousand population. If the acreage of recreation resources found in forests and wildlife refuges were included, a much higher ratio of park and recreation acreage might be justified. Actually, as of 1966, states already possessed more than twice the ratio of 65 a/1000 pop. but still were pinched for the right kind of space in the proper locations. The following table illustrates the point. The classes listed on the table are those used by BOR as being applicable to state and federal resources; Class I, High Density Recreation; Class II, General Outdoor Recreation; Class III, Natural Environment; Class Iv, Outstanding Natural Features; Class V, Primitive Areas; Class VI, Historical and Cultural Sites. Primary statistics are from the 1966 NRPA Yearbook.

STATE RECREATION RESOURCES BY BOR CLASS

CLASS	DESCRIPTION	1966-AREA	*Ratio	Acre per 1000 pop. for 190,000,000 Computed Acres
I	High Density Recreation	67,291	10	1,900,000
II	General Outdoor Recreation	2,281,927	35	6,650,000
III	Natural Environment	+30,142,298	15	2,850,000
IV	Outstanding Natural Features	671,358	7.5	1,430,000
V	Primitive Areas	1,492,796	7.5	1,430,000
VI	Historical and Cultural Sites	39,272	Small	40,000
TOTALS		34,794,942	75+	14,300,000

* Author's personal suggestion.
+ 90% Forests, Fisheries and Wild Life.

There can be some difference of opinion concerning the breakdown of the ratio as shown, but not in great enough degree to alter the general conclusion that the important shortage of area is in the active recreation categories of Classes I and II which are located with reference to population centers. What surplus areas, if any, occur in Class III which is 90% made up of the state forest and wildlife refuges which are not exclusively recreation resources. The inadequacy of Classes I and

II is a current state recreation problem. The usefulness of the ratio technique makes it apparent.

The Ratio Applied to Federal Resources

As a whole, federal resources are less susceptible to a-nalysis by the acres to population ratio than the states as has already been noted. However, National Recreation Areas, like their state counterparts do find such analysis, at least helpful if not altogether relevant. The National Park Service seeks to establish Recreation Areas, each not less than 20,000 acres and usually much more extensive, within 250 miles of centers of population of about 25 million people. This makes a minimum of 10 a/1000 pop. with usual results far higher. Then, too, a more careful scouting of possible sites for National Scenic Parks, Wild Rivers, Seashore Recreation Areas continues in the regions of the country harboring large centers of population – and a number of qualified national parks are being found. This is a concerted effort to correct, so far as is practical, the natural mal-distribution of recreation resources, and in doing so there is a furtive eye cast in the direction of the ratio, acres to population.

There is one more vulnerability to the acre/population ratio and that is use by visitation – or rather over use of critical areas. If annual visitation continues to increase faster than the population, time may come when over use becomes general. Only two alternatives exist. As the old rancher says, "When the land is overgrazed, reduce the herd or get more pasture land." In our case that additional land must come from new additions to Classes I and II or we rob Class III if any of its lands are accessible. More probably, we may sacrifice the native areas within Class II – a real recreation tragedy. Logically, the ratio of land to population should be revised upward.

In actual practice, no rule-of-thumb ratio is entirely adequate for land acquisition and design purposes. A very careful "market survey" must precede both acquisition and development to ensure an efficient result. More will be said about this later.

CHAPTER 5

THE COUNTRY'S PHYSICAL RECREATION RESOURCES SUMMARY

God help the boy who does not know where
All the woodland berries grow,
Who never sees the forests glow
When leaves are red and yellow.
Whose childish feet can never stray
Where nature does her charms display —
For such a helpless boy I say
"God help the little fellow."
Author Unknown

The Nationwide Plan

The problem of securing an orderly and adequate nation-wide system of park and recreation services is a concern shared by professionals in the service and the general public alike. A number of federal agencies have a special interest in public recreation and one in particular, the Bureau of Outdoor Recreation, has an exclusive interest in devising, and helping to achieve, a nation wide recreation goal. Others, as a part of their total function, also aid; of these the Department of Housing and Urban Development is the most potent because of its effect upon urban improvement and urban development. Both BOR and HUD administer grants-in-aid for acquisition of land and its development. BOR funnels its aid through the states which in turn are encouraged to add additional aid to their political subdivisions. To be eligible for aid, the local and state proposals must conform to state-wide recreation plans. HUD dispenses grants-in-aid directly to metropolitan complexes and their component parts. To be eligible, projects must conform to the plans of some agency involving a greater geographical scope than the applying city or village. Consequently, there is a comprehensive attempt to provide a system orderliness and competence to most of the future attempts aimed at developing a nation-wide system of recreation resources. While it is true that individual operating agencies can acquire and develop such land as they please, if they pay all the costs, the bait of grants-in-aid is proving too great an inducement to ignore.

Local plans, regional plans, state plans and national plans still require the application of knowledgeable talent to devise

the component parts of any nation-wide effort. No single person or public agency can be expected to be endowed with enough
know-all, see-all expertise to successfully cope with the very
complicated matter of public recreation in all of the intricate
and varied situations. Nevertheless, BOR is attempting to establish broad guidelines for nation-wide planning. It has provided the states with a pattern to follow in preparing a state-
wide recreation plan: inventory the public and private recreation resources of the state, determine what, where, and how
much resources are needed to satisfy the potential recreation
requirements of the people, and the difference between what is
available and what is required is the deficiency that needs to
be fulfilled.   Presumably the pattern applies to federal and
local agencies as well.   To do this work results in the setting
up of a junior BOR in every state. Since the pattern is followed
locally as well as state-wide a uniform approach to recreation
planning is evolving.

Zoning and Classifications

The unknown factor in the pattern's formula is the "what,
where and how much" resources that are needed – which, in a
way, brings us right back to where we always have been. It is
where the research by individuals in many places can help out.
The simple process of inventorying what is available often
opens the way toward a more enlightening analysis of what is
needed.   BOR has adopted a system of resource classification
that is a great aid.   Its six classes of physical recreation resources enumerated on p. 77 tell the story which in more am-
plified form is published in the Recreation and Park Yearbook.*
The idea of use zoning, while not new, (it has been used in municipal land-use planning for decades), is now applied to whole
systems of parks as well as to individual parks and forests
that are large and varied enough to accommodate more than
one use – a situation on a smaller scale not unlike that of many
large city parks.
The zones of use in municipal neighborhood parks and
community playfields are usually easily defined even though
the neighborhoods and communities are of uncommon shape
and of unequal population density. The characteristics of the
population within the zones of park influence are readily available from the census data. What the socio-economic groups
of the population do for recreation and how often they engage
in their recreation pursuits have been fairly closely observed
_____
* Recreation and Park Yearbook, p. 40   National Recreation and Park Association.

by park and recreation personnel over a period of many years, rather than by statistical count and systematic personal interview. This is how the rule-of-thumb ratios of acreage to population and other relationships have been developed; and they have worked reasonably well for averages and for guides to area requirements. Area facility requirements have been chosen to fit population characteristics as personnel have interpreted these wants to be from personal observation and from the rule-of-thumb relationships above referred to. So the question of "what, where and how much"has not been a particularly hard problem to solve. However, with population metamorphosis in the city now in an accelerating stage, more care may have to be given to area and facility determination in urban situations. Even in years past a more precise analysis has usually been made at intervals of a few years.

In county, state, and federal situations the problem is different mostly because of the wide range of age groups using the resources, a similar wide range in the socio-economic status and the large areas involved within the radius of influence. For a complete job of appraisal and estimation in these cases, it is necessary to take precise census of population characteristics within the zones of influence and to carefully question people regarding their recreation preferences, the frequency of involvement, and their criticism of present conditions. This is an expensive and time consuming process.

As a substitute, a number of planning agencies have utilized information of a like nature gathered by ORRRC. It was found that people of certain socio-economic characteristics had certain preferences for certain kinds of recreation activity and engaged in them at certain frequencies. They tabulated the statistics and fashioned so-called "profiles". For example, a family with an income of $10,000 annually would picnic together so many times a year, swim some other frequency per season, camp so often, and so on. These "profiles" were made to apply nation-wide and not for any one location. By applying this information to the specific population characteristics of a specific county or state situation, data on preferences and frequency of use can be estimated. This operation may not yield precise results, but this method is far better than any rule-of-thumb method, or, as was so often the case, the "hunch" method of pure speculation.

The adoption of a general system of use classification by BOR has given strength to the value of classification systems in general at a time when the validity of such a system, particularly when applied to municipalities, was beginning to lose

favor with some planners probably due to the many complications encountered in its application.   BOR's system can be
applied to city park systems as well as to others, but since
practically all of a given city's parks will fall in BOR Class I,
the classification loses much of its value.   Therefore, cities
will continue to rely on one of the old classification systems
of which the Dallas one found on p. 27 is typical.   Likewise,
counties are more apt to use their own systems for their own
planning and administrative purposes. The system of the Forest Service was shown on p. 71 and the National Park Service
has its own. These do not detract from the BOR classification
which provides an over-all method of classifying all recreation
resources in a single system; rather, it suggests the need of
something which is specially adaptable to a specific agency.
Particularly is this true to determine area requirements for
certain uses, − and sometimes the degree of sophistication of
the facilities to be provided.

Amount of Area Required

In the states and in the federal arena, it is a matter of
judgment as to what is a native recreation resource of a high
enough standard of excellence to qualify as a national or state
scenic park − one that is worthy of preservation for all time
just as it is.   It is also a matter of judgment as to how much
of a single site or how many of them there are. Consequently,
measuring the quantity needed by the application of a ratio of
acres to population has little significance.   The previous portion of the text points out the non-uniformity of both state and
federal resources of this class occurring in any one state as
compared to another and also the difficulty of determining even
the acreage of recreation areas by the ratio method because
portions of the great scenic parks and forests may be properly
used for more intense recreation without jeopardizing the
preservation of any of the superlative virtues.   Nevertheless,
until more precise methods are in general use, there remains
some value (if judiciously applied) to the old rule-of-thumb:
45 a/1000 pop. for state recreation areas, (65 a/1000 pop.
total over-all) and 10 to as high as 20 a/1000 pop. for counties.

Attention is Focused on the Urban Situation

In chapter one, there was noted a continuing progression
and retrogression of certain factors pertaining to recreation

resources and service as attention moves outward from the central core of urban complexes. One of the factors only touched upon is the degree of intensity (and urgency) of the problem of supplying enough recreation facilities and services. The really sore spot is in the central city itself. The least urgent and the easiest to solve are the federal situations, with state and county problems falling between the two extremes. It is easy to see why the greatest progress is being made in the non-urban regions. So huge do the urban problems of all kinds seem to be, that some urbanologists are looking outside the central cities to solve the urban ills. They see more possibility of making the non-urban areas so attractively made into new towns that the movement into large central cities may be slowed up if not halted. There is no question that mammoth changes (some good, some not so good) are going on in the cities in physical aspects as well as in moral and psychological ways.

But whatever improvements in conditions are made outside the cities, the cities themselves must be "reborn". Two-thirds of our cities have never improved their ratio of parks to population to accommodate the era of neighborhood and community services. They never attained the 10 a/1000 pop. ratio. The danger now is that a paucity of parks and recreation services have been tolerated for so long that the present situation may be considered normal. The social unrest tends to refute that premise. In 1944, Liebert H. Weir, one of the past eminent authorities on park and recreation service, a field secretary of the National Recreation Association, predicted in one of his municipal surveys that cities would have to open up their crowded condition or strangle. The author well remembers the temper of the times: Weir's prediction seemed the pronouncement of an over-enthusiastic advocate of recreation and parks. Somewhat later, Mumford, Tunnard, and others emphasized the importance of social amenities and green spaces to offset the harshness of asphalt and concrete, traffic congestion, and air pollution. New businesses and office buildings in our cities are lately making some concession to the green-open-space point of view with the planting of lacy foliaged trees along the streets, some open space embellishment around the buildings, pedestrian malls on shopping streets and even a small rest park or two. But still the neighborhoods, communities and city as a whole are inadequately equipped with parks. A large central park, regardless of its acreage, does not supply a city with enough large city park area. Cultural and sports centers and museums are fine, but are not substitutes.

A Case in Point

The little verse at the beginning of this chapter about the poor little fellow who does not know where woodland berries grow, was taken from the 1890 annual report of the President of the Minneapolis Board of Park Commissioners. The commission was only seven years old, but a good record of park acquisition had taken place, at least by 1890 standards. A city of less than 200,000 had attained a park acreage of 1306 – 6.5 a/1000 pop. The president reported with pride:

"Thanks to the enterprise and generosity of the citizens of Minneapolis, her children now own some of the brightest jewels nature ever bestowed upon a favored people. They can roam through their own woods, sail and row on their own lakes, wander by the side of their own running brook, rest in their own beautiful gardens, ride or drive on their own roads for miles through picturesque and varied scenery, picnic in quiet glens within sound of the music of the beautiful waterfall made sacred by the song of our great poet, * and in winter take in new life when skating on the well kept ice of their own skating ponds. This great property is theirs forever, it belongs to the rich and poor alike, it will be the most valuable heritage of their children and their children's children. They will, through their ownership, be better men and women, and through it be lifted to a higher plan of intellectual, moral and physical life. "

Over the years, Minneapolis has kept pace in park acreage with the population growth. Its more than 5000 acres of parks (more than 10 a/1000 pop.) includes good neighborhood and community facilities in almost all parts of the city; it has bordered its rivers, lakes, and streams with parks and parkways; by present day standards it is one of the better park systems of the country.

Good as the Minneapolis system is, it has its deficiencies: not enough park area around its lakes, more large city parks are needed in some parts of the city, a few more neighborhood facilities, considerable re-design and reconstruction of present parks, a higher standard of maintenance. But the most striking deficiency as compared to the much more modern system of 1890 is the relatively small percentage of native landscape – where woodland berries and flowers grow. (There is a very good wild flower garden the attendance of which is apt

* Longfellow and Minnehaha Falls

to smother it in time.) In 1890, and even in 1915, native area under public control was of such extent that the public clamored for it to be "improved" for greater use. Gradually over the years native shrubs, many species of native trees, and most wild flowers have disappeared. "God help the little fellow."

What has happened in Minneapolis, has happened in all core cities to a greater or lesser extent. Some may argue that to retain more than a sample of native landscape (or a man-made replica) in the face of the vicious competitive forces that vie for space and money, is a hopeless and unrealistic objective. To argue against the desirability of such an amenity is pointless and present day social unrest may augur the day when the objective will be quite real and quite necessary.

A Stray Thought

As a passing observation to the prospective park and recreation administrator, the many points covered in the foregoing chapters bring one face to face with technical, social, and political situations, which, to handle with understanding judgment require a broad general knowledge of American life, not the least of which is how people may live together in close quarters and what social amenities are necessary to make life not only tolerable but happy and culturally constructive. The answer to the problem of recreation areas and facilities is found in the study of people – their hopes, wants and habits. And that means a broad education in humanities and philosophy.

CHAPTER 6

THE MAKING OF A PARK PLAN

"Whatever the various meanings of the word park - to the cottager of Chaucer's time watching the deer over the paling of the manor woods, to the courtier of Louis XIV philandering through the braod alees of Versailles, to Mr. Humphrey Repton and Prince Puckler-Muskay, to the East side urchin of today grasping his chance for play in Seward Park — it always suggests to us some kind of a green space with turf and trees."

"Forty Years of Landscape Architecture"
Professional Papers of Frederick Law Olmsted

Preliminary to Chapters 6, 7, and 8

It was noted in Chapter 1 that the administration of park and other recreation resources required the use of a rather extensive number of specialists, – professionals, scientists, technicians, skilled and unskilled workmen. The administrator obviously cannot be a specialist in all the ramified functions within his department; he must assign duties, receive responses, consider findings of investigations, make decisions and delegate responsibility in as broad terms as possible. Otherwise he will become bogged down in detail with little time to think and to plan strategy of operation.

Nevertheless, the administrator must have some knowledge of the specialized fields under his command at least to a degree that will permit an intelligent appraisal of the value of the specialized operations. Three of these special fields most often discussed among young executives – planning, budgeting and organization – are given some treatment in the following three chapters. The discussions are not complete but enough detail is given to expose the nature of the functions, how they are handled, and what an administrator may look for to appraise the efficiency. Other departmental functions may be touched upon from time to time in other chapters. In all cases the future administrator should look for generalities rather than specific details, (better left to the specialist), keeping in mind that the broader the horizon of knowledge, the better equipped he becomes to make the far reaching decisions.

The future administrator (and present ones too) must always have in mind the central purpose of all recreation resource operations: to provide a service that will afford the

greatest opportunity for the life enrichment of the user and encourage him to utilize his leisure time for the development of
his own potential and the betterment of society. Only a radical
change in social values of civilized people can change that.

The Making of a Park Plan

To make a plan for an individual park, even a small one,
is a very technical matter. It looks disarmingly simple to
make a layout for the ball diamond here and the tennis court
there, and the hard surface area, playground apparatus, horseshoe courts, building, wading pool or swimming pool in various
other locations, and to put them together so that they form a
decent pattern. Be assured that while this can be done on paper and look reasonably simple, much more needs to be done.

The student will feel that this sort of simple operation
may be learned in a short time – certainly within the scope of
one semester. Such is not the case. If a student has a background in simple architecture or the use of drafting instruments and the techniques of delineation; if he has studied surveying and the techniques of topographical mapping; if he has a
background in plant materials and simple engineering construction; if he understands all that is being taught in this course
pertaining to park administration of recreation resources; if
he understands the technique of simple research; if some landscape planning has been included in his curriculum, then he is
prepared to begin a course in park and other recreation area
design. Until then he is not ready.

This should not be entirely discouraging – the graduate in
Landscape Architecture and the graduate in Recreation or Forestry are no better off. The landscape architect has the skills
of planning, delineation, and representation, the Forestry student in the preservation of forest ecology and timber production and other techniques, but none is a specialist in park design or recreation resource administration. The Recreation
graduate and the Park Management graduate, the Forestry
graduate, and the Engineer can provide to the planner the special insight into park and recreation service which the planner
does not have. Pooling their talents and working together they
are capable of producing good results. In short, the creation
of a sound, functional, beautiful park design is a cooperative
effort involving more than one professional.

Park planning is, therefore, a specialized field in the
overall operation of the park and recreation organization. The

park administrator must recognize that fact. He must necessarily be very close to the planning operation, but he need not
be a specialist in that operation. In view of this, no effort
will be made in this chapter to give detailed instructions in
park planning. There will be included, however, some discussion on resource material, relationships in the design process,
and some general criteria for judging the worth of the final
plan.

Description of Some Basic Resource Material — Particularly Plans

There are two general definitions of a plan:

1. A plan is the representation of an object drawn on a single
    plane.
        A single map is a plan, but a single map as a final
    product is seldom sufficient in park administration.   It
    may be a step toward the final product or it may be one of
    a series of maps the whole of which may suit the purpose.
    A floor plan of a building likewise reflects only one piece
    of the total information we need to judge the worth of the
    project, to construct it, or to operate it.

2. A plan is a method or scheme of action.
        A budget is a plan of action: the action involves ex-
    penditure of funds.
        A report may encompass a plan of action or it may
    be only a part of a plan of action.
        A plan for construction of a building includes a num-
    ber of plans (called working drawings) and a descriptive
    report (called specifications).
        Plans for the construction of a park or other recrea-
    tion facility include working drawings, (often simply called
    plans) and specifications.
        A plan of operation for recreation facilities includes
    maps of parks and a report of instructions as to methods
    of maintenance and use of the properties after the park
    has been constructed.
        An organization chart is a plan of personnel respon-
    sibilities in the operation of an organization.
        Other examples are numerous.

In speaking of plans we often use the expressions "plats"
and "maps". A plan of a piece of land is usually called a plat
(generally applied to a land subdivision or property survey),
or a map.

Plans may refer to operational plans or plans of physical things for actual or proposed construction or execution. In this chapter we will deal mostly, but not exclusively, with plans of construction. Reference will be made to "plats" showing property ownership and "maps" showing land characteristics. Reports in connection with these plans will usually be strictly reportorial (reporting facts), analytical, and descriptive (specifications).

Property surveys on which land plats are based are made by land surveyors registered by the state and authorized by law to practice in a particular state. Civil engineers are also legally registered (as are architects) and are often also registered land surveyors. Land descriptions as a basis for plats and for the conveyance of land titles can be made by land surveyors, but before they are used in legal instruments, they should be verified by lawyers specializing in title investigation (title search or examining title abstracts) because the exact wording used is often necessary to insure contiguity of adjoining parcels, and for other reasons. Land descriptions as used in deeds can present some rather tricky problems; consequently, the employment of both lawyer and land surveyor is often advisable.

Land plats or the information for making them are usually obtainable in the office of the county register of deeds.

Topographic maps show land topography (variation in land heights), location of physical characteristics such as woods (sometimes individual trees with size and species given, for example, 24 inch elm), lakes, water courses, buildings, roads, trails, power transmission lines, underground utilities, (sewer, water, and drainage lines) and all other features that will clarify the character of the land. Land plats and topographic maps are sometimes superimposed on each other; this combination is the most basic material for the park planner.

Sometimes suitable topographic maps can be purchased, but often special topographic surveys and maps must be made. Even when maps can be purchased they usually have to undergo processes which will either reduce or enlarge the scale to fit a particular requirement.

The most complete and accurate of purchasable maps are those of the United States Geological Survey. These are available for most of the country. They show complete topographic information as well as geological characteristics of the underground with appropriate texts. Sometimes the maps of only the earth's surface may be purchased separately.

The United States Department of Agriculture sells aerial maps which are aerial photos and show what can be seen from the air. Their accuracy depends upon how much overlay or duplication of adjoining photos takes place. These are excellent for reconnaissance work.

Local aerial survey companies can often provide aerial maps. Usually these companies can also supply topographic information on the maps, the land elevations being supplied by a stereoscopic procedure. They are available in various scale sizes.

Other government agencies – state highway departments, county highway departments, planning commissions – can often supply basic maps. These agencies can also supply plans for future development of their particular phase of work.

Other informative maps, particularly those pertaining to the ecology of a region, can usually be obtained from the state conservation or natural resource department. These maps show soil conditions, lake and stream characteristics, forest areas and tree species, wild life distribution and characteristics, mineral resources and others.

Universities (land-grant colleges in particular) may also have similar maps as well as maps showing the results of special studies related or important to park administration.

Developing a Plan for a Park

The general planning process consists of these major steps: (1) the preparation of an investigative report; (2) topographic survey and map; (3) the preparation of diagrammatic sketches; (4) design of a preliminary plan; (5) the preparation of working drawings and specifications; (6) the report and plan for the method of maintenance and operation when the construction is completed.

Park Plans a Part of Departmental Policy

A park plan may be considered a declaration of intent to do something at some future time. That something must be a part of the total purpose of providing that kind of recreation service which that particular public agency in that particular level of government is organized to provide. The plan of a park, (or other recreation facility) is a declaration of policy just as thoroughly as is any written document. The things called for in that plan must, therefore, be consistent with the policies of administration because it is a part of such policies.

For plans that have the immediate prospect of execution into finished jobs, the whole previously named six steps must be carried through. For projects which might be included in a five-year program, the steps up, through, and including the preliminary design may be sufficient. For projects more remote than five years, it is possible that the steps may not go much beyond the making of the diagrammatic sketches. In all these cases, estimates of cost should be included, but these again are in the several stages of exactness depending upon how soon the project is to be carried out.

In all cases, the park plan, however sketchy, should always carry with it a declaration of intent of how it is to function. This statement may be in general terms for projects quite remote in time, but for projects being carried out promptly, this statement should be quite exact.

A plan for the development of each park in the whole system of parks having been made, there then emerges a total declaration of intent of how parks individually, and the system as a whole, is expected to be developed. This total plan of development becomes a part of the total future policy of the board or the department and must be consistent with the development plans of each of the other divisions of the department, with the standards of requirement nationally accepted, with plans for future financing of development, maintenance and operation, methods of administration, and all else that goes to make up the total operational intent of the entire department.

From what has been written of the BOR and the nationwide plan and of HUD and its regulations, it is obvious that any plan for acquisition or development of a whole park and recreation system, or of a single part of such a system, must be consistent with the federal requirements as a matter of both prudence and the necessity of qualifying for grants-in-aid.

It has been noted before that the making of a park plan, that is, the design of an actual park, is a cooperative procedure requiring the talents of expert planners, the engineer, recreation director, the maintenance supervisor, and perhaps a number of others who will have a hand in either operating or maintaining the project after it is completed. There are also administrative policies that are woven into each plan, such as the standard of excellence, the durability of construction, the method of handling certain types of recreation services, and similar considerations and there are still others that in the ultimate, may have an important influence on the suitability of the plan. All of these should be consulted.

It would be a mistake if the governing body of the park department were not apprised of the whole volume of plans for proposed development. Final and formal approval may not be necessary until the project is about to be executed, but preknowledge of the intent of all of the plans ought to be given to, for instance, members of the park board or anyone who is superior to the director of parks and recreation. Inasmuch as this declaration of intent is a part of the declaration of policy of the entire level of government in which we are operating; the city, state, or for that matter, the nation. This calls for coordination with the plans and aspirations of other departments of that level of government. In the city, that means that the urban planners must be aware of the existence of such a plan and must have knowledge of the overall policy intent and be able to refer to specific parts whenever that becomes important in the development of a city plan. If a total city plan is developed, the agreed upon park and recreation plan becomes a part of the total city plan. The county and state situations are analagous.

Investigative Reports or Analyses

In all cases in this discussion it is presumed that the particular park or other facility which is about to be planned fits into an overall park plan involving the city, the county or metropolitan region, the state, or the federal government whichever has control of the park district in which this particular park lies, it is essential that this park and the purpose for which it was acquired be related to the entire park system of which it is a part. It is from that point on that the investigation proceeds.

This report, or analysis of conditions, is a listing of, and comments on, all matters that are needed to make a facility plan which properly accommodates itself to the uses it is expected to get. Obviously, there must be an analysis of the characteristics and recreation habits of the people who live within the zone of influence of park and who will use the facility. Some reference to the methods of doing this has been made on page 81. The contents of the park and the space needed for each item are determined from this analysis.

The site must be visited, not once but perhaps often, preferably with the topographic map in hand. At this time, all information about the site which has a bearing on the arrangement of facilities within the proposed park and which has not been shown on the topographic map must be noted – ground cover, soil inspection, how drainage runs, highways and roadways bordering or near the site, the character of buildings in the vicinity, presence of water supply, power lines, municipal sewer lines, etc. It is probably necessary to visit local public offices for information on underground services not apparent by site inspection, future plans for roads and highways, building zoning regulations, police and fire protection, etc.

The following are some suggestions for specific information for each of the major classes of parks.

Neighborhood Parks and Community Playfields: A knowledge of the exact character of municipal recreation program for which these parks are essentially used becomes the first thing to be determined. This is followed by population analysis including trends of growth, age groups, ethnic groups, social and economic groups. Make note of any trend in possible change in the population characteristics, present and proposed land use of the area which this park is to serve, the age of buildings and structures, the possibility of rehabilitation and redevelopment; land values may or may not be important enough for special attention. The relationship of the location of this park to the area which it serves and to schools, streets and highways, (all present and proposed) are to be noted. In considering the recreation program (a necessary element in the investigation) certain local basic policies must be known: is swimming being provided by natural beaches, by pools, and if by pools, are there fewer large ones or more smaller ones; does the department favor wading pools or spray pools; what is the policy as to the function of buildings in both neighborhood parks and community playfields; to what extent are school buildings and school grounds available for community recreation; must provisions be made for skating either on artificial rinks or natural ice; what recreation functions and what is the space required for those activities that are peculiar to this city? Other similar and related matters pertinent to the investigation will suggest themselves as the process continues.

Large City Parks: These are susceptible to many uses and the tendency over time is to utilize every "vacant" area with some special facility such as a building, (outdoor theater, museum, auditorium, even fire station or municipal parking lot) or an active play area. This eroding process changes the original intent of the park; its original plan and charm are violated and there is little left for native or simulated native landscape. Many of these alter uses should have a home of their

own. Be careful not to crowd too many diverse uses and too
little landscape into the original design.

As to the investigative report, what special features does
this site have – stream, lake, waterfall, hills, valleys, woods,
special views, archaeological or historic items, and so forth.
What is its relationship to other similar parks in distance,
zone of influence, other land uses in the vicinity, access, location of streets and highways? Is it necessary to provide for
neighborhood park or community playfield within this larger
park area? Is this area large enough to be suitable for such
special uses as zoos, arboretums, garden centers, museum
sites, day camping, picnicking, swimming, tennis or athletic
centers, stadiums, outdoor theaters, golf, parkways? Which
of these areas must be provided for and which other uses may
it be adaptable for if found advantageous? What is the probable zone of influence of each of the functions? What will be
the attendance at the various use areas, and how will that attendance be distributed by the hour on peak days, by the days
of the week, by the seasons of the year? Compare the required
space with the available space and make suitable adjustments
of number and kind of uses or adjustment of maximum capacity
permitted. Most of the information required for community
playfield and neighborhood parks such as population characteristics, zoning, types of buildings, and so forth will be needed
within the zone of influence of this large city park.

County or Metropolitan Parks: Area use-zoning is more
apparent in these parks than in city parks where the zoning is
apparent only when the idea is applied to the entire park system, although in reality and on a small scale it exists in the
smallest park. In county parks, however, the planner is conscious of the need of applying zoning to all parks; in fact the
classification system itself is a zoning process pertaining to
the entire park system.

The investigative report is based on the assumption that
the county's parks are classified as to preserves, active recreation parks and historical and cultural sites. It is also presumed that a ratio of permissable developed area to native
area has been established as park district policy. In such an
over-all view of the entire park system, a determination of
the radius of use must be made for all parks, or an origin and
destination analysis of the park users. If this has not been
done, it becomes the first objective of the present investigative report. The radius of influence, the distance and origin
of the user, the socio-economic characteristics of the population within this zone of influence and their habits of recreation

are not easy or inexpensive to determine. Reference to this process and possible short-cut approximations has been made on page 81. It should be realized that several studies have been made applying a process to a specific location and many more will be made in the future. So the admonition here is to refer to these investigations and apply the improved principles to the situation. In any event, some determinations, however approximate, must be made.

As previously noted, sometimes the suburban towns have difficulty in providing large city parks so the county or metropolitan district has filled in the gaps.

If the county of metropolitan district policy prescribes that the park now being planned is in the nature of a large city park acquired to complement the park system of suburban communities, then the investigation is similar to the investigation outlined above for large city parks. More likely, the park district policy prescribed for this particular park includes functions more typical of the usual functions of county and metropolitan parks: uses similar to those of a large city park will be prevalent, but in a more spacious environment of a more native character; hence more information on the ecology of the area, character of soils, tree and shrubbery growth, topography, geology, water characteristics become essential. More information is required on accessibility, distance to centers of population, presence of highways and county roads, probable radius of influence, and the general nature of everything that is within that radial zone. Inasmuch as this park is probably outside of the service area of municipal utilities, factors pertaining to them become important, – the source of water supply, the possibility of sewage disposal, accessibility to electric power and possibly even to natural gas. The same investigation as to space required for the functions that must be performed, the adaptability of this piece of property to other functions and how much space each will require needs to be made.

County parks of the preserve classification are the insurance for retaining native areas of the county for a long, long time. Hence it is necessary to preserve these areas. This is done, it is hoped, by permitting only about one-fifth to be developed for active use. This is one of the reasons for the acreage to be in thousands instead of in hundreds. Because of its size it can be readily zoned for areas of various intensities of use. The prime native areas will have lowest use density, and access to it will be limited to horseback riding, hiking,

and possibly a parkway or scenic drive with no parking areas
except for small turn outs for outstanding views. This sort of
arrangement makes compliance with low density use almost
automatic.

Assuming one-fifth of the park is to be developed for active use, that portion can also be zoned variously from high
density use to medium; the former would include the swimming
beach and boat launch with adjacent area for high density picnicking while the latter zoning would include overnight camping and incidental picnicking.

In making the investigative report, appropriate areas for
these use-zones may be noted as a preliminary suggestion to
the planner with the reasons for making these suggestions.

The active recreation parks do not carry the same burden
of perpetual preservation that the preserves do. By their very
nature of being largely developed, they protect the preserves
from suffering, the native areas from being encroached upon
by active use. Consequently, these recreation parks can be
in hundreds of acres instead of in thousands and can be quite
fully developed, keeping in mind that the lure of all metropolitan parks is the sense of space in a natural setting one gets
here that is difficult to find in city parks. The zoning concept
is here present the same as in the preserves except that the
low use density of the preserve may be present very little if
at all. Allocation of these density zones may be made in the
investigative report as mentioned before.

State Parks and Other Recreation Resources:

State parks are of two general types – (1) those that are
unique and, consequently, resource based, the areas which
need to be preserved in their native state, and still to be made
accessible, and (2) those state parks which carry the classification of state recreation areas, the main purpose of which is
to provide outdoor recreation in a natural environment readily
accessible to centers of population. It is presumed that the
state policy has determined which functions are to be performed by the particular park being investigated. It will have
been determined previous to the investigation what proportion
of the total area of the park should be left native or made native in character and which proportion of the park might be
devoted to the active types of recreation appropriate to state
parks. As was true in county parks, the character of soils,
tree growth, vegetation of all kinds, geological features, the
characteristics of lakes and streams, possibilities of water

supply and sewage disposal, presence of wildlife (state policy will have been determined whether hunting and fishing are to be permitted), the necessity of control measures for wildlife, highway accessibility, distance from centers of population, estimates of probable use of the various possible outdoor recreation facilities are all matters of concern. Archaeological and historical treasures must be thoroughly documented as to exact location, and all information pertaining to the events which make this site significant must be investigated.

State parks are not the only class of recreation resources available on the state level. State forests, wild life refuges, some national forests, reservoirs of the Corps of Engineers and the Reclamation Service are also present. Then, too, a greater array of recreation pursuits must be dealt with: hunting, fishing, motoring for pleasure, overnight accommodations are examples. Privately owned facilities either complement or compete: hunting and fishing camps and preserves, camp grounds and resorts, and ski runs are examples.

These facilities and recreation pursuits complicate the preparation of an investigative report and all of these should be carefully noted. But their presence need not discourage the necessary process of determining the socio-economic characteristics of potential clientele: who they are, how many of them, how often do they come, how long will they stay, how much space will they need for various purposes, and the degree of sophistication they might expect in the accommodations. Zones of influence of the individual facilities being planned should be determined in much the same way as in other cases, but there may be more factors to contend with. The general principles heretofore outlined remain unchanged.

The factor of preservation of the native and unique resources of the state is more pronounced and of greater importance than it was in the county situation. Greater attention must be paid to the ecology of plant and animal life in the face of human invasion. Hence the extent of subject matter contained in the investigative analysis is greater than in any of the city or county settings.

National Recreation Resources: There is only one National Park Service. Since its organization in 1916 it has been functioning and has developed its methods of preliminary investigations for proposed acquisition and facility development quite thoroughly and systematically. Many examples of its reports are available. These should show the young administrator the process on the national level and provide suggestions for carrying on investigations in his own field. He will notice that in all NPS investigations great emphasis is given to the native recreation assets even for potential Recreation Areas, and to the desirability of including all those assets in a given area within the boundaries of the proposed acquisition.

In general, the planning of national parks and other recreation resources parallels the procedure outlined for the states with expected increase or decrease of emphasis on certain factors: lesser percentage of developed to total area, element of preservation more pronounced, a greater number of use-zones in any one park. Although the radius of influence of national scenic parks is nation wide, experience has shown that the bulk of the visits (because of repeaters) come from within 200 to 250 miles of the park. Scenic parks are where nature put them − resource based without reference to centers of population. But National Recreation Areas are usually located where there is a population of about 25 million within a 250 mile radius. Hence the socio-economic status and recreation habits of the population within the 250 mile radius of influence will determine the use pattern of Recreation Areas and will greatly influence the use pattern of the traditional National Parks like Yosemite and Grand Canyon.

Other federal recreation resources are of as great a variety and exceed in numbers those of the states. Again, the principles of determining the factors governing planning (investigative reports) are the same as in previous cases. Both on the federal and the state levels, a tie in with the nation wide recreation plan of BOR should be made.

Summary of Investigate Reports: In summary, the investigative report provides the necessary instruction for the planner to make his plan by providing these elements:

√   The purpose for which the park is provided.
√   The uses to which the park is to be put.
√   The probable amount and character of the various uses and, consequently, the space required for each.
√   The source of expected attendance: from which directions, at what times, and in what amounts.
√   The permanency of the present pattern of use, as to use character, quantity, and timing.
√   The land characteristics (topography, biology, etc.).
√   Special foundation conditions for buildings and other structures, soil conditions for vegetation, soil conditions for sewage disposal systems, possible underground source for potable water supply assuming public utility services are unavailable.

√   And all departmental policy statements that affect park planning; some general description of any program for organized recreation or park interpretation, nature programs, etc.

√   Any other information which will help the planner determine space requirements and space location.

As a part of the planning process the investigative report will probably consume almost as much time as the preparation of the preliminary plan, and the time required increases as the attention proceeds from neighborhood parks to the great national resources. In cases where the park site and its environment are well known because of previous experience with that locality, short cuts may present themselves either by eliminating some elements of the formal report or by investigation of only those elements which present themselves as the preliminary plan is being prepared. However, such short cuts are not recommended to anyone except the most experienced planners and even in those cases its continued practice is fraught with possible gross errors.

In the determination of probable amount and character of use the proposed facility is to be planned for, an analysis of the socio-economic status of the expected users, matched with what these kinds of people expect and require in the way of recreation facilities form the basis of any such approximation. The necessity of precision in this analysis is greatest in the metropolis and less so in the cases of federal resources. Information and methodology at this writing may be sufficient to approximate requirements for state and national parks, but in planning recreation facilities for urban living much more precise information is needed. Urbanologists, (including sociologists and psychologist specialists) are busy finding out what social amenities (including parks and recreation services) are necessary, not only the minimum that can be tolerated but what in kind and quantity are needed for happy urban living. This fitting together of socio-economic groupings and recreation needs must go on in many situations if the more or less intuitive or rule-of-thumb methods of the past are to be improved upon. In preparing investigative reports on urban proposal, the closer the ideal can be reached the more successful will be the result.

The Drawing of the Plan

The first stage of the actual drafting process consists of several cut and try attempts at producing a diagrammatic sketch in which each of the functional space areas is blocked out, the size of those spaces having been determined from the investigative report. This is usually done on an overlay on the topographic map of the site. No attempt is made to fill in the details. Even at this first stage, consultation between the planner and the administrator is important because of the functional relationships between the various areas set aside for each of the functions. A number of diagrammatic sketches of this sort will be produced before one is chosen as the basis of the preliminary plan. Some of the more important criteria to watch out for are listed below in each of the major park categories.

1. As to Neighborhood Parks, 10 acres more or less. The athletic field should fit the topography as closely as possible in order to avoid excessive grading and to permit the salvaging of as many trees and other useful, scenic features as possible. If the building is to be used as a skating shelter, it should be close to the athletic field presuming that the athletic field will be flooded for skating. However, that location ought to be far enough away from home base to be safe from batted balls. If the athletic field is not to be used for skating, the building may be removed a little farther from the athletic field but still in its general proximity. Faulty foundation conditions may influence the placing of the building to more suitable locations and this in turn will have an effect on the location of the athletic field and related facilities. The building will function as a shelter building with toilet facilities and probably headquarters for both playground leader and maintenance man. Facilities for the smaller children should be in the vicinity of the building for closer supervision. These facilities include general hard-surfaced area, apparatus area, wading pools, etc. Play areas for larger age groups such as basketball, volleyball, horseshoe, tennis, shuffleboard, bowls, etc., can be a little bit farther away from the building. All lawn spaces should be located to make their limited use and preservation (devoid of paths and worn out spots) almost automatic through proper design of traffic ways. The overall aspect should be susceptible of being developed into a pleasing pattern – a real aesthetic asset to the neighborhood.

When neighborhood parks are adjacent to schools and the grounds of both can be planned as one, certain other guides may be noted. First it must be determined if a separate park building is necessary or will the needed conveniences be provided in the school. If a separate building is required, sufficient dispersal space should be allowed between school and park to permit placing of the facilities for smaller children convenient to the park building but close enough to the school for convenient recess use. The athletic field can be a reasonable distance from the school but not too far. Provision for some auto parking is necessary for teachers and public use. Some of this parking can be used for recreation day times and some evenings, but provision for blocking off a part of it is necessary. No other parking area is necessary because this is a park that is "walked to" and not "driven to".

2. Community Play Fields, 20 or more acres. The space allocation in this situation undergoes the same process as in the case of neighborhood parks, but there is more athletic area and also the possibility of other elements such as community building including gymnasiums or large social room with several club rooms, swimming pool which may or may not be developed in conjunction with the community building, auto parking areas, a separate tot lot area, some area devoted to neighborhood picnicking, and quiet unorganized use, more chance for plantings. The relationship of the "functional blocks" of the diagrammatic sketch has more possible patterns than in the neighborhood park case, and hence the greater importance of operational advice or criticism to the planner. It should be kept in mind that recreational functioning in both neighborhood parks and community play fields are paramount to topographical and horticultural features some of which may have to be sacrificed to permit good operation. Nevertheless, the final design should present a very pleasing pattern which again will be an asset to the entire community; hence the diagram should be susceptible of being developed into such a scheme.

3. Large City Parks, 100 acres or more. Scenic beauty and topographic interest dominate the large city park. Every effort is made, therefore, to preserve existing features of this sort. Provisions are usually made for a variety of special uses both in kind and in number such as the neighborhood park, a central athletic area, zoos, golf courses, sites for buildings, horticultural displays, etc. Each of these uses constitute a separate block in our diagram. Each should be segregated and yet placed to not interfere with an overall aspect of spaciousness and scenic interest. Necessary roadways should be kept to the minimum. Obviously, large auto parking lots will be necessary but ought to be placed to serve more than one purpose if at all possible.

In the large city park the planner will assume a more dominant role than in the case of community play fields and

neighborhood parks. Important considerations here are the
proper placing of access points, the circulation of traffic, the
preservation or development of a pleasing landscape while
serving a variety of unsupervised recreation activities.

4. County Parks and State Recreational Areas, hundreds
to thousands of acres. These parks are much in the nature of
the large city park with diminishing amounts and variety of
recreation facilities and increasing amounts of spaciousness
and native areas. Picnicking, camping, boating and water
sports, winter sports in appropriate locations, native hiking
trails and bridle paths, are the usual recreational activities
provided for. Again the investigative reports will determine
the space requirements of each of these activities, which are
incorporated into the blocks of our diagrammatic sketch. These
are either concentrated in one rather large general location
that separate the park from the native areas, or they are provided in several locations which do not destroy existing scenic
and wilderness features. Preservation of these features comes
into the picture here a little bit more prominently than in large
city parks but still does not assume the importance that it does
in what was previously conceived to be traditional state parks.
Area zoning based upon intensity of use is effective in these
plans.

Important things to watch out for include traffic circulation (which should be reduced to as few roadways as possible),
the care with which estimates of space have been made, the
possibility of enlarging these spaces in case the estimates
prove to be low, and the keeping of developed areas to about
one-fifth the total area of the park. The whole should be consistent with the biological facts contained in the investigative
report and should insure a beautiful landscape.

5. Traditional State Parks, hundreds to thousands of
acres. These parks which were selected for their unique characteristics bring preservation of the native assets to the fore.
Here preservation is the dominant purpose of any plan. Consequently, in blocking out areas for possible use, none of the
preserved areas are to be encroached upon. Roads, parking
places, picnic areas, and the like, must be located and limited
to leave the native assets unimpaired.

There is more leeway for expression of the 'planners'
imagination in the larger and more native of the state and federal holdings than there is when planning city and county parks.

Use-zoning has more apparent application in allocating various use-densities; it is not unusual for large state and federal parks and forests to include two, three, or more of BOR's resource classifications.

Possibility of introducing parkways and scenic highways in state and federal properties has appeal especially in satisfying the large interest in motoring for pleasure – sightseeing. Historical and cultural sights may be linked by such means with parks and private motels, resorts and other such accommodations and attractions to improve the tourist interest of a region. On a larger and more comprehensive scale, some thought provoking studies have been made of regional development for recreational, industrial, and residential complexes of, for example, whole river watersheds, with the hope that all three interests may live together in peace and harmony to the advantage of all.

Development of the Preliminary Plan

The next step in the design process is the preparation of the preliminary plan. This is based upon the diagrammatic sketch and consists of filling in the details of the various blocks of the diagram. It is here that the ingenuity of the planner can be exercised with some freedom of his own expression. In consultation with operating specialists he can exercise his imagination with form, color, texture, and materials to produce a variety of pleasing visual experiences. Freedom of expression is highly desirable but it should not constitute a license to go "hog-wild" to the extremes of color and form. Sensible restraint is necessary and that may become an important function of the administrator. His good judgment may have to limit the extent to which experimentation takes place.

The preliminary plan should go through a very extensive and critical analysis by all those who will have anything to do with the operation of the park upon its completion. For city parks, this is the time to bring in the recreation directors and the play leaders, the maintenance superintendent and his specialists in turf management, horticulture, building maintenance, the engineer as to practical construction and the use of materials, and not infrequently, representatives of the using public. The preliminary plan becomes the final picture of the ultimate park and will be altered only by minor details encountered during the preparation of working drawings and specifications.

Working Drawings

The final stage in the design process is the making of the working drawings and the preparation of the specifications, prior to the letting of the contract. The planner has now turned over his preliminary plan to the engineering staff which now indicates by drawings how the preliminary plan is to be executed. Plans will show all underground construction such as sewers, both sanitary and storm drains, water supply and water lines, electric lines, all in their exact location and proper depths. It will show all the physical features such as roads, walks, curbs, tennis courts, hard-surface areas, fencing, playground apparatus, and whatnot, all specifically located. It will give the detailed elevations, often down to a 100th of a foot. It will show cross sections at various locations indicating the exact amount of earth to be moved, and where it is to be moved. It will show the locations of all plantings by the preparation of a planting plan usually done by the Horticulturist in conjunction with the original planner, or by means of special specifications. It will indicate the depth and the kind of soil to be used in each case, what areas are to be seeded or sodded, what kind of playground apparatus will be installed and where. In total the plans and specifications will describe in detail exactly how the park is to be constructed. The plan should give sufficient detail for any contractor to be able to state a price for which he is willing to construct the job.

Although the county, state, and federal parks are not as compactly developed as are the local parks, correspondingly detailed plans and specifications are necessary to permit intelligent bidding by contractors. Because of the magnitude and variety of facilities, separate working drawings may be necessary for water supply and distribution, sewerage facilities, electrical supply and distribution, roads, buildings, horticultural ornamentation, and so forth.

Operation After Construction

The finest plan and the best of construction can be nullified to a small or large extent by operation which misinterprets the plan. Also a similar effect results if the planner has not taken full account of how the park is to be operated. Consequently, a complete planning package should include a manual of operation which outlines the main functions of the park, the activities for which it is designed, maximum capacities of areas, what to do in case future expansion is necessary, how each area is to be maintained, and special manufacturers' instructions for use and maintenance of products. In short, the operations manual should contain the results of all conferences which went into decisions for planning, together with such special instructions as may be necessary to convey administrative policies.

Planning Procedure Summarized

1. The making of the investigative report.
2. Inspection of the site with the report and topographic map at hand.
3. Making of several diagrammatic sketches and the final selection of one as the basis for preliminary plan.
4. The preliminary design.
5. Working drawings and specifications for construction.
6. Manual of Operation.

Chapter Summary

The main purpose of this chapter has been to discourage the making of a park plan by an amateur. A rather detailed description of the process has been made to indicate that the job is not a simple one and that it is a job for professionals, actually more than one professional. Small departments having but one administrative head may have to forego the luxury of professional guidance but they should avoid that necessity as much as possible. If they are pushed into the corner of necessity, the foregoing may provide some clues for the making of a plan, but it certainly is a long way from constituting a course in planning. The criteria given, however, may aid the administrator in constructively criticizing plans which are made by professionals. The administrator who has both planning experience and park theory is in an admirable position to have his department produce excellent plans, but this is an exceptional case. Good planning is always possible when talent is available and is thoughtfully guided.

" . . . . organizations have a life cycle . . . . a
supple youth, a time of flourishing strength, and a
gnarled old age" . . . . but they "need not stag-
nate . . . . can renew themselves" if the art of
renewal is known.

> John W. Gardner

The operation of a park and recreation service at any and all levels of government is dependent on a systemized banding together of the many talents and people who possess those talents in such a way as to act as a unit. Briefly it is called personnel organization.

Viewed comprehensively, the whole personnel will include elected officials, and administrative appointees above the rank of the park and recreation administrator, as well as employees under the direction of the latter. In this chapter primary attention will be paid to the employees.

The political makeup of the governing body is a part of the general political organization of the level of government within which the park district operates. The relationship of the park authority to the whole organization is usually consistent with the political environment in which the operation takes place. Out of that political environment, statutes and city charters have been adopted which set forth the powers and duties of the park authority. It is the state of affairs in which the administrator finds himself and he has no influence on the form it takes – at least in the beginning. Years of experience may lend authority to his voice in altering those laws or in the enactment of new ones, but that process the author deems to be too advanced a function to be dealt with in this elemental work. Anyway, the form of park authority has much less effect on the basic principles of park administration than the caliber of people in office. So attention will be centered on the organization of personnel below the level of the legislative body. However, a brief listing of the principle types of governmental organization in which park departments may be found is not at all amiss.

See supplement in Appendix, p. 262.

Organization of Personnel

Types of Governmental Organization

Without discussion on the merits of various types of organizations above the chief executive level, the student should at least know that the types have no relationship to population classes or to sections of the country. Some of the more prevalent types include the following:

1. The Mayor-Council type of city government, either a strong mayor or weak mayor, in which there may be several boards for various city functions, one of which governing boards is a park and recreation board. Such a board usually, but not always, has the power to select its own chief executive, known either as superintendent of parks and recreation, director of parks and recreation, manager, administrator, or some other suitable title. Where the board does not have authority to choose its own chief executive, such an executive is usually selected through a Civil Service system. Usually such a board has governing powers, but there are some with only advisory powers.

2. In the Strong Mayor type of government, some boards may be advisory only and in some cases there is no board at all, the chief executive of the park and recreation department reporting directly to the mayor.

3. The City Manager type of government has a chief executive for the entire city operation who is chosen by a City Council. In the operation of parks and recreation there may be an advisory board or there may be no board at all, the chief executive reporting to the City Manager.

4. City organizations of the foregoing type or modification thereof in which there are separate departments for parks and recreation with full governmental powers.

5. A Commission type of city government in which usually several commissioners and a mayor are elected, each commissioner given certain municipal assignments one of which will be parks and recreation. Usually there is no park board; the Superintendent is usually a Civil Service appointee.

6. Park districts organized under special legislative acts or pursuant to general state laws usually have complete governing authority and consequently select their own chief executive.

7. State park departments usually operate without a commission, are usually associated with divisions of state forests,

game and fish, drainage and waters, and similar functionary divisions, usually under one head known as the Conservation Department, The Department of Natural Resources, or some similar designation. The top authority may be either a commission or an individual known as a Commissioner. In such a case, the State Park is a division of the Conservation or Natural Resources Department of the State Government. In some states and in some counties, a park and recreation department may be a subdivision of the state or county highway department.

8. The National Park Service is a division of the Department of the Interior reporting to the Secretary of the Interior. Recreational functions are carried on by other agencies of the Federal Government. Each is a division reporting to its appropriate Cabinet Secretary. Planning, (other than site planning), coordinating outdoor recreation services, and Federal Aid to States for outdoor recreation, are vested in the Bureau of Outdoor Recreation in the Department of the Interior.

The advantages and disadvantages from the point of view of the park activities involving each of the foregoing types of organizations are not matters of discussion here. It is assumed that the young park and recreation executive is going to have small influence upon the type of organization in which he finds himself. Consequently, the succeeding discussion will be on organization of the personnel, beginning with the chief executive.

The Essential Functions of the Whole Personnel

Whether in a one man organization, in a small organization of only a few people, or in a large organization of hundreds of employees, the following are the functions that will have to be performed and for which some special knowledge and training is required. The list could be expanded by going into more detail, but the list is reasonably complete.

> Administrative functions
> Legal matters
> Real Estate and land economics
> Planning and research
> Engineering, construction, traffic control, etc.
> Maintenance of grounds, buildings and equipment
> Biological matters, including horticulture, floriculture turf management, arboriculture and forestry, entomology

Interpretation of recreation resources, recreation leadership and promotion, public entertainment

Police and ranger service

Operation of special merchandising and marketing services. (Sometimes called revenue producing operations.)

Public relations

Liaison with other agencies

Budget control, accounting and clerical

If present, such other services as zoos, aquariums, planetariums, observatories, museums, sports stadiums, outdoor theaters. None of these will be included in the following discussion but each may require a manager or director with supporting personnel.

Assignment of Function to Personnel

The assignment of functions to individuals depends to a great extent upon how many individuals there are, or in other words, how large the organization is.

1. In Small Cities. In towns under 25,000 population, the chances are strong that the chief executive will be working alone with probably one clerk. The chief executive in this case will be either the recreation or park specialist. Inasmuch as this individual will have to perform all of the functions outlined above or see that they are performed by somebody else, (the street department or otherwise), he is apt to be selected on the basis of his proficiency in the functions the village needs most. Often this turns out to be the graduate of a school of Recreation, because the maintenance of grounds can be taken care of by some other department of the village government. However, in other instances it may be a graduate of a school of Park Management, because the function of playground director can be performed by a high school coach or similar individual. In this case, it will be noted that the graduates of either park management or recreation are very apt to have a "blind spot" which is one of the difficulties of operation in a small organization.

In towns of 25,000 to 50,000 population, the chief will probably have an assistant, together with some clerical help. He is now beginning to require specialists in park maintenance, inasmuch as he will have under his direction neighborhood areas and possibly playfields or even large city parks. Even in the two lowest categories, (those under 50,000 population), it is important for the park manager to understand the necessity of engaging qualified professional help to supplement the personnel of his own department.

As the size of the community grows, the intricacies of the personnel organization increases. For further study, an organization suitable for a city upwards of half million population, or for a metropolitan park system will be assumed. In the latter case as with a state park system, there will be a greater emphasis on the interpretative programs (naturalists and so forth) and less emphasis on the recreation programs, police, etc. In the case of state and some regional parks, the practice of horticulture may lean heavily toward silviculture and toward ecology. Otherwise, the organizations will be similar.

2. General Types of Personnel Organization. Sometimes types of organizations are distinguished by the following: (a) the staff-line type in which orders that originate at the top are transmitted through assignments to subordinates, each of which controls all the functions within an area of the total operation; (b) the functional type of organization in which the whole operation of the organization is divided up into functions with subordinates in charge of each function; and (c) a combination of the two types above-mentioned in which the line type organization is modified by receiving services of a functional nature from other divisions.

Because of the many kinds of specialists involved in carrying out the total responsibility of the park and recreation organization, and because of the necessity of quickly getting orders from the top straight to the bottom, a combination of line and functional organization is usually used. Smooth functioning depends upon close cooperation between division heads as well as careful allocation of duties and frequent inter-staff visitations. Frequent communication between divisions in such an organization is essential to good operation of the whole department.

3. Organizing Into the Main Divisions of the Department. The functions enumerated on page 108 (The Essential Functions of the Whole Personnel), may be grouped and organized in many different ways. The student will have no trouble in assembling a number of park organization charts from different sources. They will be almost as varied as there are numbers of park and recreation departments. The park department in each case has analyzed its own requirements and its peculiarities of politics, civil service requirements, personnel resources, and the job to be carried out, and so they

all differ. Rarely will one find an organization chart which will fit one's own needs. Charts do, however, provide suggestions. In this course the time will not be taken to indulge in chart exploration, but attention will be given to more generalities, logical possibilities, and a few specifics.

The initial process of personnel organization is to group the enumerated functions into a few major categories, each of which may be assigned to possible assistants. The actual number of major categories depends somewhat upon the magnitude of the job to be done, but generally three to five groupings will suffice. Some logical divisions, all under the chief executive, are as follows:

Type A. Secretary having charge of the records, general office, budgets, real estate, public relations, and possibly special services.
Engineer having charge of plans, construction, equipment, and related matters.
Division of Maintenance having charge of the maintenance of grounds and buildings and horticulture.
Recreation having charge of the recreation program, athletics, golf, permits for the use of grounds, music and entertainment.
The foregoing excludes police and law. Police must be included if it is a function of the department and not a function of the general city, county, or state police. Legal matters are usually handled either by the city attorney, county attorney, attorney general, or by a private legal firm. Only in very large organizations is there enough legal work to justify the employment of full time counsel.
Chief and Assistant Chief handle administration and liaison matters. This is also the case in Types B and C.

Type B. Secretary or Comptroller, having charge of records, the general office, budget control and accounting, real estate and public relations.
Engineer or other having charge of planning, design, construction, maintenance, and horticulture.
Recreation director having charge of programs, sports, golf, entertainment, and special merchandising services.

Type C. Secretary or Comptroller, as above.
Engineer having charge of planning, design, and construction.

Maintenance having charge of grounds, buildings and equipment.

Horticulturist having charge of the greenhouse and nursery, street trees, and turf management.

Recreation director having charge of playgrounds, sports, entertainment, permits, golf, and related matters.

Promoted and supervised recreation in the cities becomes less prominent in the counties, still less in the states, and almost non-existent in federal agencies. On the other hand, interpretive programs in the cities consist only of minor nature appreciation activities, but increase in the counties, the states, and find their greatest development in the federal agencies. Hence the function of recreation as discussed above, becomes the more appropriately named interpretation in the non-urban agencies.   This substitution may be taken for granted in this whole discussion of personnel organization.

The greater areas of jurisdiction of the non-urban agencies make distances between parks greater than they are in the cities.   In consequence of this, it becomes expedient in County, State, and National Park (and other) Service to divide their operations into regions and/or districts.   In such cases a region will comprise a number of park holdings, each park having a park superintendent who has the maintenance and operation responsibilities for his park.   These duties do not include such general functions as financing, planning, construction or administration all of which are carried on at headquarters.   Regional directors are regional supervisors.

In large cities, a similar regional or district organization is in operation.

In the past decade, the trend away from separate city park and recreation departments has resulted in a combined department of parks and recreation with still two separate divisions, one park and one recreation.   This is not complete integration and has these objectionable features:

√   Such a division of responsibilities perpetuates an undesirable professional rift in an otherwise unified park and recreation service.

√   There is no clear-cut division between the two functions.   The division must be arbitrary and the assignments very much detailed out to be understood.

√   It does not take into account the many other functions which are performed for both these two divisions, e.g., legal services, real estate, accounting, etc.

√ Possibilities of conflict are greater where overlapping functions may occur, e.g., in public relations work. This will be increasingly noticeable as the study of divisional organizations progresses.

4. Organization of the Staff. Sometimes an assistant chief or deputy chief is interposed between the chief executive and the division heads; at other times the division heads report directly to the superintendent or chief executive. Regardless of how that is handled, a line of succession should be established extending to at least three persons. If the chief is off the job for any reason, a previously designated person will act in his stead. If the second in command is off the job, a third pre-designated individual assumes the top spot. Illness, vacations, out-of-the city business may easily cause two of the top individuals to be away at one time.

The executive staff usually consists of the chief, his assistants, and the division heads. For staff meetings, appointment should be made from the staff of someone to compile agenda, call meetings, take minutes, and distribute minutes, unless it is the policy to have only informal staff sessions without records being made. The actual functioning of the staff will be discussed in the succeeding sections.

With the aid of division heads, the details of the organization are completed, after which an organization chart is prepared and distributed. Such an organization chart is essential for a clear understanding of the responsibilities assigned to each individual or group of individuals and becomes a standing order with which everyone in the organization should be familiar.

Possible Divisional Organization

Secretary or Comptroller having charge of an office manager, chief accountant, real estate section, and the public relations section.

The office manager will have charge of the general office, its discipline, the assignments of clerks, stenographers, stenographic secretaries to division heads, machine operators, and secretary for board minutes. He may or may not have charge of auditors and bookkeepers, depending on the duties of the chief accountant.

The chief accountant or assistant comptroller will have charge of the accounting procedures, the compiling and controlling of the budget, and may or may not have under his direction auditors, bookkeepers, and bookkeeping clerks who otherwise might be under the direction of the office manager.

Real estate section will have charge of appraisals, real estate negotiations, and land records. A portion of the land record function might be carried on under the Engineering Department, but under the actual direction of this section.

Public relations includes the assembling and publishing of house organs, bulletins, and publicity releases. It maintains contacts with news agencies, and makes arrangements for speakers at public functions. In very large organizations the public relations section and its functions may be of enough significance to warrant the status of a division. In that case the public relations official becomes a division head and a part of the executive staff.

If the operation of special services and the merchandising of salable goods is a part of this division, a word of caution is in order. Inasmuch as these functions require auditing to insure that all monies taken in over the counter actually reach the city treasurer's office and to prevent or expose other fraudulent practices, it would be improper to have auditing a part of this same section.

Engineering Division, having charge of plans, construction, and equipment and including planning by the engineering staff and the construction done partly by the departmental crews and partly by contract.

Office crew, headed by a landscape architect or civil engineer and having charge of landscape architects, engineers, draftsmen, stenographers, clerks, specification specialists, estimators and cost analysts. In some cases these specialists may be grouped into subsections of preliminary planning and analysis, clerical, working drawings and cost estimating.

Field crew, headed by a civil engineer or land surveyor having charge of land surveying, construction supervision with various helpers such as rodmen, chainmen, and others all known as engineering aides.

Equipment crew, headed by a mechanical engineer or automotive mechanic having charge of all automotive and stationary equipment. The organization will consist of mechanics, helpers, janitors, dispatchers, and clerks.

The equipment crew may just as logically be under maintenance as under the engineer, depending upon the talent available. If the entire organization is large enough it is desirable to have this section headed by a professional mechanical engineer rather than an automotive mechanic. If this is the case, such a professional can handle other matters such as electrical installations, air conditioning, and so forth.

Sometimes the functions of planning are separated from construction on the theory that whoever plans and specifies (the architect or the engineers) should not construct (the contractor). One should prescribe and supervise and the other should execute. In such a case the planning division, headed by a professional architect or civil engineer versed in landscape and urban planning, is distinct from construction headed by a civil engineer not necessarily so specially trained. In that situation the planning section must prepare a master plan for the entire park and recreation system, including acquisition and improvement of each of the parcels, prepare preliminary plans for projects ready for execution, prepare working drawings and specifications of those projects, estimate the costs and supervise the letting of contracts, supervise construction, prepare long range plans and estimates of cost for capital expenditures, make models and other visual aids for public interpretation.

As mentioned previously, land records are frequently kept in the engineer's office under whose direction the land surveying actually takes place. Even in those cases, however, the real estate man can still supervise the keeping of those records.

Because of the mechanical and engineering functions so frequently encountered (sewers, drainage, buildings, pavements, fencing and layouts) it is not wholly out of order to assign the maintenance functions to the engineer. This, however, is seldom done. The arrangement is illogical because horticulture poses a problem unless horticulture is a separate division.

Maintenance Division, having charge of the maintenance of grounds and buildings, shops, and automotive equipment. The central shops will usually be the headquarters for the division chief, but otherwise the organization may be according to geographical districts or by separate functions.

The central shops will be headed by a shop foreman with janitors, storekeepers, and yard men.

There may be a separate organization for maintenance of buildings and structures which will include electrical crews, painting crews, cement crews, plumbers, carpenters, etc.

If automotive equipment is in this division it will probably be headed by an automotive mechanic having with him other mechanics, including automotive mechanics, mechanics for the care of lawnmowers, sprayers and miscellaneous equipment, and a dispatcher to schedule the equipment. Automotive equipment may otherwise be a responsibility of the engineer.

Maintenance foremen, having charge of miscellaneous crews for such things as pavements, the maintenance of sewers, fences, playground and other miscellaneous equipment.

Maintenance of grounds and buildings throughout the park system, (that is, the general housekeeping functions), may be patterned in two ways, to wit: parkkeepers may be assigned to individual parks throughout the system or parkkeepers may be assigned to only the larger parks with traveling crews maintaining or performing the housekeeping functions in the many smaller parks. There are advantages in having parkkeepers at individual parks because of the greater service they can be to the public and the more information they acquire concerning the various neighborhoods. The disadvantage is one of cost, for seldom can the cost be justified except in large parks. These housekeeping functions include grass cutting, the clearing of walks, the opening and closing and cleaning of toilet buildings, and a minimum attention to plantings. Often there are district supervisors overseeing the housekeeping functions in the several geographic areas of the entire park district.

The care of trees and shrubs is a part of the horticultural functions which may be a section under maintenance or may be even a separate division. In either case horticulture will include the horticulturist, foremen and crews of tree trimmers, operators of spraying equipment for trees, weeds, mosquitoes; a turf specialist, a florist to handle the greenhouse and gardens, a nurseryman to handle the nursery, and possibly an entomologist.

Division of Recreation, having charge of recreation programs, sports, golf, use permits, and entertainment.

In the past, a usual form of organization included a chief or recreation director with two assistants, male and female. Under present circumstances this is seldom the practice.

The permanent staff usually consists of supervisors in the following categories: playgrounds, city-wide sports – men, city-wide sports – women, community centers, golf course managers, sports stadium director. Community centers operating the year-round will, of course, have their own permanent staff. Each center will be headed by a community center director.

Craft and activities specialists may be part-time or full-time, depending upon the volume of work. They will direct activities in music and entertainment, nature appreciation, arts and crafts, drama, dancing, and pageantry wherever these activities take place. In other words, they are in a position to travel from place to place. Included in this group will be a sports and feature writer separated from, but correlated with the public relations section, the principal duties here are to keep the news agencies acquainted with sports and playground activities and to report the results of competitive games.

Part time help will include playleaders, lifeguards, attendants at bathhouses, golf courses, and elsewhere, playleaders at community centers, and sometimes sports officials such as umpires and referees.

The clerical force will be permanent and include stenographers, clerks for the purpose of issuing permits, handling schedules, sometimes keeping team records, and mimeographing. There should be included here one chief bookkeeper assigned from the Accounting Department to compile and control the recreation budget.

The recreation division usually engages in, sponsors, or organizes city-wide sports leagues and other sports not organized into leagues such as skiing and speed skating, for competitions all of which result in champions being declared. Custom has decreed that champions may be awarded something besides an emblematic trophy, e. g., a team trip to play other sectional winners or to sports meets in other cities. Expenses are involved which in many cases the municipality or park district is not empowered to pay for, even though team and individual entrance fees have been charged to pay for officials, incidental expenses, travel, meal and hotel expenses for winning teams. Once those fees have reached the treasurer's office, the aforementioned expenses cannot be legally paid.

In order to obviate such difficulties it has been possible for some recreation divisions to establish a quasi-public organization frequently known as the Municipal Athletic Association with close ties, and perhaps veto powers resting in the recreation director but otherwise governed by a board of directors selected by participating leagues and teams. If such an organization exists, certain precautions are necessary. It should be established with the full knowledge and consent of the park and recreation authorities. Its financial operations should be audited by a private certified public accounting firm, and it should have an agreement with the Park and Recreation Department about use of facilities. Its legality should be assured by the Legal Department.

In the operation of community centers and other buildings the operation of soft drink machines, candy bar machines, and similar devices emerges to a surprising extent and with surprising informality as to arrangements. The local community center director often permits such an installation with the proceeds assigned to some of his club work. In each case authority for such installation and for the use of the net proceeds ought to be authorized by the governing body.

Police. The chief arguments for having a division of police within the Park and Recreation Department are: (1) police work within this department is a specialized branch of police work requiring special training which will not be given by a general Police Department, (2) a more complete control within the Park and Recreation Department is possible so that police work can be integrated more readily with the rest of the park and recreation services.

The principal argument against this arrangement is that all police functions ought to be under the direction of one Police Department with assignments being made to the Park and Recreation Department where necessary. When this practice is followed, the Park and Recreation Department is inclined to believe that it gets the least competent men of the Police Department assigned to it. With proper co-ordination of the Park and Recreation Department and city or State Police Department, a very satisfactory separate park and recreation police division is completely feasible and in the writer's opinion more desirable.

Assuming that the Park Department has a separate police division, it must be kept in mind that the service is a 24 hour service seven days a week, accomplished with men working only 40 hours a week. The division is usually headed up by a captain or lieutenant with sergeants and patrolmen reporting to their superiors. In this case the captain would be acting as the chief, the lieutenant as the assistant chief, the sergeants would act as supervisors, and patrolmen are the actual workers.

Only in the larger parks will there usually be a foot patrolman assigned and then for only certain hours a day. The rest of the organization will be assigned to squad or patrol cars. Because of two-way radios, squad cars can patrol a great deal of territory and still respond to calls almost any place in a very short time. As a result, they can easily co-ordinate their work with the Police Departments of either the city, county, or state.

Whether patrol cars should carry one or two men is a matter of opinion. Certainly there are many circumstances in which two men are essential and one man is at a tremendous disadvantage, e.g., serious accidents, possible drownings, criminal assault. However, to use two men for relatively few emergencies when one man can do the business is a waste of manpower. A careful analysis will disclose situations in which a one man patrol beat is adequate and others where two are more frequently necessary.

Some of the patrol cars will cover a definite beat, may have to interrupt their patrol to be present for a couple of hours at a special function, or they will be required to handle the crowds and perhaps do some temporary traffic work. All of the parks for all seasons of the year need not be patroled 24 hours a day. Experience will indicate the most feasible way of handling this situation.

Patrolmen may be assigned to special duties such as in the investigation of outbreaks of vandalism, a specific crime, the analysis of the character of special crowds, census counts, and otherwise.

In summary as to personnel organization, the manner of divisional assignments is not nearly so important as the qualifications and adaptability of the individuals involved. As can be seen from the above, there are certain groupings of functions into divisions which are logical, but in each case several variations are possible. While the makeup of the organization is flexible, once it is determined it can be considered to be fixed and the assignments definite and adherence to those assignments religiously kept.

Operation of Staff and Personnel

All the preceding discussion, that is, the consideration of
the nature of park and recreation management, and the make-
up of the park and recreation system, and the organization of
personnel leads up to the functioning of that personnel in carrying out the job of providing a park and recreation service to
the people of the park district. How do we best use the tools
at our disposal to accomplish our final purpose?

We might visualize our undertaking by imagining that all
of the assets in land, improvements, personnel, including the
board or other superior authority, as being on board a ship
headed for a port on a distant shore. That port is our goal:
the best and most appropriate park and recreation service possible. If our established policies are in one direction we will
be heading for Port A, if another direction, Port B, or even
still another, Port C and so on. But we will have a definite
goal and a definite port to seek. On this voyage we will be
buffeted about by various elements and we will have to steer
our way through various obstacles. The lack of sufficient funds
will blow us in one direction, public apathy may increase our
drift, sudden prosperity may blow us in the other direction.
Possible collision with other vessels of state, the presence of
restrictive laws, and temporary court decisions all may veer
us to one side or another. But always we try to get back on
the course toward our goal.

The captain of that ship is the park and recreation administrator or chief executive, by whatever name known. He has
on board his board of directors representing the owners to
whom he is responsible, and who may influence orders or even
prescribe that Port B rather than Port A is the final goal. Our
purpose, however, is to see that the ship as a whole works in
unison and seeks the most desirable port. The captain, being
the professional, will do all in his power to keep the ship operating without friction, to keep it on course and, if possible,
direct it toward the most favorable port.

The Chief Executive

As captain of the ship, the park and recreation administrator must possess a solid professional background. In addition, he should possess those qualities of leadership which will
cause his associates to willingly accept his decisions, not because of a show of power, but because of good example, and

recognition of his competence. He should possess practically every good quality there is in the book and at the same time have enough minor vices and frailties to be human and, consequently, to be tolerant to a degree and even occasionally quite humble. To some, the qualities of leadership come easily and to others it is more difficult. All can improve their potential by a constant broadening of their knowledge of subjects included in their basic university education. This requires constant study beyond the professional realm, not only through reading but through personal contact with people.

The development of leadership calls for well prescribed specifics to any one individual; generalities are often misdirected. Besides, they may be slanted in directions which are favorites of the advisor. Taking such a risk the writer suggests a review of the following:

1. Contrary to the situation in past generations the present day public administrator cannot afford to be an autocrat. He must be forceful, but he cannot habitually impose his will because of the authority he possesses. He must earn compliance through the good will of his associates. He must be decisive, but only after hearing all the evidence. His fairness must be apparent. His judgment must be based upon sound professional knowledge and an appreciation of human values.

2. Helpfulness, courtesy, and kindness must be constantly practiced. No one in our society is self-sufficient. All depend upon others for some part of their existence. A lot of people on occasion depend upon us; we depend upon a lot of other people. In such an environment it seems only sensible to conclude that if we are to receive aid from others we must build up a credit of helpfulness toward others. Therefore, the chief executive should be one who is ever ready to be of help and assistance in all of his contacts – contacts in society, in business, in professional organizations, in church, and in civic affairs.

3. Because a park and recreation service permeates all through society, the manager of such a service organization, either personally or through other personnel with whom he is in daily contact, must be associated with a great many organizations. The manager should carry his share of the load in this respect and should attempt to carefully choose those organizations in which his kind of ability is most needed; for again he is not merely a hanger-on, he is a helpful worker. He should beware of being only a name on a masthead – a "front".

4. There must be a genuineness in his desire to be helpful. A false front is soon recognized and the "help" takes on
the character of a bribe. As the poet says, "The gift without
the giver is bare."

5. Confidence is an essential element in leadership but
overconfidence and snobbishness are definite liabilities. Because the chief executive possesses human frailties, it is
occasionally desirable for him to back off and to appraise himself objectively. A wife can sometimes do this very well.
Close friends can help. Accept criticism so as to be modest
and tolerant; but criticism should not destroy solid confidence.

6. Most people are good citizens and most people are
friendly and helpful, but they are all human and on occasion
most anyone can participate in a sharp deal. The ignorant and
the incompetent are the more likely transgressors. In spite
of the desire to be always helpful, the park manager must be
of sufficient keenness of mind to detect chicanery and unethical
motives early in the game. Forewarned is forearmed and the
good administrator will know what to do about it. An aggres-
sive exposure of the sharp deal, however, is seldom the correct procedure.

7. In all actions and consideration, the eye of the park
administrator must be kept on the final goal. Even though he
may be momentarily off course, he should bide his time and
get back on course as soon as conditions will permit.

This list could be extended but the foregoing suggests
enough to permit its expansion by individual analysis.

At the risk of seeming naive, the writer is inclined to suggest thoughtful consideration of time worn attributes of leadership: (1) the incorporation of "copy-book" virtues into a
sincere belief in the supremacy of noble goodness: idealism,
(2) the emulation of a hero's attitude of courageous adventure –
a willingness to step into the unknown with a confidence born
of a solid knowledge of the known. In sum total, here is the
suggestion of a child-like faith in the triumph of goodness over
the forces of evil as manifested by a courageous and skillful
white prince over the treachery of the prince of darkness.
Unrealistic? No. Rather it is an inspirational and satisfying
attitude as opposed to a "cynical" or even a so-called "realistic" viewpoint.

The Board or Superior Authority

Considerable thought and attention must be given by the
park administrator to the Board or other authority establishing

the general policies under which he operates. It should be kept in mind that the men who are elected to such boards or even an individual acting in the capacity of superior are either lay persons or persons not especially versed in the operations of park and recreation departments. It can be assumed that they have the genuine interest of the operation of the department in mind; what they lack is a special knowledge of parks and recreation. Consequently, they need a great deal of help in acquiring that information. Generally, they have other business or professional interests occupying their time in making a living and can devote only spare time to park and recreation activities. Consequently, information given to them must not be in overwhelming doses. The information should be brief and concise and specifically informative.

Personal contact with superiors should be brief unless invitation to the contrary is received; but personal contact can be frequent, even if it is no more than a telephone call so long as such calls do not become a nuisance. Regardless of the relative social status of board members and the chief executive the latter should recognize his official place. He should not be forward, but should permit the board member to make the overtures in all social intercourse. The ideal relationship should be one of mutual respect, friendly helpfulness, and a happy relationship that comes from a mutual genuine interest in a common undertaking. The relationship between the chief executive and his superior authorities is a prime concern; a good relationship is of great value in unifying the commanding operation of this "ship" of ours.

Staff Operations:

In small organizations, (50 to maybe 100 people), the chief executive may be capable of making all, or almost all, major decisions of administrative policy without more than superficial consultation with subordinates. The larger the organization, the more complex the department's relationships become, the more important it is for the chief executive to have the benefit of ample discussion of issues with subordinates on administrative policy matters and even on policy recommendations to the legislative body. Staff operation is also a means of keeping the entire supervisory team aware of departmental problems and objectives – a means of getting the entire organization to pull together as a unit.

The Executive Staff

The executive staff consists of the chief executive and his assistant together with his division heads, making in all about half a dozen persons. On occasion others may be invited to sit in. The chief must decide early whether he will call his staff together at regularly stated times or whether the meetings should be periodic when matters of staff significance are ready for discussion.

1. <u>Meetings</u>. The frequency of meetings is a matter of individual choice. Regularly held staff meetings have the advantage of frequent contacts which is a desirable objective. No excuse is left for letting things go beyond appropriate times for decisions. On the other hand these meetings can be perfunctory because there is little time for full discussion; they become time consuming because of their frequency, and might militate against efficient operation.

Calling irregularly scheduled or periodic meetings when matters have accumulated worthy of discussion has the advantage of the meetings being purposeful, more interesting and thought provoking; they clear the air more completely, create a closer bond of fellowship, and tend to do a better job. The disadvantages are that too long a time can elapse between staff meetings because they last longer, scheduling of time is more difficult, preparation must be more carefully done, records must usually be kept, and the day's routing for division heads is interrupted.

In the opinion of the writer the periodic staff meetings are preferred in spite of the disadvantages, provided that no 30-day period elapses without a staff meeting. In addition to the staff meetings, there should be opportunity daily for division heads to confer with each other and each with the chief executive. This can be accomplished by extablishing an office hour at which all division heads are expected to be available. This may occasionally cramp a division head's style but infrequent exceptions can be condoned.

2. <u>Mechanics of Staff Meetings</u>. If staff meetings are held at frequently scheduled times it may not be necessary to take minutes and record decisions. Such meetings are usually brief and their frequency minimizes the necessity of note taking. However, if meetings are periodic the mechanics should be better organized. The assistant chief can usually be held responsible for making up the agenda under the direction of the

chief, to arrange for a time and place, and to see that the suitable notice to division heads is given. Some other staff member may be appointed to take the actual minutes of the meeting and to have them transcribed and delivered to each of the participants.

The chief will preside at the meeting but otherwise the discussion is democratic throughout. The consensus is noted by the chief who usually accepts that as the final decision but, of course, he does have veto power and the final decision. The atmosphere of such a meeting should be entirely relaxed, the cue for such is usually given by the chief. If he is friendly and in good humor, that will be reflected in the discussion. Every opportunity should be given to be entirely frank about everything with chances for misunderstanding or the grating together of incompatible personalities minimized to the greatest extent possible. The stage for this may have been set by previous social contacts and an occasional good fellowship session.

It is at a staff meeting where the policies of the board or other superior authority are transmitted and aired and where the chief may obtain suggestions on policy which he may transmit upward.

3. Suitable Subjects. The following list of appropriate subjects for consideration at staff meetings is presented as being suggestive rather than complete.

The budget. This will involve free discussion between division heads about the relative merits of divisional requests and since decisions are usually arrived at by consensus of opinion, the pros and cons of all division requests causes the subject matter to be viewed in a purely objective way. The main items of the budget will divide themselves into such things as the ordinary housekeeping items that recur year after year, recreation programs which may be expanded or contracted, depending upon various conditions, and nonrecurring items such as major repairs and lesser capital expenditures. The latter items can be varied from year to year but consistent neglect over a period of years becomes expensive. Although the same items do not occur annually, there are items of this nature in almost all annual budgets.

Somewhat in connection with the budget discussion is discussion pertaining to the expansion or contraction of service to be rendered. This is usually dependent upon available funds, but may depend upon a number of other factors.

The formulation of recommendations for staff attendance at professional conferences held out of the city or out of the district.

A review of operations in any one or all categories periodically during the season or at the close of the several seasons.

The plans for an in-service training program and the assignment of duties to carry out that program.

The discussion of current matters presently before the governing body, which discussions lead up to definite recommendations by the manager.

Discussions as to various methods which may be employed in unifying the operations of the entire department; in other words, getting the entire crew to pull together.

Long range finance plans both as to capital expenditure and as to current operations. This may lead to suggestions for a change in laws by some legislative body.

Any modifications in the organization chart.

Matters which normally come under the heading of labor-management relations including matters which may involve the Civil Service.

Preface to Departmental Operations:

The following discussion on departmental matters is presented to introduce the student to some of the possible detailed operations and the selective way in which an administrator views these operations so that he may be aware of the policy and objectives of each without his having to know all the techniques involved. The chief executive cannot possibly be up-to-date on all the detailed operations of his department, but he should be aware of the efficiency of each, and that all divisions combine to supply a unified operation. In this discussion the student will also get a general idea of the ramification of the whole department without investigating each one. Every department involves many techniques that are largely acquired through experience and in in-service training.

Maintenance Division

The work of the maintenance division consists mainly of routine, seasonal operations, and a few which involve special work which may not recur the following year. Some of the seasonal functions applying to park organizations in the temperate zones of our country include the following:

Spring operations usually begin in late March or early April. However, if horticulture and greenhouse operations are included in this division, the growing of plants will have begun a month or more earlier. In the snow belts, the melting of the snow calls for the cleaning of roadways and lawn spaces of the debris accumulated over the winter, and the preparation of lawn areas for the coming growing season. Buildings will be inspected and clean-up paintings and repairs accomplished, all preparatory to the gradual use of these buildings – first the toilet buildings and proceeding through the various kinds of buildings to the bathhouses which probably come last. Athletic fields are put in shape for play; playground equipment, having been repaired during the wintertime, is now reinstalled and that which has not been removed is cleaned up and gotten ready for use. Grass cutting begins early and is continued throughout the season. The installation of beach equipment and marine facilities are included here. In summary, everything is done in the spring to prepare all facilities for summer's intensive use.

The summer season is the intensive use season and usually begins early in June, quite probably about the closing of the public schools for summer vacation. Bathhouses, pools, and beaches and boating facilities are already in use. The summer season is one of continual grass cutting, picking paper and debris from all areas – parking areas, picnic areas, neighborhood parks, playfields, everything. Painting and minor repair of buildings can continue through the summer season. Pavement and other road repair is done now. The peak of the season may be reached in July. From the middle of August on, the process of dismantling gradually begins.

By fall, athletic attention has switched from baseball and softball to football, soccer, and similar field games. The recreation program has been shifted from summer playgrounds to school buildings and playground activities after school hours. The community center recreation buildings gradually begin their indoor activities. As the weather gets colder, the removal of leaves, the taking in of moveable equipment, the preparation for snowfall with the installation of snow fences, the draining of pools, the cleaning up of roadways preparatory to winter, all become matters of prime importance. It is very possible that a lull in activities may take place at the end of the fall season or the beginning of the winter season.

Winter activities, usually beginning in December sometime, include the preparation of skating rinks or the making of

ice on skating ponds, the clearing of them, and the maintaining
of them throughout the winter season. These jobs use most of
the man power. Preparation of ski runs, sliding hills, and
other winter sports facilities is also taken care of. The recreation program has now shifted definitely to indoor activities
including the use of school buildings for basketball, probably
some craft work, and social activities. These same activities
take place in the Park Department's own recreation buildings.
Snow removal becomes a problem. The overhaul of summer
equipment and the manufacture of some items is a winter activity. Toward the end of the winter season there may be again
a lull which may call for a reduction of man power on a seasonal basis.

These routine chores are often carried on by regular seasonal assignments, but weather conditions and other factors
may require temporary shifting of these assignments. In consequence, the superintendent of maintenance has a constant
job of scheduling personnel for various days of the week and
sometimes various hours of the day. Heavy rains or storms
or other weather conditions may come any time of the day or
night requiring great flexibility in the operation of his man
power. It is very likely that the peak of the summer season
will find him short of man power so that nonrecurring jobs
cannot be scheduled at this particular time. Inasmuch as this
season is also one in which there is a constant public demand
for little special jobs, the superintendent of maintenance is
often hard put to satisfy these demands. It is not until the
peak of the summer season is over that the maintenance division is in a position to undertake some of the major repair
items which are on the list to accomplish. No doubt one or
two special crews has been doing special work during the summertime. Now the maintenance superintendent is in a position
to draw some of these off and add additional man power to do
major repair work.

The various building trades are part of the maintenance
organization. There is much routine work for carpenters,
plumbers, cement finishers, and electricians, involving minor
repairs to equipment and to buildings occasioned by the breaking of windows, faulty doors, failure of lighting equipment, the
breakage and plugging of plumbing equipment, etc. There are
also some seasonal jobs such as the draining of toilet fixtures,
golf course water lines, the re-equipping and redirecting of
athletic field lights, and beach lights. Then there is a gradual
shift from outdoor to indoor work for carpenters and painters,
and cement finishers.

If the operation of automotive and other equipment is a part of this division, it will be occupied with the scheduling of equipment for its daily use. Major repairs will be done in the off-season periods and field repairs during the operating season. For example, all mowing equipment will receive an annual overhaul and reconditioning during the winter season, and only field repairs or major breakdowns taken care of during the operating season. The same is true of all automotive equipment.

If horticulture is a part of this division, it, too, has its seasonal aspects. Greenhouse operations include the growing of plants during the appropriate time preparatory to placing them out into the gardens for display purposes. Inasmuch as both annuals and perennials are involved, the starting of annuals is at appropriate times of the year while perennials may be propagated either during the growing season or in the off-season in the greenhouse, depending on the species. Propagation may take place through cuttings or from seed and the plants may be grown for display purposes indoors, either in the greenhouse or at park buildings. Greenhouse operations may include a display conservatory where exotic plants are grown, in which case there is a year-round maintenance job in this connection, as well as in the preparation for special seasonal displays.

The operation of the nursery involves the growing of plants of the woody type, shrubbery, trees, etc. While this operation has its seasonal aspects, it also requires long-range planning, for certain species may be in the nursery for a period of 10 years before they are actually used in the field. The techniques involved include budding, grafting, transplanting, propagation from cuttings, experimentation in the development of hardier species.

The planting and the care of all plants, trees, shrubs and flowers is of concern to the horticulturist. The detection of diseases, insect infestations, is done by continuous inspection. Proper applications are made of insecticides as well as growth inhibitors, fertilizers, and other aids of plant life.

The maintenance of trees, (those in parks as well as those on streets), is another responsibility of the horticulturist. A regular program of pruning, spraying, and surgery is usually carried out in almost all seasons of the year except perhaps just prior to and during the planting season.

The operation of the maintenance division exposes to view all of the varied operations of the department affecting its physical properties. The variety of crafts, skills, and duties makes this function of park operation susceptible to all sorts of confusing situations if the divisional organization is not carefully made and assignments carefully made and scheduled. It involves the greatest number of men of any division and consequently, is the object of greater attention in the fields of communication and inservice training. It also is the source of most of the problems of labor-management relations. It deserves an unusual amount of attention by the park manager and his assistant. Indeed, the assistant may possibly be specifically charged with the responsibility of overseeing this division.

Some of the more important concerns of the administrator in the operation of the maintenance division include the following:

Make sure that the organization of the division is such that all functions are adequately provided for, including provision for emergency response.

See that there are sufficient cost records of individual operations to disclose any inefficient operations. Craftsmen in this division are prone to experiment and to manufacture where the purchase of manufactured goods is more economical and to grow things which can be more readily and economically purchased.

Check on the operations of the stores to see that supplies are adequate, that obsolete items are not stocked, and that odds and ends of materials and tools are not stored over long periods of time, eating up space and taking time in inventorying and record keeping.

See that matters of departmental policy filter through to the many workmen in this division that come in contact with the public.

See that the items which are budgeted to be performed in the current year are properly scheduled for completion so that everything does not pile up for the end of the season.

See that public complaints are promptly and courteously attended to.

Recreation

Basically, this is the division for which all others are provided – the division that should express and demonstrate the objectives of the whole department. This statement applies to all tax supported recreation agencies in all levels of government. Recreation is the common denominator of all efforts at providing those services to the people – local, state, and national. *

A division of recreation usually refers to a municipal operation because public recreation was born and reared in that kind of environment. Its purpose was incidental to living and not a fundamental requirement of life as it is today. Today recreation points the way to a constructive use of leisure time. Its "guidance" techniques are as applicable and necessary to the unorganized, free-time sort of recreation, (hunting, fishing, touring, exploring) as it is to a well organized, year around both-sexes-all-age-group type of operation that is encountered in the usual municipal operation. Imagination and innovation is what is required in the relatively new field of so-called outdoor recreation. (Witness the touring service of Auto Clubs, travel agencies; the guidance of sports reporters on fish and game; ski instruction; the interpretive programs of the National Park Service; camping and mountain climbing instruction.)

Recreation divisions of municipal departments are usually headed by university graduates with a B. S. degree in Recreation from a school of Health, Physical Education and Recreation. They are competent in play leadership, programmed recreation, the techniques of arts and crafts, the fundamentals of the performing and visual arts, sports and athletics. They have some good recreation philosophy, sociology and techniques of communication. Those with advanced degrees have much broader understanding of the great responsibilities and opportunities of recreation.

Hence, for the ordinary municipal operation, the administrator can assume that the usual programs which aim at providing fun, play, satisfying craft work, and some dancing and dramatics are well in hand. What the administrator needs to concern himself with is the appropriateness of the guidance programs being offered as they relate to the current needs of the several classes and age groups of people being served.

A well-rounded recreation program should include activities which are of general interest to, and participation by all age groups and both sexes at all times of the year. The thing to avoid is the adoption of programs catering to only a comparatively few people, unless it can be shown that such programs

* Refer to discussion of recreation and leisure in Chapter 1.

are the only programs which will appeal to the specialized group and then only if they can be given within reasonable cost. The park and recreation administrator and the recreation director, should concern themselves with this average unit cost from which any great deviation ought to be avoided. This unit attendance cost might be in the neighborhood of 10 to 15 cents. Deviations might cause some items to be three or four times this figure, while other mass activities might be very little. The higher cost may be justified by programs involving experimentations, with the expectation that additional and increased attendance will reduce the unit cost. There are often other good and sufficient reasons for higher unit costs in some instances. User fees sometimes bring high unit cost activities down to average unit costs.

The late L. H. Weir attempted to determine the fundamental instincts of people, which instincts he thought ought to be susceptible of satisfaction through recreation programs. He was inclined to judge the worth of a program by seeing how many of these instincts could be experienced by a given service. These are reproduced here for references purposes.

1. Provision for physical activities.
2. Constructive, creative facilities for handcraft and handcraft art activities.
3. Opportunity for learning of the natural world.
4. Experiences in communication, such as conversation, discussion, debating, public speaking, story telling, writing, etc.
5. A chance to express feelings and mental concepts in beautiful ways, such as in music, graphic and plastic arts, dramatics, dancing, etc.
6. Opportunities for people to mingle together in social intercourse, picnics, celebrations, etc.
7. Without the state being mixed up in religion, there should be provided opportunities for communion with a higher power outside one's self.

More recent writers — Brightbill, Butler, Meyers, and others — have extended and improved on that sort of examination and improved the analysis with greater detail and precision.

Still more recently, the objective of these has been oriented toward social betterment of the neighborhood or community somewhat in coordination with the efforts of the voluntary social welfare agencies — especially in poverty areas. But by and large, municipal programs (sometimes conducted by school departments) are stereotype programs of organized play. Such programs fall short of involvement in the social and recreational needs of children, youth, and adults. Both here and in the areas of so-called outdoor recreation, a greater manifestation of imagination in relating the recreation process to the aspiration of constructive use of leisure time is needed.

Before leaving this discussion, it should be noted that there is little in the education of the play-leadership type of recreation that prepares one for business operations or the sensitive operations of government. Therefore, it is prudent to add to the staff of this division one versed in business affairs, budget preparation, and budget control, for there are many small business operations that often are handled very casually otherwise.

Engineering Division

Invariably, this division is headed by a professional engineer who is properly licensed. Those in his employ who exercise independent judgment in the making of plans, drawing of specifications, etc., likewise, are professionals. These training and experience requirements insure a high caliber of performance in the great majority of cases. In other words, the individual operations are executed according to good general professional practice.

Matters of concern to the park administrator, however, do include these:

See that there is proper coordination of the operation of the division with the other divisions of the department, particularly in regard to the service that can be rendered to other divisions. These include the drawing of specifications for equipment and machinery in consultation with the appropriate mechanics and division heads; the drawing of specifications for materials and supplies of a construction nature but used in, for example, the maintenance division; consultation with others in regard to the care of pavements, care of sewer and water lines, the repair of bridges and structures where engineering may be involved, etc. Occasionally, the Engineering Department will be charged with the special investigation or survey involving not only technical matters but some involving park managerial judgment and political acumen which will require

attention by the park administrator. Having some general knowledge of the engineering functions, the park administrator should request justification for the engineer's
judgment in such matters as estimating, the use of certain materials, and the propriety of engineer-contractor
relationships.

Public Relations

When the park department's operations are large and varied, the public relations function may be important enough to
assume the status of a separate division and not be a section
of some other division. Its broad function is to provide public
information service and to present to the public a picture of
the character of the entire department.

The functions ordinarily performed include the production
of brochures describing the services the department renders,
bulletins on various subject matters, publications circulated
within the department in the form of departmental news, aid
in preparing speeches and articles for publication; the taking
of pictures and the preparation of slides, movies; the preparation of feature stories for news agencies such as magazines,
newspapers; arranging for public appearances before audiences,
radio and TV; maintaining smooth communication between the
department and the various news agencies — newspapers, radio and TV, the making of an annual report of the department's
operation from material collected from the various divisions
under the direction of the park administrator.

All of these functions need to be performed within a well
thought out program which has been the result of executive
staff discussion, approved by the administrator, and adopted
by the governing authority. Without such a definite program,
none of the foregoing functions ought to be performed. Simply
letting a public relations director loose on the general operations of the department is a poor investment in time and money. The program should be just as carefully drawn and budgeted as a program of dollars and cents expenditures.

Preparation of the annual report deserves more specific
attention. Annual reports of park departments the country
over are of various shapes and sizes, degree of attractiveness,
cost of production, extent of circulation, and variety of content.
This disparity of uniformity probably stems from a desire to
do too many things with one publication: (1) The recording of
history requires a detailed description of the happenings of the

year on virtually each piece of property. (2) Managerial observations certainly form a part, and, viewed over the long
pull, will give greater appreciation of the objectives of the
department than anything else. (3) Then there is the desire to
describe the salient characteristics of the department together
with considerable statistical matter. (4) Certainly, there will
be included an annual report of the financial transactions of
the previous year.

Taken separately and considering historical obligations
first, a complete description of all transactions, philosophical
observations, and financial affairs is a desirable document,
but is one that is of more value in the archives of the department than it is for general distribution. The general public
will be more interested in an attractive four-page affair than
it will in a large document. Even such a brief annual report
will find limited circulation.

The second type of general information can again be done
attractively showing in various degrees of detail, the facilities
and the programs available to the public. These will require
wide distribution.

The make-up of annual financial statements poses some
interesting problems. Professional accountants will invariably
begin by attempting to draw up a statement of assets and liabilities – a balance sheet. In this we encounter the first major
difficulty: that of capitalizing the value of park properties.
To be sure, we can keep track of the expenditures for land,
place a valuation on donations, and add to these the cost of
improving park lands, but that does not give us a true picture
of the present worth. Improvements become obsolete and expenditures for new improvements added on to the old simply
distort the picture. No accepted way of valuing in dollars and
cents park property has yet been devised. The mere presence
of a park enhances property in its vicinity and to compare private land values to obtain the values of adjacent park land is
an erroneous procedure. We come down to the fact that the
balance sheet will disclose the flow of cash but gives a poor
picture of the net worth of the organization.

Statements of income and expense, if drawn simply enough,
provide the public with the essential financial information.
Park departments frequently operate in a number of different
funds. Attempts to consolidate all of these operations into one
statement may be an interesting accounting exercise, but it
can be very confusing to the taxpayer. A great deal of thought
can profitably be given to the makeup of financial statements.

Annual reports are of considerable interest, not only to the home team but to park departments elsewhere and to public libraries where such information is used for reference purposes. A desire to fill this need can frequently complicate the issuance of annual reports. Those that are attractively produced and are of substantial size are the ones more apt to be chosen by reference libraries.

Just a word about statistical material. Without reference to the same material of the year before or five years before, or without reference to some other operation, or some other city, or park department, statistics can have relatively little meaning. Statistics should be given with some reference by which the statistical material can be valued or measured.

CHAPTER 8   BUDGETS

A false balance is an abomination to the Lord, but a
just weight is His delight.

Proverbs: 11 - 1

Budget is such a common term that presumably everyone understands its meaning; and yet a discussion of budgets is an ever-popular subject particularly at meetings of young park administrators. These young people have been in the business just long enough to know that the term budget can mean different things to different people, and there arises a degree of confusion. The discussion of this chapter seeks to clarify the subject matter without getting into a complete dissertation of budget compilation, analysis, control, and integration with accounting procedure. Each topic is enough involved to warrant special study. Enough will be discussed so that an administrator will know how budgets are compiled, how they can be used in the management of his department, and in what ways and to what degree the adoption of the budget may constitute operating authority.

According to the dictionary, a budget is (1) an estimate, often itemized, of expected income and expense, or operating results for a given period in the future; (2) a plan of operations based on such an estimate; (3) an itemized allotment of funds for a given period. The compilation and adoption of such a budget, consequently, may contain all three of the above ingredients, or only one of them, or parts of two or more. This accounts for the confusion in the significance of the term, budget, as used in ordinary conversation.

When the legislative body adopts a budget, it, in effect, is saying to its chief executive, or administrator, "Here is how much money we expect to take in; here is how we expect to spend that money; and when we adopt this plan of income and expense (budget) for the coming year, that adoption is your authority to do one of these things:

1. Expend the funds as nearly in conformity to this plan as your judgment dictates, so long as you do not exceed actual income. Of course, any great deviation from the budget or any actual deviation from the implied *intent* of the budget you will be expected to submit to your superiors and to receive confirmation of your proposed course of action – or,

See supplement in Appendix, p. 267.

2. Expend funds in the various categories up to, but not in excess of, the detailed estimates unless further authority is obtained – or,

3. Expend funds as provided for in paragraph two, but for only a three-month's period, or until a review is made of operations up to the end of that quarter and revisions made for subsequent quarters. "

Trouble usually results when the intent of budget adoption, as provided for in the three foregoing plans, is not clearly set forth – when there has been no clear-cut understanding between the legislative body and the chief executive as to exactly what is intended by the adoption of the budget. The first step in budget matters, then, is to determine just exactly how much authority the adoption of the budget extends to the administrator.

The paragraph one plan provides the greatest leeway for the chief executive of any of the plans. It implies a great deal of confidence on the part of the legislative body in the chief executive; and it gives the chief executive great latitude in operation. At the same time, it places the responsibility of suitable fiscal control squarely upon him.

In the second plan, the authority to expend is greatly curtailed; and in this case, the legislative body has actually made an itemized allotment of funds for the given period. No opportunity for transfer of funds between categories or for exceeding the total amount is within the discretion of the chief executive; he must go back to the legislative body for further authority. In this case the legislative body is attempting to hold a greater control over the acts of the chief executive and in doing so, of course, limits to some extent the dispatch with which the functions of the department can be carried out.

In the third case, a still further restriction is placed on expeditious operation through budget adoption by providing for the expenditure of funds for only a limited period of time. In the example given we have used a quarterly period of time; this might easily be semi-annual, or otherwise. This is the most stringent kind of restriction of the authority granted by the adoption of the budget and greatly hampers the operation of the department.

In case one, the budget is an estimate of income and expense, a plan of operation, and an allotment of funds. Cases two and three are modifications and restrictions on the above. In all cases, the actual plan of operation is not complete until the actual budget of income and expense is supplemented with

a budget of actual things to be done in terms of units of accomplishment, or man-hours of work, or units of materials and
supplies to be purchased. To provide this, some further discussion about the make-up of the budget is desirable.

*Insofar as the budget is a plan of expenditure, as well as
a plan for anticipated revenue, the items in that budget correspond to accounts carried in the accounting procedure. Usually such procedures require accounts for (1) the expenditure
of personal service (payrolls) in the various categories and
(2) the expenditure for the various classes of materials, supplies, manufactured goods, contracts, and such other things
as are classified as "other than personal" expenditures. This
sort of "personal,"and "other than personal" compilation may
or may not coincide with the needs of the executive for the
management of his operations. He may be more interested,
actually, in how much is expended for certain operating functions, such as the maintenance of roads and park areas of
various kinds, preparation for celebrations, the costs of constructing various items of improvement, the moving of facilities from one place to another, the delivering of supplies, and
various other functions which utilize combinations of personal
service, supplies, and materials. Hence, from his standpoint,
a compilation of the budget by functions, rather than by "personal" and "other than personal" items, may be more advantageous.

Not infrequently, even a third compilation is desirable for
a large system in which the amount of money expended for each
of the various parks becomes a desirable bit of information.

In reasonably large systems the job of compiling a budget
which is not only an itemization of income and expense and an
allotment of funds, but also a plan of operation – in such a
system, the complete compilation is an intricate correlation
of "personal"service and "other than personal"service, hooked
up to functional procedures or operations, as well as to the
costs allotted to individual locations, all of which must tie into
the accounting procedure for accurate control. Fifty to a hundred pages of typewritten and tabulated matter may easily be
necessary to support a budget of income and expense covering
only one or two pages of typewritten material. An examination
of some of this material may be of particular interest.

At this point it should be noted that public park departments frequently carry on operations financed by several different funds; for example, general tax funds for ordinary operating purposes; one or several capital expenditure funds

* See pp. 146, etc.

financed by the sale of bonds; separate funds for the operation
of revenue producing activities, such as refreshment stands,
refectories, restaurants, golf courses, and so forth. The
question immediately arises whether there should be one overall budget for all of these funds; separate budgets for each; or
separate funds for some, and combinations of others. Funds
financed by the sale of bonds, which have been authorized for
a specific purpose, must be accounted for separately and,
consequently, must have separate budgets. The operation of
revenue producing activities might be combined with functions
of the operating budget which are financed out of general taxation unless special commitments have been made for disposition of the revenue of one or more of these revenue producing
activities. In the latter case, the budget and accounting must
again be separate from other funds. Generally speaking, from
the operational and managerial standpoint, it is better to have
a separate budget for revenue producing activities, using only
the net results – profit or loss – as part of the general operational budget. Inasmuch as both methods are used, any comparison of operation budgets between cities ought to note whether
the gross income from revenue producing activities, or only
the net income, is used to augment tax receipts, and also
whether the total expenditure includes the gross expenditure
of revenue producing activities, or none at all. Comparison
of statistics between cities without this correction being made
is, of course, misleading.

For the sake of simplicity, in this discussion we will assume that the general operating fund does not include the gross
expense of the operation of revenue producing activities and
that the income is largely from taxation, augmented by only
the net result of the operation of revenue producing activities;
also that the expenditures, in consequence of the foregoing, do
not include expenditures involved in the operation of the same
revenue producing activities. We can therefore concentrate
our attention upon the compilation of budget for the general
operating functions of the department.

Referring now to the first form of compilation into two
general categories, "personal service" and "other than the
personal service", the personal service section will probably
account for two-thirds of the total expenditure of the department. It is divided into the various kinds of personal service
which the department employs, all the way from administrative
and supervisory help through clerical, labor, various crafts

(carpenters, painters, mechanics, plumbers, etc.), recreational leaders, etc., etc.* Such a listing does not indicate where or how this personal service is used; and from a strictly managerial standpoint, it is insufficient.

A similar situation exists in this same compilation, wherein the "other than personal" service category is itemized. The subdivisions in this category include such things as outside consultant service; the communications services of postage, telephone, telegraph, etc.; travel and transportation service, including auto allowance; binding and reproduction services; rental service (buildings, grounds, equipment); cleaning and waste removal; utilities; repairs; departmental supplies of many kinds; building materials; road materials; agricultural and gardening materials; awards and indemnity; insurance; and perhaps some minor capital outlay. As in the case of personal service, the amount spent for each of these items is not allocated to functions of performance; and, again from a managerial standpoint, they are insufficient.

We come now to the second compilation in which budget expenditures are broken down into functional operations, each of which is a combination of both personal service and other than personal service. Such a breakdown, combined with the compilation above mentioned, improves the control considerably. The subdivisions contained in this compilation are maintenance of parks, parkways, and playgrounds (if this is itemized according to parks, it provides the third compilation spoken of in the first part of the chapter); rehabilitation of grounds and installation of recreational facilities; walk and curb repairs; special road repairs; special building repairs; special park and parkway lighting repairs; special repairs to storm drains and water lines, (in each of the foregoing special accounts, each of the items is nonrecurring year after year; but the total item is recurring; this group of items is subject to variation from year to year); winter sports; greenhouse and nursery operations; operation of bathhouses and boatdocks; recreation promotion and supervision; operation of playgrounds and neighborhood community centers; general administration of the department; engineering; planning; police; stores; care of tools and equipment; and other items applicable to the specific park system in question.

These two compilations should be supported and supplemented by an enumeration of the units of work** expected to

* See p. 144.
** See pp. 146-147.

be performed in each of the foregoing categories of Compilation Two, together with the location at which such work is to take place. For instance, in the category of special repairs to buildings, this should be accompanied by a complete list of the buildings which are to receive this service, together with an estimate of time and material required to do each individual job. This, then, becomes the program that is the plan of operation for that department, or that division. The budget recites that Building "A" is to receive painting in such and such areas, outside or inside, or both; and certain alterations, and possibly a new roof, are to be provided. Each item is estimated in terms of man-hours for the various crafts to be used, together with costs of materials. In the case of the painters, for example, the summation of such items all the way through the budget constitutes the plan of operation and the allocation of funds for the painters for the entire year. The same would be true of the plumbers, the carpenters, and all other crafts.

Another example: In the case of road repairs, the budgetary item is supported and accompanied by a list of roads which are to be repaired, together with an estimate of man-hours of various types of personal service required, together with an estimate of the amount and cost of materials required to do each job. Here again, the summation of these items, so far as general labor is concerned, will constitute the man-hours of general labor which is required for the entire year and will support that particular item in the budget Compilation Number One.

Still another example: The items of recreation supervisory service, playground operation, and the operation of community center buildings, will indicate which buildings and which playgrounds are to be operated for the year and what the season of each will be – that is, when they open and when they close – if there is a season. Again, the summation of the man-hours of work in each of the personnel categories will correspond to the amount of money set aside in the two compilations above referred to. Materials and supplies costs will also add up to the total set out in the compilations.

In summary, then, the budget is a listing of income and expense, compiled in more than one way, for both operational and accounting control and will also have the statements of the amount of work to be performed in each of the categories, together with schedules, in certain cases, for the seasonal operation. The adoption of a budget of this sort constitutes an estimate of income, a plan of expenditure, and an actual plan of operation for the entire year. Such a budget facilitates the entire park operation and, if properly managed, permits various division heads and supervisory help under those division heads to be responsible for a certain section, or subdivision, of each of the categories involved in the entire budget, all of this, of course, within the limitations established by the legislative body.

The rigidity with which budget allocations for individual items is adhered to depends upon how much leeway has been given by the legislative body and how much leeway the chief executive has delegated to his subordinates. It also depends upon unforeseen and unpredictable incidents within the operating year. In any event, when the adoption of the budget has taken place and anyone in the entire organization encounters something which ought to be done and was not provided for, he approaches his superior for authority to digress. If the superior has that authority, it will be limited to minor variations within his own budget, but certainly not to the extent of increasing it. He may be able to forego doing one thing for the sake of doing some other thing, or he may not. There should be some limited leeway in each case, the degree depending upon how much leeway the chief executive himself has. The significant point remains, however, that the adoption of a budget is the adoption of a plan of expenditure and a plan of operation with flexibility limited to such a degree as the legislative body sees fit.

The following tabulations illustrate the various ways compilations of expenditures are made, as was discussed in previous pages. This is condensed from budget of Minneapolis Park Board.

Compilation No. 1

ESTIMATED EXPENDITURES
By Accounting Codes

PERSONAL SERVICE $2,283,100

    Divided into 27 categories, such as
Administrative, Clerical, Engineering,
various building trades, Maintenance
Labor and Supervision, Horticulture
(Labor and Supervision), Recreation
(Supervision, Play Leaders, Attendants),
Mobile Equipment Operators, and others.
Each item can be supported by number of
employees, hours of work, exact length
of season, thereby constituting a plan of
employment.

CONTRACTUAL SERVICE   556,735

    Expert and Consultant, Communications and
Travel, Printing and Binding, Rent, Cleaning, Utilities, Repairs.

MATERIALS AND PARTS   188,230

    Office, Chemical, Household, Recreation,
Building, Maintenance, Agriculture.

OTHER CURRENT CHARGES   8,340

    Insurance, Indemnities, Membership Fees, etc.

MINOR CAPITAL OUTLAY   28,595

    Building and Plant Equipment, Construction,   ──────────
Equipment, Furniture and Fixtures. $3,064,050

Compilation No. 2

ESTIMATED EXPENDITURES
By Operating Function

MAINTENANCE OF PARKS, PARKWAYS $ 957,000

A third compilation (No. 3) breaks this figure
into expenditures for each individual park.

SPECIAL MAINTENANCE AND
IMPROVEMENT ACCOUNTS   235,650

These are items that do not occur each year,
although others may take their place. They
include Grounds, Recreation Facilities,
Shoreline Repairs, Walks, Roads, Buildings,
Drains and Sewers, Park Equipment, etc.

WINTER SPORTS   332,850

Skating, Hockey, Ski Slides, etc.

HORTICULTURAL   178,100

Nursery, Greenhouse, Gardens, Forestry.

BOAT DOCKS, BATHS, BEACHES   121,750

Individually itemized.

OTHER OPERATING ACCOUNTS   16,850

Tennis Center, City Wide Sports Fields.

RECREATION PROMOTION AND SUPERVISION   503,850

Administrative and City Wide, Community
Centers, Playgrounds, Concerts, Central
Stores.

GENERAL ACCOUNTS   700,000

Administration, General Engineering, Park Design and Research, Police, Care of Tools and
Equipment, Purchase of Tools and Equipment.   ─────────────

                                                 $3,064,050

Note: Each item of this compilation is supported by estimates of cost
and units of work to be done (See Compilation No. 4).

Example of Compilation No. 4

This supports the item of Special Building Repairs ($65,000) which is part of SPECIAL MAINTENANCE AND IMPROVEMENT ACCOUNTS in Compilation No. 2 and which has a total for all such accounts of $235,650. Other items in this category have similar supporting estimates, the total of all of which is $235,650.

SPECIAL BUILDING REPAIRS

PERSONAL SERVICE

111	Maintenance Labor (465 hrs)	$ 1,545
114	Plumbing Labor (15 hrs)	65
141	Carpenters (1,220 hrs)	4,940
142	Cement Finisher (450 hrs)	1,850
143	Electricians (290 hrs)	1,300
144	Mechanics (13 hrs)	50
145	Painters (7,000 hrs)	27,300
146	Plumbers (25 hrs)	125

TOTAL PERSONAL SERVICE . . . . $ 37,175

OTHER THAN PERSONAL SERVICE

541	Advertising	10
552	Rental of Park Equipment	540
582	Contract Building Repairs	16,700
599	Misc. Contract Service	200
602	Small Tools	65
603	Shop Supplies	25
609	Misc. Operating Supplies	25
653	Plumbers Materials	160
654	Painters Materials	6,320
655	Electricians Materials	1,000
656	Carpenters Materials	2,720
658	Cement and Concrete	60

TOTAL OTHER THAN
PERSONAL SERVICE . . . . $ 27,825

TOTAL ESTIMATE $ 65,000

The program will follow the attached schedule as closely as possible, although the listing does not necessarily indicate the priority of the projects. See next page for program.

Note: The hourly costs used here include general items such as cost of vacations, sick leave, etc.

Compilation No. 4 (Continued)

The said listing is in the following form:

PROPOSED PROGRAM OF SPECIAL BUILDING REPAIRS AND IMPROVEMENTS

LOCATION	CARPENTER	PAINT	PLUMB.	ELEC.	CONTRACT	MASON	TOTAL	
	$	$	$	$	$	$		
AUDUBON PARK								
R Paint Wading pool		$200					$200	R
BRYANT SQUARE								
I Tile Floor in office & craft room	190						190	I
R Elec. outlets in office				100			100	R
I Cabinets in craft room	200	59					259	I
R Rewire lights				350			350	R
							$899	
CALHOUN LAKE								
I New Roof for boathouse	630						630	I
R Paint Mast		250					250	R
FOLWELL PARK								
I Cupboards, Kitchen	150	60					210	I
R Touch-up painting		190					190	R
R Paint flag pole		100					100	R
							$500	
FRANKLIN STEELE SQUARE								
R Paint Wading pool		200					$200	R
HOLMES SCHOOL								
R Paint Wading pool		200					$200	R
JACKSON SQUARE								
R Paint Wading pool		200					$200	R
KEEWAYDIN FIELD								
I Kitchen cupboards	120	35					155	I
I Storage cabinets in craft room	150	60					210	I
R Paint window and door frames		200					200	R
I Soundproof ceiling							200	I
I Gas convert, stand-by heat (School Board)	600						600	I
TOTALS (6 pages later)	$9,450	$32,918	$350	$2,660	5,000 $16,917	$2,705	$65,000	

Note: R = Repair, I = New improvement - Other items of the "Special Maintenance and Improvement" accounts have similar programs.

Note: In separate memos, each of the above items is divided into personal and other than personal components, each coded so they can be woven into the compilation by codes on p.

CHAPTER 9   POLICIES–IN GENERAL AND ON RELATIONSHIPS

Michael Haider, Chairman of Standard Oil of New Jersey, commenting on the value of nonprofessionals on his Board, "Their unfamiliarity with the oil business can be useful just because they will ask a question to which we think we've known the answer a long time."

Policies in General

In making decisions, it is very difficult to weigh the pros and cons of a subject without having some idea of the historical background of previous decisions made under similar circumstances or without knowing what the current local and national practice is in regard to similar matters. A knowledge of previous decisions and current practices would help a great deal because these decisions no doubt were made only after many discussions on similar subjects everywhere. If these decisions could be shown on a graph, they no doubt would fall in a band somewhat above and somewhat below a median line which might be called policy. What is policy?

In the dictionary a number of definitions for policy may be found, but the one which is most applicable here is "settled or definite course or method adopted and followed by a government, institution, body, or individual."

Policies are not immutable laws or rigid rules. In toto they indicate a settled course – a course which can change with the times. Decisions made contrary to a policy should be considered deviations from the "settled course", probably marking a turn in the road. Deviations are, therefore, important enough to ponder carefully as being just what they are; a turning away from the old way of doing things and not just a momentary exception to a general rule. Deviations from the general policy should be made only with a full determination that the new way is distinctly better than the old – that the policy itself ought to be changed. To make a step away from a set course with the expectation that the next step can be made back onto the old course is a pretty optimistic viewpoint to assume. One deviation leads to another. Hence, it is of prime importance that in some way or other, the first point of deviation from the settled course must be promptly detected. Before a decision at that point is made, a review of the possible consequences should take place.

See supplement in Appendix, p. 271.

A simple example can illustrate the point. A community center director has had policies laid down to him as to the use of his building for certain times and events by groups or clubs which are not a part of his program. Suppose that on some off hours a small group, not included in the permissible users of the building, approaches the director and asks permission to use the building because it is not being used at the moment. They reason that the group is not a large one, they will not use it very long, and they advance other plausible reasons. The director sees nothing wrong with it at the moment, even though it is in violation of the rules, but he thinks it is safe to make an exception in this case. The building is used in that manner and no unfavorable consequences followed, so when a second situation of that kind arises, another exception is made. This may be followed by a second group which argues before the director that Group A used the building on such and such an occasion and why can't Group B use it under similar circum-stances – and the director consents.

Similar exceptions to the stated policy may be repeated many times over a period of months before the director's su-periors actually know about the situation, and then only be-cause a decision is asked for on a most flagrant violation of the established policy. The whole inconsistent application of the existing policy is disclosed. It is now very difficult to get back on the original path without embarrassment to the park department as well as to the organizations involved. If a re-view of the situation had been made at the time of the first de-viation, the whole unfortunate subsequent experience could have been avoided.

It is possible that at the point of the first deviation a re-view may lead to the conclusion that an actual change in the policy is advisable. This results in an orderly change which is altogether different than having the matter drift to an unfor-tunate conclusion.

It has previously been stated that policies are not immu-table laws, implying thereby that some deviations may be pos-sible; it has also been stated that one deviation from a policy leads to another and to expect that after one exception to the policy a single simple step back onto the old course can be made is all too optimistic a viewpoint to take. The reconcili-ation of these two statements is a very common administrative dilemma; it confronts everybody from the community center attendant cited above to the top administrator. Much of the success of the administration of the particular function mo-mentarily at hand depends on how well judgment and finesse are exercised in resolving this dilemma. Being fallible human beings, all of us are sinners to some degree; our good reputation rests upon the small degree and the little extent of our sinning, as well as upon the acceptable standard in which we are operating, also to what extent these shortcomings may be offset by exceptionally good performances.

Deviating from the established policy, like sinning and lawbreaking, is fraught with danger. Policies, therefore, may be closer to rules of conduct than simply broad guides of behavior and bases for decision. Policies should be made within a framework that is humanly feasible of attainment and socially and politically acceptable. Periodic review and revision are necessary to keep policies current and meaningful. The time of first deviation from the settled course of procedure should be the automatic signal for "stop, look, and listen" – a time for review and possible revision of the established policy. The first deviation should not be ignored.

Inasmuch as the making of decisions in the absence of reference material is difficult and very often inconsistent, the enunciation of policies is of prime importance. But policies are often distilled from many small decisions made over a long period of time, may have evolved imperceptibly by habit and may or may not be in written form. A new employee, or an old employee in a new position, finds out such things by making unfortunate errors of judgment. The whole operation of the department would be much better if there existed in each department a "book" of general policies.

It is helpful for the purposes of this text to consider policies to be of two general classes: (1) Legislative Policies which are formulated by legislative bodies or by individuals above the rank of PR Administrator, and (2) Administrative Policies which govern methods of procedure within the Legislative Policy framework, and the formulation of rules and regulations to insure compliance with established policy.

Legislative Policies emanate from the laws which create the Park and Recreation Department and enable it to function. Within this legal framework the legislative authority adopts rules governing its own legislative procedure*, ordinances governing the use of park property and general policies governing the operation of the department. * *

---

*   For sample see Appendix p. 307.
** For sample see Appendix p. 294.

Although the Administrator may take part in advising the legislative body about the formulation of Legislative Policies, his special province lies in establishing Administrative Policies, rules and regulations for daily operations of his department, all within the policy guide lines laid down by the legislative body.

The two general classes of policies facilitate the compilation of policy manuals. Rather than having one unwieldy, large book of Policies and Manual of Operation, separation of subject matter into two classes makes the whole more understanding.

The discussions on relationships which follow may be considered to have been derived from both Legislative and Administrative Policies, they being the net result of decisions of both the commission and the chief executive. It is also from the suggestions contained in the following discussions that policies may be formulated – some legislative and some administrative as may be appropriate to any department under consideration.

Policies in Relationships

A park and recreation department in any of the levels of government will have many relationships with other governmental agencies as well as private agencies in allied fields. There also will occur relationships of importance between divisions or division heads within the same department. If the department has a legislative and policy-making board, important relationships will exist between the legislative body and the chief executive and his staff.

Established and well-recognized policies in governing these relationships are important aids in the efficient and friendly operation of the department. Both the relationships and the policies which might occur in connection therewith are too numerous to compile in one volume which presumes to cover all levels of government and all geographical areas. Enough is included in the following discussion to enable the student to get some concept of how these relationships may be treated and to recognize policies when he sees them stated. The student should recognize, however, that as regards the former, there frequently exists opportunity for differences of opinion for any given set of circumstances and that there may be alternative and more applicable statements in various special circumstances.

The Chief Executive and His Legislative Body, With Some Comments as to Procedure

Every Park and Recreation Department is established by some law, state statute, park district law, municipal charter, or in the case of the federal services, the Congress. If the powers and duties in connection therewith have been assigned to a legislative body like a Board, that Board will probably have adopted rules and regulations for its own conduct and in doing so has prescribed duties and powers for the chief executive, all as part of legislative policy.

Within the limitations stated in the "Rules of the Board,"* the Administrator is expected to operate the department. However, the statement of duties and authority in the Rules are probably so broad that further clarification is desirable. This clarification comes about by either an elaboration of the original statement (an extension of the Legislative Policy Statement) or by a period of experience in dealing with matters of administration during which time the administrator is testing the limits of his authority in dealing with departmental affairs without specific legislative guidance. In other words, the Administrator seeks to exercise as much authority as he can within the general legislative policy without incurring the displeasure of the Board itself. The legislative body is just as apt to invade the province of the administrator as the reverse situation.

Obviously, there is going to be some difference of opinion on some issues as to the appropriateness of the Administrator's action, which in time, may cause modification of the original policy statement. It is well, therefore, to anticipate as many of these possible conflicts when the policy is first adopted than to wait for emotions to becloud sound judgment as differences arise. There are PR departments that never do draw the line between legislative and administrative prerogatives, letting the matter work itself out during changes in personnel – not a really happy solution.

Matters Properly Before the Board

Matters requiring action of the Board probably originate in three ways: petitions and communications from the general public, reports of its officers, and by members of the Board

* See p. 307 of appendix.

speaking from the floor under the heading of new business. A typical functioning may be as follows:

Citizens wishing the Board to act on certain matters which cannot be disposed of by the Chief executive and his staff because of lack of authority, are informed that they can lay the matter before the Board in the form of a petition or communication. Sometimes they will appear before the Board in person, but generally speaking, this is discouraged (unless a public hearing on the subject is called for later by the Board) because such impromptu appearances interfere with the orderly procedure of the Board and the scheduling of matters to be brought before it. Also, the subject matter is usually prematurely discussed because no investigation has been made, making it difficult for the pertinent points involved to be brought out and logically discussed. Ordinarily no citizen should be entitled to speak before the Board without the consent of the Board. Occasionally, the Board may give its consent as a matter of courtesy to visiting V. I. P.'s or to anyone for some brief and noncontroversial matter.

The chief executive and his staff are always acting under Board direction, deriving all of their powers and authority from the Board. Much of this is in general terms as provided in the rules of the Board, the adoption of the annual budget, the approval of plans for new construction, and similar matters. Nevertheless, these and many specific items require Board approval. Consequently, the chief executive or other officers of the Board sometimes present matters for Board action through official reports.

Under the heading of new business, any board member is entitled to present any matter to the Board for its consideration. For the sake of both harmony in Board procedure, and good public relations, Board members should show discrimination in the subject matter brought to the Board's attention in this manner. Details of administration which could be taken up privately with the Administrator or his staff ought to be avoided. For example, "Why wasn't the skating rink cleared on a certain day?" "One of my constituents has complained about how the tree in front of his house was trimmed," that he "saw loafing on the job," and hosts of similar questions and complaints. These can be readily handled by the Superintendent and his staff. However, if Board members do not get satisfaction from the Administrator on repeated occasions, the subject matter can be brought before the Board and investigation made. It is well to keep in mind that if open criticism between Board members or between Board members and staff members occurs in open Board sessions at which the public's eyes are focused and their ears attuned by the presence of newspaper reporters, the effectiveness of the Board's influence of public matters suffers. Every effort should be made toward frank, private discussion which may eliminate misunderstandings in open meetings, thereby permitting complete harmony and decorum to prevail.

Matters which are appropriate for Board members to bring to the attention of the Board include: items pertaining to new projects which ought to receive special attention, subject matters which require special investigation, and in general, matters pertaining to policy and legislation which is the broad function of the Board. Even on these matters prior consultation with other Board members and sometimes even with the executive officers may point out the most orderly and expeditious way to resolve the subject matter.

Usually in carrying out the intent and purposes of the law under which they are operating, the Board has assigned to its chief executive officer, and his staff, all administrative matters and has retained for itself all legislative matters and matters of general policy. * It is important that these areas of activity be carefully followed. While frequent conversations take place between individual members of the Board and the Administrator and his executive staff, it should be fully recognized that the actual orders to the Administrator come from the Board as a whole and not from its individual members. It is equally important, on the other hand, that the Administrator and his staff recognize that action on policy and on legislative matters, or on any other matters, are paramount to the individual opinions of members of the executive staff and should become wholeheartedly the attitude of the entire department. The Administrator should have ample opportunity to make recommendations to the Board involving all matters, even including suggestions as to future policy, but once the Board has acted, that action, be it in accordance with or contrary to the recommendations, must be accepted wholeheartedly as the conclusion of the entire department.

While the rules of the Board may establish certain procedures for the operation of committees and for the conduct of Board business generally, the time available to individual members of the Board to attend meetings necessarily requires

* See P. 305 in Appendix.

certain deviations not only as to meeting dates but as to the orderly presentation of some matters. When that becomes necessary, however, it should be the policy of the executive staff to keep the Board members individually informed so that the spirit of the orderly procedure outlined in the rules of the Board can be carried out.

In his relationship with the Board and with his executive staff, the Administrator ought to have an understanding with both the Board and his staff members as to how frequent and on what subjects direct contact between Board members and staff members may occur. Generally speaking, there should be easy communication between them. However, it should be thoroughly understood, especially by the staff members, that no conversation of significance should be withheld from the chief executive. Occasions do arise when Board members like to pry, or shall we say spy, to see if some rift cannot be nurtured between the chief executive and his staff for the purpose of discrediting the chief. The staff member, on the other hand, feeling that a ready line of communication has been opened with an influential individual, thinks he can further his own prestige by aiding in the discrediting of his superior. This is a good way for a Board member to "divide and conquer". However, with suitable staff organization and staff operation, such situations can be avoided. In any event, it should be noted that the circumstances above described are more the exception than the rule. Generally, the entire relationship involving the chief executive and his executive staff with the Board as a whole is a friendly one.

In summary, policies in regard to the relationship between the Park and Recreation Administrator and his governing body may be expressed as below; the spirit thereof might apply to any authority superior to the chief executive.

1. Although the general duties of the governing board are to adopt legislation and broad policies and the chief executive is to operate the department within the law and the general policies, it is desirable that the lines of authority and responsibility between the two be carefully drawn.

2. Even though the responsibility for adopting broad policies rests with the governing board, the chief executive, being a professional in his field, should be permitted to make recommendations as to policy as well as to matters of operation.

3. Once the governing board has acted and has established policies, those policies must be wholeheartedly accepted by the Administrator and by his executive staff.

4. In transmitting orders from the governing board to the chief executive, it should be understood that those orders come from the board acting as a whole and not from individual members.

5. Attempting to place himself in the position of the individual board member, the administrator will do all in his power to keep individual board members informed of significant operations so that the board member is in a position of supplying responses to questions from his constituents.

6. In regard to social contacts, the administrator should take cognizance of his relative position and allow the individual commissioners to take the initiative regardless of the relative social and financial status of the individual member. The administrator shall do all in his power to keep the friendly associations between himself and individual board members the same for all members.

7. In general, the administrator should recognize that while he is presumed to know more about the field of park and recreation operations inasmuch as he is a professional, he should also recognize that the individual board members are interested and very likely enthusiastic supporters of public parks and recreation even though they are without professional training in that respect. Therefore, the professional should do all in his power to improve the specialized knowledge of the board members, but at the same time accept decisions of the governing body as coming from the electorate which in the final analysis is that body of citizens for which the entire service is being provided.

Relationship of Administrator to His Executive Staff

Stated about as succinctly as the author has seen the role of the manager expressed anywhere is this observation by Robert S. McNamara, Secretary of Defense (1962) as quoted in the Magazine U. S. A. 1, May, 1962 issue –

"The role of the public manager is very similar to the role of a private manager; in each case he has the option of two major alternative courses of action. He can either act as a judge or a leader. In the former case, he sits and waits until subordinates bring to him problems for solutions, or alternatives for choice. In the latter case, he immerses himself in the operations of the business or governmental activity, examines the problems, the objectives, and alternate courses of action, chooses among them, and leads the organization to their accomplishment. In the one case it's a passive role; in the other case, an active role....... I've always believed in and endeavored to follow the active leadership role as opposed to the passive judicial role. "

In the case of park commissions it is more appropriate for the board members to assume the judicial role; the administrator the active leadership role.

1. The general attitude of the manager should be such as to create within his executive staff a spirit of unity and mutual cooperation, a relaxed but business atmosphere, and an esprit de corps aimed at operating the staff as a unit. That unity of purpose should permeate the entire park and recreation department.

2. The manager should recognize the need for continual professional self-improvement of his staff members and should encourage them to participate in the affairs of professional organizations applicable to each and to see that they get opportunity for carrying their share of the responsibilities in such organizations.

3. The manager should see that staff meetings are held with reasonable frequency and with definite purposes but not so often to nullify their effect. He should see that an organization is perfected for the smooth functioning of such meetings, the making up of agenda, the calling of meetings, the recording of them. In such meetings, the relaxed and informal manner should encourage full, free, and frank discussion, and if at all possible, the manager ought to accept as his, the position which represents the consensus of opinion of the staff.

4. Having confidence in the professional ability and integrity of each of the staff members, the manager should be willing to support his staff members in matters of controversy until proof to the contrary is produced.

Park Department With the Planning Commission

Relationship here is one between general practitioner and the specialist. The Planning Commission is responsible for the planning of the entire city, county, or state, the coordination of all services, the zoning of properties according to suitable land use, and in general the responsibility that the parts fit together into a sensible whole. * The Park and Recreation Department is responsible for the planning of a park and recreation system together with the designs of individual properties. When each recognizes its respective responsibilities, the two departments can work out their own problems in a well-coordinated fashion; without such a relationship, the results and the processes both are most unfortunate.

It should be added that the rapid shifting of population segments (and other factors) is becoming most confusing to the best of planners and the nice division of respective responsibilities suggested above can be obscured especially in the metropolitan complexes now developing. All planners, lay and professional and the new breed of specialists known as urbanologists, are all in need of help in determining causes and anticipating effects. In consequence, park and recreation departments must necessarily broaden their role in planning far beyond the confines and general purposes of recreation areas alone, even to the extent of including in their staffs planners of general outlook rather than special interest in recreation services.

Relationship of Parks and School Departments

The objective here is to get both park departments and school boards to agree that both parties have a responsibility in community recreation as a public service because both have facilities which are useful in the performance of that service. The basic understanding should be that the school department is primarily, if not exclusively, responsible for education and that the responsibility of the park and recreation department is to provide a park and recreation service to the people as a primary if not an exclusive function.

This understanding takes on special importance in situations which have arisen more frequently in recent years with the rapid expansion of urban growth out into rural areas. The

* In federal matters, the Bureau of Outdoor Recreation closely approximates this function.

general acceptance of the necessity of adequate public support for education has enabled school districts (whose boundaries do not necessarily coincide with village corporate boundaries) to acquire generous school acreage far in advance of actual village land occupancy. Children are transported to schools and hence school location may be almost independent of the presence of local built up areas, and also independent of local village planning. Schools may assume initial responsibility for some community recreation in connection with their physical education program. As the villages become better organized and more built up, more complete and comprehensive recreation service becomes necessary. At that point schools may have some properties in excess of purely education needs, while park and recreation departments are competing with housing and industry for adequate park and recreation land. Recreation and education are thrown together; both must discharge their respective responsibilities, but now with greater emphasis on public economy.

Both departments have physical assets which are of value in performing the primary service which is the responsibility of the other. When these responsibilities are understood and accepted mutually by the parties, then the basis has been laid for some specific policies:

1. The requirements for site location in the case of elementary schools and neighborhood parks being substantially identical, there will be cooperative planning for the selection of sites for both of these purposes. If possible, the identical sites should be acquired.

2. In the acquisition of properties, each department will understand that it will acquire for itself the area necessary to carry out its full function without overlapping onto the properties of the other.

3. When elementary or junior high school or senior high school properties are located adjacent to or in connection with park properties, the two properties shall be jointly planned to provide one coordinated, single, community asset with the best possible arrangement of facilities regardless of property lines. In case of park facilities overlapping onto school property or vice versa, permits for the use of such property should be exchanged.

4. Suitable agreements shall be entered into for the interchangeable use of the facilities so that each may carry out its primary function with the privilege of using the assets of the other.

These provisions may be followed by numerous rules and regulations and even some statements of policy to further clarify the functioning of the two departments.

Relationship of Park Department to So-Called Red Feather
Agencies or Agencies of the Community Chest, Privately Supported.

1. The spirit of mutual understanding and cooperation shall be fostered and friendly operational relationships established.
2. Conferences shall be held for the planning of facilities and operational programs for the purpose of avoiding duplication and overlapping of services.
3. Aid should be given the private agencies in the organization of athletic leagues and permits for the use of properties in connection therewith on an equal basis with but not preferential to any of the department's own activities.
4. The park department shall stand ready to aid in the training of leaders in specialized fields when such training is difficult to obtain elsewhere.

Relationships With Other Local Governmental Agencies

In this category there are large numbers of agencies with which the park and recreation department has business and with which it has numerous contacts. Such agencies include Civil Service commissions, legal departments, the treasurer's office, register of deeds, county and state highway departments, state conservation departments, health departments, and others.

In each case, the park and recreation department should endeavor to develop a friendly and cooperative relationship but without sacrificing by default its own powers and prerogatives. Suggestions as to policy methods include the following:

1. Keep the paths of communication open by an occasional call, even if there is no definite business to transact.
2. Keep in mind the responsibilities of the other agencies and confer with each of them whenever matters in the park and recreation department arise which would be of interest to the other agencies.
3. Keep in close enough touch with other agencies' planning and work to anticipate possible future contacts.

Often conferences in the early stages of planning will avoid serious conflict which might occur after the plans have been developed.

Relationships Involving State and Federal Agencies

Recognizing the increasing evidence of the inability of local governments to solve their most aggravating physical and social problems, the federal government has within recent years assumed a major responsibility to help – by partial financing, and because of financing, also by establishing policy for solving local problems. The federal government also has aided states and prodded the states to further aid local governments. Sometimes federal aid to metropolises is direct and at other times it is funneled through the states. A myriad of such programs exist.

It, therefore, becomes an essential and a new function of local governments (as well as state governments) to be aware of these programs, the requirements by which each becomes available, the bureaucratic rules and regulations that must be followed and the devious ways by which action may be stimulated.

If aid is genuinely needed and expected to be forthcoming, whole hearted cooperation with federal bureaus must be given. There will be irritating situations, rules to be complied with, some delays and frustrations, even criticism of results, but these are the price to be paid for the aid.

Time may reveal that local problems cannot be successfully and efficiently solved in Washington; that the financial aid is actually money collected at the local level by federal agents; that the inability of local governments to cope with local problems arises from at least two causes: (1) the inability to see the whole forest of situations rather than only the single trees of local ideas, and (2) the lack of sufficient sources of tax revenue. The exchange of philosophy and techniques between federal and local agencies, presents possibilities of more efficient and equitable operation.

Should such hypotheses or others of similar nature prove to be logical, the PR Administrators should equip themselves with the proper knowledge to enter into discussions which may lead to improved methods. In the meantime, it seems sensible to recognize that the purposes of the present programs are worthy ones, and that their inauguration has been an incentive to advance and an eye-opener into greater possibilities of recreation objectives. The word, then, is to cooperate.

Park and Recreation Department With the Press and the Public

1. No official meetings of the board shall take place at which the press is excluded.
2. All matters which have been officially acted upon become a part of the public record and are accessible to the press and to the public.
3. The press and the public have a right to know what the policies of operation are when those policies are fixed by official board proceedings or established by executive order.
4. Executive policies, especially if not written, are not necessarily subject to public examination. They may not be official records.

CHAPTER 10

ACQUISITION AND
DEVELOPMENT POLICIES

Acquisition in General

Parks are acquired with a definite purpose in mind, the same as are factory sites, retail stores, hotels and shopping centers. One does not simply look at a vacant lot and say to oneself, "That would make a dandy playground; let's buy it," or a wooded vale with a babbling brook running through it and say, "What a spot for a nice park! Let's add it to our system." In the chapters on the make-up of park systems, and again in the chapter on the design of a park, certain general criteria for site selection were mentioned. The most important one is that the site must be of such a size, of such a nature and of such a location as to fit into an overall plan of the whole park system of which it is to become a part. If the proposed site does not nicely fit into the scheme of the overall park system, whether it be too small, (or too large), or too flat, or too rugged, too barren, too wooded or in the wrong location, it is no good for the purpose and should not be acquired.

This applies to property that is about to be donated as well as to property that is to be paid for with taxpayers' money.

The supposition is that there does exist a master plan for the park system in question, that the plan suggests not only the skeleton, but shows the muscles of the system and is fleshed out to a definite size, shape, location and character and is not simply an indefinite blob. If such a plan exists, acquisition of properties can proceed with sensible confidence. In the absence of such a plan, any acquisition process is like the blind man pinning a tail on the donkey with just about as ridiculous results. Hence, to begin with, we have these policy statements:

A definite plan for the entire system of parks is essential. Acquisition of properties should be in the location and of the proper character consistent with that plan.

Site Selection Notes

The plan of the park system denotes the location and size of the lands to be acquired, but there is usually some small flexibility in location (very little for neighborhood parks, more

See supplement in Appendix, p. 275.

for larger parks and perhaps considerable for state parks), a
little flexibility as to size and some as to character. Here
are some points to keep in mind.
    1. Since neighborhood parks are supposed to be in the
center of a neighborhood the general dimensions of which are
3/4 mile to 1 mile square any location away from the center
reduces the full effectiveness of the proposed park. Moving
off the center as much as 300 feet may be permissible if the
difference in land costs are great. Hence, *acquire property
away from the center of the neighborhood only with great re-
luctance.*
    *Access to neighborhood parks should be complete on all
four sides,* either from streets, alleys (less advantageous than
streets) or other public ways. Avoid the situation where public and private properties have a common boundary; this leads
to conflicts, the public being a nuisance to the private property
owner and vice versa. Play lots and large parks, even state
parks can also suffer from this situation.
    *Otherwise poor land can be used for parks, but in the case
of neighborhood parks, the location is paramount to all else.*
The reclamation of a poor piece of property (e. g. a swamp) to
a good park is not justified if the location is not right or the
access inadequate or faulty. New and small towns are prone
to utilize poor properties regardless of location or access because the land developers have donated such land with little or
no value for building lots. Location and access must be right
or else leave such properties alone.
    One or two existing buildings in one corner of a 10 acre
plot may tempt the park department to omit its acquisition.
The omission will be regretted when the park is fully developed.
    The size and shape of a proposed neighborhood park should
be as prescribed in the table of standards on page 27 and in
any event sufficient to permit the development of an athletic
field of appropriate size. *If an athletic field cannot be accom-
modated, the site is not adequate.* This suggests that *some
schematic plan of development ought to be prepared before
acquisition becomes final.* A neighborhood park of a size sufficient to provide some horticultural embellishment is a distinct asset to a neighborhood whereas one of cramped design
can be a nuisance to adjacent property.
    2. In acquiring land for community playfields, and re-
gional athletic fields, there is a little more flexibility in site
location for two principle reasons: (1) the area being served

is probably two miles or more across instead of one mile or less as in the case of neighborhood parks and (2) instead of walking to the playfield most patrons use a bicycle or an automobile. Even so, *a location very close to the center of the area to be served should be selected.*

In both cases – neighborhood parks and community playfields – *the usuable ground is the flat ground.* Undulating or rugged topography, ground cover (e.g. woods and brush land) as well as water areas are of no value; indeed may be a detriment unless the total area is large enough to accommodate all the active recreation facilities without the rough ground and water area, in which case the interesting topography becomes a real asset.

Access and shape of site are just as important for playfields as they are for neighborhood parks. The possibility of acquiring neighborhood park and playfield sites jointly with school sites should not be overlooked.

3. Site selection for large parks, parkways and special use parks (golf courses, zoos, etc.) present problems of their own. Geographic location may be important in some cases, but *size, coupled with topographic and scenic values will be paramount in almost all situations.* Hills and valleys, woods and clearings, lakes and streams, upland and swampland, beautiful and unusual scenery are all sought in establishing large city parks – and county and state parks as well. Variety of scenery lends enchantment; and yet there must be present enough reasonably level and open areas for active use; e.g. picnicking.

Stream valleys and lake shores should be acquired as completely as is possible. Only an abundance of such natural advantages can justify private ownership to a limited extent. The reasons are more readily set forth than the accomplishments can be achieved. Private ownership of shorelands limits the real enjoyable benefits and hence real estate enhancement to shore owners alone; whereas, public ownership with suitable (i.e. roadway) access spreads the benefit to all the public and especially not only to those fronting the access road, but to those properties reaching some distance away – as much as a half mile or more. Real estate developers (or city fathers) can rarely see that selling a few shore properties at high prices is not as advantageous as selling many more properties (some just across the access road and many more a block or two away from the lake or stream) at an overall higher average price. An owner of a 40 acre tract having stream frontage could actually afford to donate a reasonable stream right of way for park or parkway purposes because of the benefit it brings to his remaining real estate.   This situation is advantageous to the city because of the improvement of the tax base. The alternative to public ownership is usually spotted development and an administrative problem of water control, cleanup, and possible pollution.   Conclusion – *make public ownership of lake shores and stream valleys as extensive as possible.*

The extent in depth of shorelands to be acquired depends upon the possible use and possible extent of the flood plain. If the scenic aspect of a stream from a bordering roadway (possible parkway) is all that is required and if the flood plain is narrow or even nonexistent, the public right of way may be quite narrow – one hundred to a few hundred feet.   However, if picnic grounds or other concentrated uses are contemplated, or if the flood plain is broad, acquisition lines must be drawn accordingly.   Lake shore public properties must be quite extensive for water draws people and people require space.   It does not pay to underestimate required size.

About 150 acres are required for an eighteen hole golf course. It may be crowded into less, but this is not advisable. If accessories such as driving ranges, and pitch-and-putt courses are added (and it may be well to anticipate these), additional acreage is, of course, necessary.   Availability of suitable acreage is more important than geographical location although the latter cannot be entirely ignored.   Gently rolling (not rugged) topography is desirable. Some open woodland and water areas (lakes, ponds, streams) are distinct assets. Because of the large grass areas to be maintained, soil conditions are very important. Adequate water supply and possibility of sewage disposal must be present or possible of attainment.

From 75 to 200 acres are required for an adequate zoological garden. (Avoid the mere gradual accumulation of a group of animals confined to a small space resulting in something in the nature of a menagerie). Actual site selection is a matter for the specialists in zoological garden operation and planning.

The employment of specialists or teams of specialists is advisable in the selection of sites for many of the special use areas: golf courses, zoos, arboretums, aquariums, marinas, outdoor theaters, great municipal stadiums, sites for museums, planetariums, observatories and a number of other items.

In an earlier time, parkways and boulevards* were essential elements in the park system of the city. Times have changed. The unifying effect on the whole city, the element of grandeur and imposing appearance, the locale for the exhibition of fine horses and carriages, have been supplanted by other elements in the city plan. Parkways have not entirely been done away with even in cities. Counties and even the National Park Service have built parkways in relatively recent years and are still planning for more. But today's parkways must be planned on a much larger scale. Too often, however, the acquired right of way widths have not kept pace with the need for greater scale. When horse drawn carriages were traveling 5 to 10 miles an hour, or when automobiles did not exceed 20 miles an hour, a new viewing experience was just around the bend a few hundred feet ahead. In the interim, there was time to look closely at the verdure on the roadside or the attractive homes 50 to 100 feet away. Today's 30 to 50 mile an hour pace permits no close view of small plants or fine homes close to the roadway, and if the "bend" in the road is not a half mile to several miles ahead, the road is dangerous. Our views are farther away and on a much larger scale. These viewing areas must be protected if the parkway is to preserve its intrinsic value. * Hence, *the rights of way to be acquired (or controlled) should be generous enough to protect and maintain for all time those attributes which first made the site appealing enough to locate a parkway thereon.*

In state and federal acquisitions, special attention must be given to the classification systems of B. O. R. , National Park Service, Forest Service, and others. Acquisitions should be made according to the criteria established in each of these services, keeping in mind that, for example, scenic parks of the NPS carry with them a preservation obligation which is not necessarily a provision of National Recreation Areas. Hence the native aspect, while important in all categories, is more binding for scenic parks.

Financing Capital Outlays – Acquisition and Development

Groceries cannot be bought on the installment plan, but almost everything else can. Radios must be fully paid for in

* See "Future of Minneapolis Parkways and Boulevards" in Appendix.
* Note: For the purpose of quick and general understanding of the subject, the discussion of bonds in this section has been oversimplified. Do not use it as a guide to the issuance of bonds in any specific situation. Consult the applicable laws and seek legal counsel.

a shorter period of time than automobiles, which, in turn, must be fully paid for in less time than homes. Anything that is not immediately consumed or has a life during which some value exists can be "mortgaged," thereby extending full payment up to somewhat less time than the life of the article.

In government business, consumable goods or items of current expense must be paid for out of current income. Short time borrowing may be permitted to tide over the agency pending the receipt of current income – (an easy procedure especially when the forthcoming income is from taxes which have already been levied), but there is no chance of long term borrowing to pay for current expense items. (Exceptions are the U. S. government and some states as hereinafter noted). In almost all cases, the use of the proceeds from long term borrowing to pay current expenses is illegal; violations carry stiff penalties. Generally speaking, *governmental corporations pay "cash" for consumable or current items* of the departments' budget.

Tangible items having an economically usable life span measured in years are generally known as capital goods and the payment for them is called a capital expenditure. Governments have an option as to methods of making capital expenditures: they may pay cash (i. e. out of current income) or they may buy on the installment plan (i. e. issue bonds or other securities). The choice rests upon consideration of a number of factors, but the basic one seems to be; "Will the political constituents stand for a high enough tax rate today to pay the whole cost of something that will be used for many years to come, even extending into the next generation?" Usually they say, "Let our children pay part of the cost," or "We cannot afford it today, but give us time to pay for it as we use it."

Seldom may a government engage in a complete "pay-as-you-go" procedure in spite of the presence of much argument as to the value thereof.

The net result then, is that *the usual practice is for government to pay for current expenses out of current income and to go in debt for capital expenditures.*

The borrowing of money for capital expenditures usually takes the form of selling bonds for cash. A government bond is evidence of indebtedness – a promise to pay the face value of the bond on a certain date and to pay interest at specified intervals upon the surrender of interest "coupons" attached to the bond. Bonds are classified as to type of security, time of maturity, interest rate, purpose of issue, and otherwise.

In private installment buying, the written agreement usually provides that if certain payments are not made at the times
prescribed, the seller may retrieve the capital goods sold and
the purchaser forfeits all equity in it. A government bond of
similar nature would be a mortgage bond which provides that
if the bond holders do not receive the payments called for in
the bonds, the capital goods (usually land) can become the property of the bondholders after certain legal steps (foreclosure
proceedings) have been taken. Usually, bondholders are not
interested in foreclosing on public park improvements and in
some instances, foreclosure or the enforcement of liens for
the recapture of public real estate by private parties is not
possible. Municipal corporations may, however, mortgage
real estate in the usual way, if the law specifically permits it.

The usual government bond is secured by the "full faith
and credit" of the government and its pledge to levy and collect taxes to pay the full interest and principal of the bond.
When issued in compliance with the law pertaining to the issuing agency, the provisions of the bond are legally enforceable
and the collection of interest and principal is secured so long
as the particular government is solvent. These bonds can be
sold for cash. Whether the amount of cash that bond buyers
(wholesalers who in turn sell bonds to retail buyers) are willing to pay is the face value of the bonds at the interest rate
called for, or more or less than this, depends on the market
for bonds at the time of sale as well as upon the credit of the
issuing agency which, in turn, is dependent on the agency's
history of financial responsibility.

Special assessment bonds are secured by the collection of
special assessments on "specially benefited" real estate. The
situation arises as follows: The establishment of a park (in
each of the stages of acquisition and development) imparts a
special benefit to real estate in some zone of influence. This
benefit is measurable in the actual rise of real estate values.
Special assessments are levied against the benefited real estate
in the form of taxes which is over and above the ad valorem
tax on real estate. Receipts from these special assessment
taxes are pledged to pay for the interest and principle of bonds
which have been issued to raise money to pay for the original
capital expenditure, i. e. the acquisition and/or the development of the park. Since delinquencies in tax collection do occur, there could develop a shortage in funds to pay bond interest and principle. Hence, to add to the security it is advisable

for the issuing agency to pledge itself to make good any collection deficiency out of general taxes. Special assessment bonds backed up by the full taxing power of the issuing governmental agency are as sound as any other of the bonds of that agency.

The other extreme of soundness of this sort of security is encountered when public works are financed, not by bond issues, but by the issuance of special assessment "certificates." These may be given to contractors for work performed, or to real estate sellers for real estate, instead of cash payments. Because of possible delinquencies in collection of special assessments (assuming such collections to be the only monies promised to pay these "certificates") the certificates are often not worth their face value, and are susceptible to heavy discounts.

There is great merit in the special assessment process and it has been used for many public works. A few cities and some counties have used it to finance all manner of parks from neighborhood parks to large parks and parkways. But, in the majority of localities, especially in suburban towns, the public has not been used to this method of financing park acquisition and development and so *the special assessment plan has not been widely used.*

If the proposed capital expenditure is for *some project which is to be operated at a "profit," revenue bonds may be issued* to finance the undertaking. The security may be limited to the net receipts from the operation in which case the marketability of the issue is dependent upon the probable financial success of the project. Hence, if the success of the project is a "cinch" this type of revenue bond can be successfully sold. When the project is financially more hazardous, but not entirely so, the issuing governmental agency may further secure the bonds by pledging to make good any deficiency in net income by levying the necessary taxes. Municipal stadium financing quite frequently requires the added security of the tax levying pledge of the municipality. The establishment of municipal golf courses in many instances may be financially sound enough to dispense with the added security of tax levies. Revenue bonds are a useful financial tool and are resorted to in a number of special cases, but are not extensively used to finance park and recreation facilities in general. In some cases, as a sort of substitute, the municipality may issue general city bonds to finance the project and then require the park and recreation department to deposit all net receipts from the operation of the enterprise into the "sinking fund" until the project is paid for or for a specified number of years.

All the foregoing discussion on bonds applies principally to levels of government lower than the state governments. The fiscal policy of the Federal government and some state governments calls for a different kind of operation. Capital expenditures of the Federal government and items in the annual budget and are not financed by specific bond issues. United States bonds are secured by the "full faith and credit" of the U.S. Government and are issued in various categories and under various names to supply cash as needed to finance any and all governmental operations pending the receipt of budgetary income items, whereas a municipal bond is issued to finance capital investment projects. The U.S. bonded debt is an accumulation of budgetary deficits over the years, and, of course, some part of that budgetary deficit might conceivably be caused by capital expenditures. In that sense there is a similarity between numicipal and U.S. bonds but not enough to make the foregoing bond discussion applicable to the U.S. government or to the states that operate similarly.

The student should be familiar with other characteristics of bonds. They are issued in more than one form, at various rates of interest, and for various number of years.

One form may prescribe that bonds will be issued in denominations of $1000 (or other amounts) with interest coupons attached calling for the payment of an amount equal to interest at a specified rate (say 4%) for six months or three months or twelve months, as the case may be. Payment of interest is made by the surrender of these coupons, usually at the office of the treasurer of the issuing agency. Upon a specified date of X years from the date of issue, the principal sum of the bond becomes payable. Such bonds are known by the number of years between date of issue and date of maturity, e.g., straight ten year bonds, or straight twenty year bonds, etc. During the life of the bond, the only annual payments required are the interest payments, but at maturity the whole whopping principal becomes due. Usually provision for this lump sum payment has been taken care of by accumulating funds from each year's taxes in a so-called "sinking fund" out of which both interest and principal are paid. The "non-working" capital in the sinking fund may sometimes be reinvested pending its actual need. Sometimes such "idle" funds may even be used to temporarily finance other capital projects. In practice, the financing of capital improvements and the manipulation of the sinking fund can become quite involved; many legal safeguards have been provided to insure the integrity of bond issues and to avoid slip-shod operations.

General bonds may be retired piecemeal over a period of years, say one-tenth or one-twentieth each year for the ten or twenty year life of the bond issue. These are known as serial bonds. Each individual bond is for a specified life, but the maturity dates of the various bonds are selected to make one-tenth or one-twentieth of the total number fall due in successive years. Obviously, the sinking fund for serial bonds retains money for periods of only months (the time intervening between tax collections and payment dates for principal and interest on bonds), instead of for years as in the case of straight bonds. For most counties and municipalities, *the issuance of serial bonds has an advantage over the issuance of straight bonds*.

The length of life of a bond issue usually hinges on two factors: (1) How close to pay-as-you-go financing is the issuing agency willing to consider? The closer to that plan of operation, the shorter will be the life of the bonds. (2) The economically useful life of the capital purpose for which the bonds are issued, e. g., "radios, " "automobiles, " or "houses" as were first mentioned in our installment buying analogy. Because of rapidity of technological advancements, this useful life of things is shortened as much or more by obsolescence as by physically wearing out. The trend, therefore, is to avoid long term bonds. Taxpayers don't like to pay for dead horses.

Pause for a moment now to succinctly summarize the foregoing suggested policies having to do with financing capital expenditures with money that ultimately comes from the pocket of the taxpayer.

√   A pay-as-you-go plan may be a fine idea but very few governmental agencies will find it possible to adopt it. Paying for capital expenditures out of current funds, except in small amounts is not feasible and should not be relied upon.

√   The issuance of bonds is the most reliable method of financing capital needs. Of the various kinds of bonds, general serial bonds of relatively short term – say ten to twenty years – will fit most situations better than any other form. However, other types of bonds issues may be investigated for special cases.

√   Special assessment procedures are very much worth looking into. Bonds issued in these situations ought to be backed up by the full faith and credit of the issuing agency.

√ Projects susceptible of turning an operating profit sufficient to amortize any capital indebtedness might be financed by the issuance of revenue bonds. These again, should be backed up by the full faith and credit of the issuing agency.

√ In extreme cases, mortgages (rarely mortgage bonds) may be feasible.

√ Lots of things are sometimes possible with the use of idle cash in the Treasurer's office. Sinking funds may even have a surplus over and above outstanding requirements. Investigate possibilities, but move with caution and then only upon legal advice.

√ Direct appropriation in the annual budget is the normal method of financing capital needs in the case of the Federal Government and for some state governments.

Financing by Sale of Use Rights, Tax Forfeiture, Private Gifts and Bequests and Miscellaneous Sources

Capital needs are frequently acquired with funds from sources other than by bond issue or direct taxation. Rights to use public property may produce cash; private lands may be forfeited to the state for nonpayment of taxes; lands and items of land improvement may be given or bequeathed by private parties, or money to buy land or to make improvements may be donated. These are examples of a number of ways that capital needs are met.

Land being the basic ingredient of park holdings in all levels of government, and land inherently containing, as it does, things of negotiable worth, money may be obtained by selling, leasing, or otherwise granting the use of portions of it. Excess lands, or seemingly excess lands, may be sold or leased for long periods of time. Mineral or oil drilling rights may be sold. The right to graze cattle, to farm, to cut timber, to dam streams for water power or other purposes, to use as public parking lots, to construct airstrips thereon, innumerable rights for innumerable purposes – all these are worth money. Sometimes they are valuable enough to cause prospective buyers to arouse public sentiment in favor of such sales and to lobby for them in our legislative halls. What to do?

Perhaps fortunately in the past, a segment of the park and recreation fraternity has considered all park lands to be park lands for all time to come, held only in trust by the present

administrations, not to be changed in outline, or to be exploited
by private interests or to be "mutilated" in any way whatsoever.   Such an attitude is the natural heritage of a park and
recreation administrator, who recalls the firm stand taken
against the many efforts to invade New York's Central Park
with all sorts of "gimmicks"; how the Congress directed the
National Park Service to "conserve" for posterity the wonders
of our national parks and how nobly the N. P. S. has fought off
timber barons, ranchers, power and mining interests, even
sportsmen in order to preserve inviolate the nation's parks;
how in our own day we band together and sympathize with each
other over the havoc being wrought by the terribly heavy hand
of the highway engineer and the urban redeveloper.   These
noble and courageous acts of resistance deserve emulation
today, so the safe and supportable attitude seems to be to assume that parks of all kinds are entirely inviolate and that
they are everlasting fixtures of an unchanging civilization, or
nearly so.

    Laudible as this attitude may seem to the fundamentalist,
it seems to the author* to be both unrealistic and in the nature
of a crutch on which to rest our more normal analytical ability
to make present day evaluations and decisions. It is unrealistic because if parks and their functions are everlasting, they
constitute one of the rare things in this universe that does not
change.   Also some things have happened to parks over the
years that seemed questionable at the time, or they have gradually evolved over the years, that now are taken for granted
with scarcely the raising of an eyebrow – the famed Ellipse in
front of the White House has become an athletic field; Central
Park has its cocktail lounge and dance hall; an amusement
park has been added to the park system of Westchester County,
New York, but some of its parkways are part of the State Highway System; the Outer Drive in Chicago is labelled highway;
Mt. Rushmore has been carved into forms representing some
of our Presidents; a parking garage was built under, first,
Union Square in San Francisco, and then later, under several
other of our city parks; how about the development of power of
Niagara Falls and its effect on parks on both sides of the river.
Somehow these and other innovations have been accepted with-
out much damaging effect on the basic usefulness of parks.
Realistically, changes have already taken place, and may be
expected to take place in the future.

* The student is warned that there are many administrators who hold fast to the idea that
once a property is dedicated as a park it remains so, unless the Park Department is forced
to relinquish by forces beyond its control.

It is unprogressive to rely so heavily on tradition and the judgment of our forebears as to believe that judgment to be infallible. It is equally unwise to assume that park properties may be nonchalantly disposed of, or that their commercial possibilities may be exploited willy-nilly, or that entrance for all sorts of enterprises may be gained with impunity. Not at all. What is suggested is serious reappraisal of a past policy in the light of possible new evidence, even though at first a traditionally park-partisan viewpoint is taken.

The following principles then are suggested in the consideration of possible sales or leases of park lands, or the granting of use permits for a monetary or other consideration:*

1. The decision to grant or not to grant is a decision of today — not of yesterday. History, heritage, tradition, and past policy all are part and parcel of that decision, but unless the pending matter is minor, routine, or trivial a re-evaluation of past policy is in order with a full recognition of the fact that a new or revised policy may be the result. Warning must be here given that when the crutch of tradition is discarded, the administrator must have the ability to analyze, to wisely decide and to effectively defend the new position.

2. The proposed sale, lease, use permit or whatnot must be advantageous to the park authority over the long pull. It must leave the park system as a whole in better shape to perform its function than it was before the transaction.

3. This transaction must not set a precedent which, if followed in the future, will be embarrassing, damaging, or frustrating. If repeated in future cases the result should be just as advantageous as this one.

4. This proposal, if carried out, should be for the overall public good. This asks the park administrator to judge the proposal objectively, especially if in some aspects, the acceptance of the proposal is damaging to the best park interests. Here, the administrator can defend the park interests to a reasonable extent, acquiescing only when the overall good is adequately proven.

Capital assets, both acquisition and improvement items, may come about as a result of gifts, bequests, trust funds,

* See N.P.S. News Release of November 19, 1962 in re Grand Canyon in Appendix.

endowments and other miscellaneous ways.   This applies especially to land.

Coming from private sources, the forms these acquisition possibilities take are many and varied: outright gifts of land, the establishment of trust funds from which acquisitions can be made, the outright donation of money for the purchase of lands, provisions in wills for the donations of money for lands, securities, or real estate which can be sold and the proceeds used for the purchase of park lands, and any similar device which the ingenuity of donors can think up.

Because these are donations, the donors may attach conditions to the acceptance of the gifts and conditions which must be met after the park is acquired, sometimes with reversionary provisions in case the conditions are not met.

Here are some:

√   Donation of a piece of property with the condition that the house on it may be occupied by the owner until his death or the death of himself and his wife.

√   Donation of a piece of property for public park purposes which, if not used for that purpose, reverts to the owner or his successors and assigns; or that the property must be used for a certain park purpose in perpetuity, otherwise it reverts to the heirs or successors.

√   A man deeds a portion of his property to the park district for park and parkway purposes on the condition that the remainder of his property shall be exempt from all future special park assessments.   (In one state, this was held to be illegal and of no effect because the government agency had no power to contract away its taxing power. However, if the deed of gift had provided that the owner should be exempt from special assessments up to a certain definite amount, that was held to be a legal contract.) Or that the owner may continue to water his stock in the creek or erect a windmill or have a dock for his private use.

√   A piece of property is donated with the understanding and deed provision that it shall not be added on to.

√   The property has been donated for a municipal zoo, but it is not sufficient for a zoo and additional properties to add on to it are not available for any acquisition.

√   A trust fund has been established, the proceeds of which may be used for the acquisition of properties, but the trust may be limited to such securities as to render the interest from these years later almost too small to be practical.

Such a list might be continued almost indefinitely. It be-
hooves each park department to look these gift horses in the
mouths squarely, determine whether the conditions imposed
are going to prove embarrassing or impossible of compliance
years hence, and attempt to get the provisions altered before
acceptance of the gift.

*In general, it can be suggested that where conditions are
definitely limited in time (a stated number of years, or when
some event happens which is sure to happen, like the death of
an occupant), the gift may be acceptable; but if the condition
operates in perpetuity there is present an element of future
embarrassment and even frustration in carrying out in the future the full purpose of the law; and consequently, such a condition should be avoided.*

Embarrassing conditions of gifts can sometimes be limited or eliminated years hence through the process of condemnation and sometimes other legal procedures may be effective
where the conditions are wholly out of harmony with the times.

In spite of sometime difficulties attendant to gifts of land,
a great deal of public property has been acquired that way and
the process is important enough for every park department to
take special steps to encourage further private donations.

Except in the case of donations, properties which are acquired must somehow be paid for if fee title is conveyed, but
in the process a number of methods may be resorted to for one
reason or another. Here are a few: In the filing of a plat of
land for subdivision into lots, one or more parcels may be
dedicated to the public for park purposes – sometimes the
mere filing of the plat conveys a provisional title and other
times some action on the part of the park department is necessary to complete the transaction. In either case, this is not
conveying the property in fee simple. It is a use right which
is obtained, and whenever that use ceases, the fee title stays
with the platter of the property or his successors and heirs
and only the use of the property reverts back to the original
conveyors. *The park department is not in a position, in this
case, to convey title to the property for it does not have it.*

Property on which taxes are not paid regularly reverts to
state ownership after the reversionary provisions of the law
have been complied with. Sometimes, the state may transfer
title to some other governmental agency including park districts. Almost invariably, the states, in doing so, retain mineral rights to the property and usually there is a provision that
if the property is not used for the public purpose for which it

was conveyed, the title reverts to the state. *This sort of title does not give the park district freedom of action to do whatever it will with the property, including its sale.* Incidentally, Federal participation in the financing of lands for park and recreation purposes (through BOR and HUD) may also carry conditions affecting the fee title to not only the lands thereby financed, but to the lands already owned to which the new acquisition is to be an addition. Red the fine print carefully.

Reservoir properties under the jurisdiction of the Army Engineers, and also some under other governmental agencies, are sometimes leased out or use permits given to villages, cities, counties, and states to operate as public park and recreation grounds. *The length of time of such leases and use permits ought to be long enough to justify the permittee to make respectable type improvements thereon. The lease or permit should also grant the right to govern the leased property* so long as there is no interference with the basic purpose for which the reservoir was constructed.

Property on which a museum, stadium, or other facility may be placed or is placed may be conveyed to the park district with the provision that the donors may have exclusive use of the facility which is placed thereon and in case that use ever ceases, the property remains the property of the park district. Variations of this arrangement are many. One is that the city is the owner of the facility including the land and has leased the land from the previous owner with the understanding that after 20 years or some other suitable time, the fee title to the entire facility would pass to the park district.

One park district confronted with certain limitations, legal and otherwise, which prevented it from entering into a contract for deed payable over a period of time, resorted to this device. It acquired only a portion of the property during the current year, say 1/10 of it, and paid an additional sum which would have equaled six percent of the deferred payments under a contract, this additional amount being the price of an option on all the remaining property of the owner, the option to be exercised at the discretion of the park department, piecemeal over a period of years. The option price carried with it restrictions on the use of the owner's property pending the exercise of the option.

The number of deviations of this sort of transaction is limited only by the ingenuity of the parties to the agreements — all of course by the law.

Processes of Acquisition

There are two procedures which may be followed in the acquisition of lands for park purposes: acquisition by direct negotiation with the owner and by eminant domain going through condemnation proceedings. There are also two main purposes to be accomplished: to acquire the desired property at a fair market price and to leave a record which will substantiate the fact that it is a fair market price.

1. By Direct Negotiation. In direct negotiations with the owner, there are certain advantages: process is usually quicker, face to face conversations usually result in a better understanding between purchaser and seller, minor variations in the sale can be effectuated and greater flexibility is always present. The great disadvantage is that direct negotiation is open to public criticism as to motive, as to price, and as to the possibility of so-called graft. In order to obviate this situation, park districts frequently resort to appraisal by disinterested and competent realtors before a negotiating price is arrived at. If that negotiated price shows any substantial variation from the appraised figure, full explanation ought to be left in the record.

2. Condemnation Proceedings. Governmental agencies usually have the power of eminent domain and may take any property by going through the proper legal procedure and paying the market price, or in this case the appraised price, for the property. The advantage of this method is that it is one in which the process is usually minutely provided for in the law, that it provides suitable protection for the property owner through appeals from the first appraised figure, that good and sufficient title can be obtained from owners unwilling to transfer title by deed. The acquisition is positive as to time and property described. The main advantage is that such a proceeding leaves very little or no opportunity for so-called graft or undercover negotiations.

The disadvantage of this process of acquisition is in its inexorable characteristics, no flexibility to meet an owner's peculiar situations is present, there is no variation in time element, the process is long, possibilities of delay through technicalities are numerous, and the proceeding is frequently irritating to both parties. Often it is not conducive to the establishment of good will.

A fixed policy to fit all conditions is seldom practical over an extended period of time. Direct negotiations are usually

more practical in smaller parcels of land and where price
determination is easy. When protected by a sufficient number
of reliable appraisals, large tracts of land and large numbers
of parcels may be also practical. However, when there are
large numbers of parcels covering a great variety of properties, and time is not an element, condemnation proceedings
usually produce the best result. Over a period of time, both
methods will be used. *

Land Records

*A record of all lands owned or controlled by an operating
park and recreation agency ought to be on file in every such
agency.* This is so self-evident that it should not be necessary
to call attention to it. However, there are enough instances of
laxity that have come to the attention of the writer that he feels
the need of mentioning it.

Land records should consist of the attorney's opinion of
the title, and the deeds or other evidences of ownership together with documents that satisfy the requirements of the
opinion. These are of such primary importance that they are
usually kept in a very safe place. Copies of the significant
portions of them are kept separate for ready daily reference.
Such records include: (1) legal descriptions of the land, (2)
conditions of ownership, (3) where the deeds are filed in the
official files of the government, (4) official actions affecting
the title such as street vacations, etc., (5) other miscellaneous
information bearing on the title or the dimensions of the property.

Land plats showing outside dimensions, as well as dimensions of parcels of the total, the official land subdivisions and
original government surveys are necessary. These plats should
correlate land titles with land surveys and this correlation
should be shown on the plats.

Situations Particularly Applicable to Development

A. As to Plans and Basic Data

The process of the development of a park plan preceding
the construction of the project has been dealt with in Chapter
6. The complete planning package includes: Investigative
Report, Topographic Survey and Map, Diagrammatic Sketch,
Preliminary Plan, Working Drawings and Specifications, and

* In the cases of acquisitions using grants-in-aid money, the granting agency, either Federal or State, may prescribe the process of acquisition to be used.

finally a Manual of Operation. Who is to prepare each of these?

Basic data is usually assembled by staff employees if the material is of a purely statistical or informational character. However, in the preparation of topographic maps, preliminary plans, and working drawings, choices are possible depending upon the policy laid down by the authorities. Topographic mapping as well as property surveys may be made by employees of the engineering division or the work may be contracted out. Some topographical mapping may be accomplished through means of aerial photography and that usually is contracted for or else the maps purchased if they are already on the market.

Preliminary planning may be done by members of the planning section or the work can be contracted to be done by private planners. Working drawings and specifications may be made by the engineering division, or again, the work may be contracted for.

It is not impractical for smaller organizations to contract with a park specialist to compile original data, make the original surveys as to requirements, prepare preliminary plans as well as working drawings, specifications, and to supervise the construction. This is true also of buildings, only in this case an architect will be engaged.

A department may resort to a combination of these situations depending upon the particular project at hand. For example, the engineering department may be so organized as to be able to take care of surveys, both topographic and property surveys, to supervise construction projects, but not be organized for park planning either in the preliminary stage or as to final working drawings and specifications, in which case the missing links must necessarily be done by outside contractors.

If the park district is of sufficient magnitude, it is desirable to have as many of these planning and survey processes done within the department itself. This permits a more continual process, a greater insight into the peculiarities of this particular park district, a better conception of long-range plans, and usually these plans will get the benefit of more internal criticism than otherwise. On the other hand, an occasional intrusion of outside talent will prevent the sameness of plan and developments from producing monotonous effects. In some cases, some of the engineering and planning will be done by agencies allied with the park district. These include separate planning departments, the use of public works departments, and sometimes even other governmental agencies.

While any one of these situations will produce satisfactory results depending upon the quality of personnel available, *it is generally more desirable to have as many of these functions performed by employees of the park district as local conditions will permit.*

B. Construction

Here again, choices may be made. The park district may organize itself with sufficient talent and machinery for carrying on sizeable construction works or it may choose to minimize this part of the organization and carry out all of its construction by contract with private parties. A third possibility is the combination of these two in which the department may do some of its own constructing and contract out the balance. Variations of these would include having the construction done by other agencies of the government such as the public works department or the state highway department, but these would be in the same category as letting the jobs out to private contractors.

The choice here depends very much on the same factors as the choice in the case of the preparation of plans. Considering the magnitude of some of the park improvement projects and the large investment in heavy earth-moving equipment, the park district would have to be of considerable magnitude to undertake all of its construction in all its various forms as well as its various magnitudes. On the other hand, the department must be very small if it is not prepared to carry on any of its own construction. Consequently, *most park districts will do part of the construction by force account and part by contract.* A fairly good sized park organization ought to be prepared to do a fair amount of construction itself in order to ensure the completion of jobs at scheduled times or to escape from contractors who are too busy to undertake their contracts at the proper time. Not infrequently, a department having a pretty good construction force and suitable equipment can command competitive prices when otherwise competition may not be present. This is not quite so applicable in complete projects, but in portions of the projects this advantage is not unusual. The disadvantage of having too much of a force for construction is that such a force must be kept busy all of the time for the operation to be efficient. Equipment and man power cannot be subject to frequent layoffs without the organization losing efficiency. When equipment is idle, depreciation continues. The highest quality in man power can command jobs where layoffs do not occur.

C. The Letting of Contracts

Somewhere in this discussion of relationships between Park Department officials and private business interests, there must be presented two topics of great importance to the park administrator, namely, conflicts of interest and gifts. The seriousness of these subjects hinges upon not only the legality but the propriety of certain acts which if handled in the wrong way can lead to serious impairment of the good will of the Park Department and the possible ruination of the reputation and career of individuals involved. These subjects are very delicate ones and must be handled with tact, understanding, diplomacy, and above all, absolute honesty. Because of the possible appearance of these offending situations in construction work, they are dealt with here.

1. Conflict of Interest. The law, including our local city charters, usually prohibits elected public officials from doing business with the governmental agency of which they are a member. In other words, a member of a Park Commission cannot sell or buy or otherwise do business with that particular commission. If he is a member of a firm or connected with a firm doing business with the Park Department, he must either relinquish his business association or his membership on the Park Board. Sometimes it becomes the delicate job of the park administrator to inform a Board member who has innocently in ignorance of the law gotten himself into such a position. Delicate as this task is, it must be done for the sake of the reputation of the department as well as the individual commissioner. The park administrator cannot afford to simply close his eyes to something of this sort of which he is aware.

Elected park commissioners cannot hold any other elected office which the courts have decreed or common sense will indicate are incompatible. *Incompatibility arises out of any situation in which the individual may find himself acting on both sides of a bargaining table or by being both an appellant and a judge at the same time.* For example, a member of a Park Board which on occasion must appear before the State Legislatures for modifications of the law cannot very well be a member of the Legislature also. In such a case he is appealing for a decision and he is also in a position of making the decision.

Park managers or members of the executive staff cannot be in the position of being associated in any way with a firm that is doing business or might do business with his own department or any other branch of his level of government. Some occasions may arise where this situation is unavoidable as in the case of a public employee holding property which may be acquired by his own board, In this case, he must disassociate himself entirely from the transaction, in other words, disqualify himself in that particular case. It is not unusual for men of high ethical standards to disqualify themselves from such transactions even though they may have been disassociated from the firm or from the public agency for some time.

Favoritism is akin to conflict of interests. The public always presumes that favoritism is going to be shown to relatives, close friends, and close business associates of the recent past. It is not always possible to avoid doing business with these classes of individuals, but such associations should be avoided as much as possible. Where circumstances prevent such avoidance, every precaution should be taken to ensure the fact, and the *appearance* of the fact, that the association is entirely on a business basis and that no favoritism develops.

2. Gifts. Gifts range all the way from an occasional complimentary luncheon to items of considerable value as everyone knows who reads the newspapers, particularly in regard to involvement in these matters of high government officials of the federal government. All of this is separate and apart from money bribes, the detection of which are punishable by fines and imprisonment. In this discussion, gifts refer to matters of propriety where bribery cannot be proven. The whole question before us here is where does good will friendly gifts end and influential bribery begin.

Private companies as well as governmental agencies have struggled manfully to devise codes of ethics to cover these matters. Except for a complete prohibition of the giving or acceptance of any business gifts, no general standard has been devised which will fit all circumstances and all conditions. Even complete prohibition proves to be too inhuman to be realistic. Where human kindness and human appreciation for a happy association is too prevalent to happily accept complete prohibition, guides to action become difficult to even suggest because they are easily misunderstood as justification for excesses not intended. Assuming the reader to be completely honest, (not being of the grasping and parsimonious type), to being responsive to high ethical standards, to being somewhat gregarious but having what is normally accepted as uncommonly good common sense, the following guides are timidly suggested.

First, make sure of the motive of the giver. If a business representative suggests that you take lunch with him, decline by making some polite excuse unless you know him well enough to know his motive: that it is entirely upon a friendly basis, that he knows that there is no possibility of influencing you. Even in such cases, it is well for you to make the point that you intend to reciprocate this friendly gesture. Motives are not so easily hidden that they cannot be detected by anyone who is forewarned and who hesitates enough to examine the situation in his own mind. Therefore, unless the motive is positively understood by the park manager (or members of his staff), no gratuities or business courtesies of any kind are ever to be accepted.

Secondly, not only must the motive be devoid of the expectation of a business favor, but even the appearance of a questionable motive must be asbent. For example, the business manager cannot be seen frequently in social association with contractors who are doing business with his department. This has the appearance of unholy intimacy, and suspicion will immediately rise in the minds of some people. Any association with business people must be on a general plane where others in like situations are present. The appearance should always be on such a level as to produce the impression that business associates and public officials are mingling upon the basis of mutual reciprocity where the entertainment might be at the expense of one as well as the other, where the social standing of one is in the same circle as that of the other.

Thirdly, if the motive and the appearance of motive pass muster, the acceptance of small favors can be justified. It can be recognized that pleasant business associations can induce the participants to express their gratitude in modest ways. However, there is just as much excuse for the public official to appreciate that association as there is for the man in business. Hence, *this is not a one-sided transaction by any means.*

Fourth, just how small does this favor have to be, to be acceptable? Some have said that it ought to be small enough to be used up in a day or consumed in one sitting, probably in the amount of $5 or $10 or something which you would be willing and are ready to give your business associate in return for the pleasure he has given you in past associations.

In the course of his business, the park administrator will, on occasion, be called upon to solicit funds for the benefit of some project which his department is undertaking – a convention, a campaign of some sort, (nonpolitical), or a particular public project. One of the sources of prospects of solicitation will be companies with which he has done business. Many departments try to avoid this sort of solicitation. If it is permitted, solicitation ought to be very discreetly and carefully made and complete freedom of decision must be left with the business. No pressure of any kind, no threat of business retaliation, no dictation as to the amount or any implication by word or tone of voice must be given in the request for support. The businessman must understand that his contribution, if any, is of his own free will and is not associated with his business dealings with the department.

3. Purchasing Agent. Purchasing agents are usually interposed between the manager of a park department and the actual letting of contracts or the purchasing of goods. This does take some of the "heat" off the manager in regard to some of the relationships mentioned above, but purchasing agents are not provided for that purpose. Their job is a specialist's job requiring special training in the art of purchasing. The establishment of a purchasing division enables the park department or even larger groups of governmental agencies to pool their purchasing power and to make uniform the method by which goods and services of a contractual nature are procured.

Quite often, a separate purchasing department may be established for all of the agencies of the state, or a municipality, or a county, or the federal government for that matter. Purchasing departments establish their own rules of procedure with which other agencies must comply, including the park and recreation department. Some discretionary matters, however, are left with the park and recreation department. These may include a limitation on the monetary limit of any item permitted to be purchased without advertising for bids, the actual specifications of material and services to be contracted for, whether or not the furnishing of material is to be covered by a contract or a purchase order, whether the purchasing agent is to join in the recommendations as to the acceptance of bids or the rejection thereof.

Assuming the park department has something to say about the matter, when will a purchase order suffice and when is a written contract needed? Contracts will be needed for the construction of all of a particular project. They will be required for the purchase of goods, the delivery of which is extended over a long period of time or in which the amount is considerable, or where the quotation is on a unit basis which in turn is based upon estimated quantities, (for example, the furnishing of bituminous material for a season's operation in the repair and construction of roadways, the construction of sidewalk in a geographical section of the city), but with quantities unknown until the job is finished.

Contracts will be required wherever it is necessary to ensure fulfillment of an agreement which is enough involved to warrant all the conditions being specified in writing.

The simple purchase orders which in effect are contracts may be sufficient in the supplying of most of the goods purchased and even of the rental of equipment where the equipment can be made easily identifiable.

4. Bids and Letting of Construction Contracts. Specifications accompanying plans for the construction of a project are usually given out to contractors about two weeks before the date set for the receipt of their bids. These bids are usually accompanied by a certified check of a certain percentage of the estimated cost of the job, and some deposit for the use of plans and specifications is usually required to ensure the return of these documents.

As contractors study over the plans and specifications, some questions will arise, and an occasional error will actually be noticed which will require the park department to issue memorandums of alterations to all of the contractors who have plans and specifications in their possession. These alterations become a part of the original plans and specifications.

Bids are received by the purchasing agent and opened at the specified time in the presence of contractors who wish to be present and representatives of the park department. Bids handed in after the specified time are disqualified and returned unopened to the bidder. The bids are tabulated and examined sufficiently to eliminate discrepancies, evaluate alternatives, and later to investigate the reputation and financial responsibility of at least the two or three lowest bidders. These bids are retained by the purchasing agent pending the authorization of a contract. A tabulation of all bids is transmitted then to the governing agency with the recommendation of the purchasing agent and the manager of parks and recreation.

This recommendation will be to accept the lowest responsible bid or the rejection of all bids. The latter situation may occur if the bid price is beyond the financial limitations of the department or the appropriations established for this job, or for any other reason – all because the right to reject all bids has been written into the specifications prior thereto. The best bid is usually recommended to be accepted. If some other bid is recommended, then the full reason thereof must be thoroughly explained, and the reason must be based upon conclusive proof that the low bidder is irresponsible one way or another, or that his bid is improper and did not comply with the plans and specifications.

At this point, a public park and recreation department is not in the position of bargaining with any of the contractor bidders for a preferred situation. The department is not in the position of suggesting to the bidder that if he alters this, that, or the other thing in order to reduce the amount to come within the appropriation, his bid would be accepted. This is entirely an unethical procedure and certainly is open to serious public criticism. Either all of the bids must be rejected, plans and specifications altered and readvertised, or one of the bids must be accepted.

Specifications for the purchase of equipment or even certain supplies must be drawn by the park department to permit the receipt of competitive prices. In other words, the specifications cannot be drawn to limit competition to one specific piece of equipment when there are other similar items on the market. Not infrequently, the specifications may call for a specific make of machine of a specified character and then add "or equal."

In this case, after bids are received and the favored machine is of higher cost and the manager wants that machine in preference to the machine which has bid the lowest, the manager must be in a position to prove that the wanted machine is superior either in composition by comparing specifications, or that it is of distinct monetary saving to him in the operation of his department. When this matter arises, the park manager must be very sure that his technical specialists are sound and thorough in all their arguments.

5. Supervision of Construction. Once again we are confronted with a choice as to who actually supervises construction – a choice which depends upon the policy we are following in connection with the construction function. If the construction is being done under contract according to plans and specifications prepared by the department engineer, the engineer

is the logical one to supervise construction. If the construction work is being done on a building for which an architect has been retained, the architect is the logical supervisor. If the park is being constructed according to plans and specifications prepared by a landscape architect or park specialist outside of the department, the arrangement with that specialist may or may not include services for supervision. If it includes supervision, of course, he accomplished that task, but if the supervision is not contracted for, then the engineer will very likely assume that responsibility. If the work is being done by departmental crews under force account system, whichever division or section drew the plans and specifications ought to supervise construction and see that compliance with the plans and specifications takes place.

If the work is being done under contract, the contractor usually is entitled to part-time payment usually every 30 days. Whoever is supervising the work in behalf of the owner certifies the percentage accomplished and, by various means, determines the amount of money that is due the contractor for the work accomplished. Usually there is a percentage, (about 10 per cent), withheld pending final inspection of the completed job.

Regardless of who has supervised the construction on behalf of the owner, before the completed job is accepted, it is inspected not only by the supervisor but by others in the park and recreation department. These usually include the park manager and may, on some occasions, include a representative of the board if there is a board. This final inspection is a rigid one, because at that time, full compliance with the plans and specifications is determined and every minute detail is checked. When a certificate of inspection has been properly placed before the board or final authority and adopted by them and payment ordered, there is no further recourse except any guarantee provision which may have been included in the specifications.

Because of the importance of the final inspection, the governing authority of the park department will usually have a set policy as to who is to be responsible for making the inspection and making the final certificate of acceptance. Usually that is left with the park manager, but it sometimes is left with the park manager and a representative of the board. If the park manager is inclined to delegate his responsibility to the engineer, for example, the manager still is responsible in the final analysis. It is possible that the policy laid down for the

process of final inspection and acceptance routine may vary
with the size and importance of the contract or construction
work being carried out. In other words, there may be certain
classes of construction which are left to the park manager and
others in which the board expects to have a representative
present. The presence of some definite policy is very desirable.

    6. Shifting from Construction to Maintenance. Offhand,
it would appear that as soon as the construction job has been
accepted, the jurisdiction and responsibility should shift from
the construction or engineering division to the maintenance
division. This is the intent. However, in the construction of
parks, we are dealing with growing things such as grass, trees,
shrubs, etc., that do not mature promptly, and consequently,
there is a period of time in which either division could logically
assume responsibility for overseeing the work. Therefore, a
policy should be determined as to the routine which must be
followed to place the responsibility on a completed job or partially completed job from one division head to another.

    Normally, a report of the status of the job should come
from the construction division to the park manager who decides
the right moment for placing the responsibility on the maintenance division. Incidentally, it is not at all unusual to include
a year's maintenance cost in the appropriation for construction. Also, if it is expected that possible ground settlement
or other alterations in the project may take place in a year or
two from the time of completion of the job, it is logical to reserve an amount from the appropriation to take care of re-
storing the job to its original completion form.

CHAPTER 11   POLICIES OF OPERATION

In the operation of park and recreation systems, the possible circumstances requiring determination of policy are so frequently encountered and so varied in character that the entire field could not be covered in a generalized study course such as this. Some of the more common situations will be discussed. Sometimes a right and a wrong policy may be apparant, but in most of the situations there is no clear-cut right and wrong — success, in these cases, depends upon the evaluation of local conditions and the ingenuity of the park manager and his staff. An attempt will be made to cite the usual pros and cons in these cases as guides to future decisions.

Policies Already Established by Basic "Ground Rules"

There is a basic law, charter provision, or executive mandate that is the authority for the existence of every governmental park and recreation agency. That "authority" will give the purpose, the responsibility and the powers of the park and recreation agency. It frequently will establish certain policies. These policies are usually found in the description of the purpose, and sometimes in some sort of preamble. It is essential that these laws and edicts be examined for the basic policies which they contain.

The park and recreation administrator is always subject to some higher authority — a commission or board, a single commissioner, a cabinet officer (state or federal) or a department head. In other words, the superior authority may be an organized body or a single individual.

In cases where the superior authority is an individual, the park and recreation administrator should find out what policies of administration his superior has. This should be determined early in the game before differences arise through subsequent administrative experiences.

Boards and commissions may have established policies either formally in written form or informally by habitually following a settled course and without recording the practices. In the latter case, each new commissioner and each new administrator is left to learn these policies over a period of "wait-and-see" experiences. When policies are in written form, even though not formally adopted, and therefore constituting only a record of practices, a great deal of time is saved

See supplement in Appendix, p. 278.

and misunderstanding avoided by referring to that record.   A
wise administrator will see that during *his* administration such
a record is made and kept current.

Most boards have adopted rules governing board procedures, and these contain matters of policy. If an administrator
finds that no such rules exist, he should propose a set of rules
for the board's consideration and subsequent adoption.   The
subjects usually covered by board rules are as follows. *

1. Meetings – Time and place of regular meetings, who pre-
    sides, how many members make a quorum, how special
    meetings may be called, order or business, rules of con-
    duct, process of adopting ordinances, a statement as to
    whether or not all meetings are public.
2. Officers – What officers are provided for, how they are
    elected, and what are the duties of each.   Herein, there
    may be found a paragraph or so about the chief adminis-
    trator: how he is selected, the general scope of his re-
    sponsibilities, how much authority is conferred by the
    adoption of the budget, the submission of monthly reports
    and similar matters.
3. Naming standing committees, prescribing duties, limiting
    authority to investigations for report to the whole board,
    relationship to administrator, the appointment of special
    committees.
4. Other provisions – The agenda and its significance, the
    conduct of public hearings, clarifying the authority and
    prescribing relationship of individual members to the
    board as a whole and to the administrator.
5. Amendments to the rules, their repeal and the suspension
    of the rules. Roberts Rules of Order usually govern when
    not in conflict with the law or the specific rules of the
    board as herein provided.

The law, the written policies, (or those implied by repeated practice), the rules of the board, all constitute existing
policy "ground rules. " One other document might be added,
namely, the Ordinances of the park and recreation department;
but that subject will be touched upon later.   Quite obviously,
these "ground rules" constitute the foundation on which is constructed the superstructure of departmental policy.

Matters Requiring Board Action—Effect on Formation of Policy

The skeleton of the policy superstructure to which reference has just been made, emerges from formal acts of the

* For sample see p. 307.

governing body or the decisions of a superior officer before whom subject matters have been placed. In the succeeding discussion, reference will usually be made to a board or commission as the governing authority, but more or less parallel circumstances are present in cases where the authority which is superior to the park and recreation administrator is an individual.

In the original understanding between the park administrator and his superiors there has been laid out a general area of responsibility for the respective parties. If there exists a board of commissioners, the board is expected to do the legislative work and to outline broad policies for the guidance of the park administrator, and the park administrator is expected to have complete jurisdiction over the operating affairs of the department. Like most generalized situations, there is an area of grey between the black and the white − an area which logically could become the responsibility of either party, or partly by one and partly by the other. The succeeding discussion will help to clarify some of the more common situations.

The Purpose of the Board Record

The minutes of the board meetings should show authority for all the actions which the board and its employees take. Often this is accomplished by actions delegating broad responsibility to the administrator and his staff and by the declaration of policies.

The board may adopt rules governing its own conduct and may also fix the duties and responsibilities and powers of its officers, including its park and recreation administrator, as previously referred to.

It may have authority to adopt ordinances for the proper use of its properties and the conduct of people using them. Subjects covered by laws and ordinances include: the proper use of the several park areas; the permitted hours of use; the defacement of buildings and other structures; littering and vandalism; use of beer and alcoholic beverages; improper personal conduct; the building of fires; use of firearms; hunting, fishing, and trapping; public speaking and religious services; commercial enterprises on park property; a whole series of sections dealing with traffic; another group on bathing, boating, use of water areas and water pollution; the protection of flora and fauna. The specific provisions are by no means the same in all park systems; they will reveal some general policies consistent with the local social environment of the particular park system rather than policies calling for general debate on the national level. Some exceptions may be discussed later.

The *law* will prescribe certain actions which the board *must* take. These usually involve procedures for the acquisition of property through condemnation proceedings and sometimes otherwise, or the procedure for the taxing of property for park purposes or for requesting funds, both current and capital, preparatory to direct appropriation by other departments of the government, or for the issuance of bonds.

It must approve all contracts.

It must approve the payment of all bills, although this may be modified by granting to the park manager and his staff authority to pay bills as they come due, especially those where discounts are permitted for prompt payment, and then reviewing a listing of bills and confirming the park manager's actions. This review does not alter the actual payment of any properly-contracted-for indebtedness, but it does permit a review of the park manager's judgment which, if differing from the board's desires, can be altered in future cases.

Aside from the foregoing more or less standard board responsibilities, there are other actions which carry varying degrees of authority with them.

The Administrator and His Staff Organization

Usually, but not always, the administrator is expected to obtain approval of his board or his superior for the makeup of his staff and the type of personnel organization with which he expects to function. This is desirable even though not required in order that there may be a unity of understanding as to the method of operation. Also, it indicates at least in general terms, the numbers of classifications of employees graded as to rank. In some cases, the board or superior authority may fix the number in each classification and require specific authorization to increase that number. This is a matter, however, that must be considered in connection with the authority accompanying the adoption of the financial budget.

Salaries and Wages

Unless salaries and wages are fixed by some other agency such as a Civil Service Commission, (and not infrequently when such commissions exist), authority to pay specific salaries and wages to either individuals or classes of individuals must be obtained from or confirmed by the governing authority. It is usually expected that the administrator will submit specific recommendations on salaries and wages.

The Operating Budget (Refer to Chapter 8)

The adoption of the annual budget by the board may carry with it broad authority for the administrator to undergo all expenditures authorized or enumerated in that budget, to hire all help necessary to carry out that budget, and to order all materials involved therein, subject to the normal process of the approval of all bills to be paid, the fixing of wages and salaries, and sometimes limitations as to number of employees in each classification.

Various limitations in connection with operation within the budget may be established either by policy, custom, or specific board action in specific instances. Sometimes the administrator is restricted from exceeding expenditure in one category of the budget even though savings in another are made. If there is confidence in the administrator, this restriction is decidedly impractical. There must be some flexibility left to the administrator.

Sometimes there is not just one annual budget, but four quarterly budgets or two semiannual budgets. In other words, the total annual budget is released for authority to operate every three or six months. This again is a restriction which hampers efficient operation.

Plans for New Projects

Plans for new projects are normally submitted to the board for approval, first in their preliminary form and later in the form of working drawings and specifications. Authority to request bids is requested at the same time. There are times when the approval of working drawings and specifications are left with the discretion of the administrator after the preliminary plans have been approved.

Matters Not Covered

The park and recreation manager, (administrator, director, or superintendent, by whatever name known), is confronted with all sorts of situations which require daily decisions. He must feel confident that in making these decisions he has the authority to make them and that authority has been granted to him by the board either because of custom, the adoption of definite policies, or because of his knowledge of the usual re-action of board members. If there is serious doubt as to his authority, the administrator is wise to refer the matter to the board for guidance. A new manager in a new situation involv-ing new board members finds himself in more doubt than an old hand in the matter. An experienced manager can rely upon past custom for his usual action, explaining such to the board at the proper time. However, a new man in an established department will find it politic to get more frequent guidance in these matters. The student will recognize, in this situation, a comparison with the President and Congress of the United States. A strong President and a weak Congress will find a greater responsibility being borne by the President and on other occasions the opposite is true. So it is with administra-tors and their boards and commissions, and sometimes with an individual who is the administrator's immediate superior.

The writer's suggestion is that the able manager assume as great a responsibility as his board will permit him to as-sume − up to a point. When the manager has succeeded in making practically *all* the important decisions with the board willing to approve without much discussion, the manager is on his way to becoming an autocrat, and that is not good. An autocrat manager loses his ability to think objectively and his decisions tend to become personal whims. His board is not questioning him enough or in the manner that their constituents might question him, and the manager loses his ability to de-fend his plans, not infrequently because they have become in-defensible.

On the other hand, a weak manager afraid to assume re-sponsibility and take independent action is of small account. Associate him with a weak board and the park and recreation service is apt to become deplorable.

A board whose members seem to be so strong-willed as to want to assume all administrative responsibility and are continually nagging at the manager and his staff members, in time will find themselves without a competent professional and the job which lay board members can do will again be inferior.

This entire relationship is a test of the executive ability, tact, and diplomacy of the manager.

Discussion of Some Operating Policies
Common to Many Situations

Neighborliness and Cooperation

Neighborliness and cooperation are intangibles woven into the spirit of the department in such a way as to constitute a policy of attitude. The larger, the stronger, the better equipped, the more technical know-how it has, the more should a park organization help those in less fortunate circumstances. Something has happened in recent years to remove some of the luster from that glowing thought. Competition for space, for money, and the fierce pride in local autonomy all but make enemies, for example, of the central city and its suburbs and suburbs are lined up against its neighboring suburbs. Sometimes a neighbor may not use another suburb's properties without paying more for this use than local citizens — a sort of tariff barrier has arisen between communities. The central city and its suburban towns expect the metropolitan or county park systems to provide those things which urban areas have difficulty providing for themselves; and all of these, towns and county alike, look further upward to the state to supplement local effort; and in turn, all expect the federal government to do more than it is doing. Much energy is being lost squabbling with each other and the practice ought to be stopped. Greater cooperation coupled with a greater sense of self-reliance bring about a more uniform and satisfying service throughout the several governmental levels. Help from above is, indeed, present, but every park administrator ought to recognize that this sort of "incentive help" will not wholly satisfy the needs of his district. Each district must still rely upon its own sound plans and must possess the aggressiveness to execute those plans. Nevertheless, helping one's neighbor helps all.

Attendance at Professional Meetings

When the board authorizes any of its members or executive staff to attend conventions in a distant city, there is always a segment of the public that believes public officials are going to a gay party at public expense. Sometimes, unfortunately, this can be true. The proper policy on this matter should ensure public benefit equal to or more than the expense involved.

Improved methods of organization, operation of equipment, and processes are emerging constantly from hundreds of manufacturers all over this country and foreign countries as well. Many professional meetings are held annually at which men attempt to explore and evaluate possible improvements to their operation and to see what is going on someplace else. All of this is of real value to the professional and the work he is attempting to perform in his own bailiwick. These meetings are likewise of inspiration and a source of greater knowledge of park and recreation services to nonprofessional board members. Much good emerges from these meetings and that good ought to be taken back home, reported in written form, and the report distributed to appropriate staff members and board members.

Not all of these meetings and conventions are of national scope and national importance. There are many sectional and local meetings of similar nature – the expense of attendance at which is much reduced. This might make possible the attendance of those whose expense to attend national conventions would not be justified. Sometimes the board is willing to grant the manager discretion within limits in permitting attendance of employees at such meetings.

There should not exist the spirit that authority to attend meetings is granted simply as a reward either for past performance or simply for membership on a board. The policy should be to authorize attendance in cases which will yield specific valuable results; i. e., (1) either those attending the conventions ought to bring back information and material of real value, or (2) men possessing special leadership qualities and technical know-how that is of value and inspiration to the entire profession should be sent to the convention to contribute to the general welfare and, incidentally, to add to the prestige of the local community.

Fees and Charges

For what services, if any, does a park and recreation department make a charge? There have been more discussions locally and nationally on this subject than on almost any other policy matter confronting park and recreation departments.

It will be recalled that the justification for the various levels of government providing park and recreation services is founded on the responsibility of government to promote the general welfare. Specifically in the case of parks and recreation, it has been well accepted that this function is so broad in its application and so general in its distribution of benefits that it comes well within the general welfare provisions. Having that thought in mind, a large number, if not the majority, of municipal park departments established a no-charge or no-fee basis for its services unless that service was a special one provided for a special class of people who found government more capable of rendering their specialized service than private enterprise. Here are some examples:

Golf courses were established and the golfers were expected to pay the costs of that service. There was confusion at first because some departments concluded that golf was a logical form of recreation and ought to be subsidized by the government and the fees charged were either very little or nothing at all. Most park and recreation departments considered this to be a specialized service and made appropriate charges from the beginning. Others justified a lower fee because golf courses, as beautiful open space, contributed to the general welfare even if golfers were not present, hence, to some extent, golf ought to be subsidized. Presently, if public golf is subsidized at all, it most likely escapes the usual amortization charges devolving upon self-supporting and self-liquidating enterprises.

There has never seemed to be any question about making a charge for refreshments and other saleable merchandise. However, there is a difference of opinion as to providing firewood, charcoal, and similar picnic accessories. Charging for attendance at swimming pools has been quite general except for younger children. Parking the family car is generally free, but parking on a pay basis is gradually increasing, especially where the parking fee becomes the means of collecting a fee for use of beaches and picnic areas.

Making a charge for general revenue purposes has come into being in recent years particularly in state park operation. State legislatures, harassed on all sides by mounting expenses and increased requests for funds, have been rather niggardly in appropriating funds for the expansion and operation of state park systems. Managers, confronted with almost impossible operating conditions, have advocated that a nominal charge be made for each person or automobile that visits the state park. These fees are sometimes used for capital expenditures, and sometimes for general operating purposes. The practice of charging has apparently been accepted by the residents of the states in which it has been tried. If success continues, the practice may be extended to many more states.

However, this practice raises the fundamental question of propriety in the minds of the fundamental theorists. Indiana long ago resorted to fees and charges probably on the grounds that state parks in themselves constitute a special service. The general demand for, and accessibility to state parks now raises the question as to whether or not that service is general enough to promote the general welfare of all people and therefore to justify the service on a free basis. This theory is that all people should be taxed because of the general good that arises from the mere presence of the park, regardless of any special benefit that might accrue to the user.

All in all, there seems to be no set of basic principles on which decisions concerning the making of fees and charges can be based. There are, however, some pertinent facts that should be kept in mind in rationalizing the appropriateness of any proposal for imposing a fee or making a specific charge:

1. It has been firmly established that park and recreation services may justifiably be supported by general taxation – established that when charges are made for that service, under some circumstances the operating governmental agency may be operating in a proprietary, and not a governmental capacity, and in so doing, sacrifices liability immunity granted to governments when acting in their governmental capacities.

2. The mere presence of a park may impart a benefit even without being entered upon. In some instances parks may enhance the value of nearby property and thereby justify the levying of a special tax on that property. The *use* that is made of some parks may, on occasion, be detrimental to adjacent private properties.

3. The public does not obtain all its recreation from public parks and recreation services. Some recreation services available to the public are attractive enough to command sufficient price to be profitable to the entrepreneur. The propriety of tax supported recreation entering into this sort of business is a debatable issue.

4. Some recreation services offered by privately supported welfare agencies sometimes demonstrate such a wide general appeal and offer so much general benefit that government may be justified in enlarging its repertoire of services to include those services that have enjoyed such

wide public voluntary financial support. That has happened in the past with the result that the "floor" of tax supported service has been raised. This is one of the forces that is continually at work to raise standards. Minority pressure groups constitute another force. Activities which are the subject of these moves to raise standards are susceptible to the application of special fees prior to their inclusion in the tax supported category. Where tax support ends and special fee begins remains the debatable issue.

5. In view of the foregoing point 4, neither the extent in money nor in variety of services that warrant tax support has been determined except momentarily. Both the amount of money and variety of service at any one time and in any one place is the temporary result of a continuous conflict between taxpayer groups and user groups.

Some further insight as to when to make a charge for services may be found in examining the matter in the separate spheres of city, state, and nation. The underlying problem is the same in all cases but the degree and frequency of making charges may vary. Historically, municipal services were originally considered to be wholly tax supported; there was practically no tax support for national parks; there always was a difference of opinion as to state parks. Time has wrought changes but tradition is still discernible: National and state parks now have tax support but fees and charges are more frequently encountered here than in municipal systems. There may be more logic to these current practices than mere tradition would indicate and for that possible additional logic we need to examine the degree of use that the several classes of parks get.

It has been previously noted that the equivalent of the whole population uses municipal parks once every week or two. Such general participation in a park and recreation service suggests a justification for broad tax support. To be sure, some modifying factors are present but the eligibility for tax support remains very prominent. The use of state parks by the equivalent of the whole population is once in three to four months, or roughly one-tenth as much as municipal parks. Visits to national parks by the equivalent of the whole population are only once every two or three years, or about one-eightieth the frequency of municipal parks.

Does this imply that the justification for tax support for state and national parks is only one-tenth and one-eightieth respectively of the justification for tax support on the municipal level? Hardly.

There is at least one other important factor to consider — long ago the Congress and the states concluded that the preservation of their unique and historic areas warranted tax support at least to the degree of securing title to them. Where *use,* as distinguished from *preservation,* is the dominant service offered (e. g., in recreation areas) the foregoing reasoning has some appeal — not conclusive enough for general acceptance, but intriguing enough to someday pursue further.

Some very general conclusions as to when and for what, fees and charges are justified, now may be timidly suggested. (1) Seldom make charges on the local government level. (2) Be very careful about making charges for state and national parks where *preservation* is the dominant purpose. (3) Be frequent in making charges at state and national parks where *use* is the dominant function. (4) In all cases, be sure that *some* benefit accrues to the taxpayer for the payment of his tax. (5) Aside from the foregoing, the specific services to be charged for and the fee should be matters of local choice, experimentation, and finally public acceptance. *

Amount of Tax Support

It has been previously stated that the extent and variety of services that warrant tax support are by no means standardized. Also it has been suggested that the administrator might do well to examine costs per attendant unit in deciding the eligibility for tax support of that particular activity. Are similar correlations valid in arriving at the *amount* of tax support park and recreation services should enjoy? Even though no such standard measurement of tax support can be justified, an examination of current practices may prove at least interesting.

On the municipal level, the 1961 Yearbook of the National Recreation Association will be the reference. ** At the outset, it should be realized that although the reference is the best available, the statistics are not always comparable as between cities, and the actual figures are not always precise. We start out from an imperfect reference point, so the results are indicative but not exact. The cost of tax support that cities give to park and recreation operation and maintenance ranges

* Both the federal and state governments now impose entrance fees for parks. The practice is not so all-inclusive for entrance to forests, reservoir lakes, or wild life refuges.

** The 1966 Yearbook of NRPA contains a greater variety of information but because of the greater complications of Metropolitan political subdivisions, the amount of tax support for each is not so easily available as in the 1961 edition.

from $1 per capita to $10 per capita. In cities having populations in excess of 100,000 the per capita appropriations run from $2 to $3 in the South with a very few important exceptions. Comparable figures rise to $4 to $6 as we go North into the Middle States and New England; from $5 to $8 on the West Coast. The largest cities of the country also run from $5 to $8 per capita, regardless of geographical location.

There are no statistics reliable enough to yield municipal appropriations in terms of attendance. On the other hand, the most significant statistics on state parks are those based upon attendance.

"State Park Statistics – 1961," a publication of the National Park Service, is also the best in its field, but is plagued by faults similar to those of the National Recreation Association publication. It shows that the cost per visitor for operation and maintenance is 22 cents which may be offset by revenue which reduces the cost to 14 cents net. The corresponding per capita costs would be 33 cents and 21 cents. If frequency of use were a logical way of measuring tax support, the appropriation for state parks should approximate say one-tenth of about $5 or 50 cents instead of 33 cents or possible 21 cents.

This sort of investigation might be carried on with the National Parks, National Forests, Army Reservoirs, etc., but aside from being an intriguing mathematical exercise, it will aid little in our search for a base on which to formulate policies for tax appropriation. Oh, a city *could* declare that it will limit appropriations for park and recreation services to, say, $5 per capita. * (Indeed, that approach has already been taken.) A state could approximate its appropriation for state parks by multiplying anticipated attendance by, say, 13 cents. In both cases, additional income and added service could be realized from fees and charges. ORRRC suggested a system of fees and charges for outdoor recreation to supplement tax appropriations. Did ORRRC anticipate this sort of approach? Techniques are as yet not sophisticated enough to permit general acceptance of this idea. Maybe some day more precise statistical data, some method of evaluating the ever-changing factors involving standards of services, and the determination of a few other elusive factors, will produce some meaningful mathematical formulae. But not now. Cut and try, hee and haw, pressure against resistance, propaganda and fact, all work on the present scene to produce temporary results good only from day to day.

* Hennepin County, Minnesota once was permitted a levy of only 18 cents per capita for park operation.

Who Operates Revenue Producing Businesses?

The activities included here are those that are ancillary to the primary function of parks. They are services that make the recreational experience of the park visit more enjoyable and more complete and a charge is made for them. The sale of refreshments, meals, souvenirs, and other merchandise, the rental or use of equipment, the furnishing of overnight lodging are examples of an almost endless array of special services. Who shall make the capital investment and who shall operate these businesses – the park and recreation agency or private individuals or companies?

The simplest of these businesses involves the sale of refreshments, souvenirs, and incidental merchandise. Advocates of self operation by government usually cite these advantages:

1. The department has complete control of the service at all times. It can rectify promptly any complaints. It can provide service during hours when profit is questionable. It has complete control of personnel, of quantities and quality.
2. If a private operator can make a profit in this operation it stands to reason that the public agency can make that profit plus the license fee the private operator pays to the public agency. In other words, the public makes more money.
3. Self-operation by the department eliminates any chance of the establishment of private vested interests on public property.

Those advocating private concessionairs make these points:

1. Believing that private operation can be more efficiently done than public operation, they charge that the public makes more money by private operation.
2. The department is relieved of many bothersome details in the matter of hiring personnel (no Civil Service requirements), purchasing regulations, and similar irritations.
3. Where initial investment is required, private operation enables private investment without public appropriation.
4. As rebuttal to departmental operation, the private concessionaire believes that quality and hours of service can be adequately provided for in a well-drafted contract.

Examples of successful operations are numerous for each of the systems. The writer is inclined to favor departmental operation unless local restrictions are too severe. If concessions are let out to private operators on bid, there are some minimum precautions which ought to be made:

1. The private operator ought not to have the opportunity of establishing any vested right on park property. Admitting that this can be provided for in contract, the wailing that private concessioners can do when this matter is enforced, all too frequently makes the public agency appear to be persecuting them. However, instances can be cited, where even termination of contracts of previously agreed-to dates have been extended time and again on the plea of the concessioner until he has virtually acquired vested rights for all practical purposes. If he is permitted to make an investment on public property, rigid contractural provisions ought to be made as to its depreciation and valuations at stated times in case the public agency wishes to buy that interest. This whole situation is fraught with so many unfavorable possibilities that too great a caution cannot be taken to avoid any possibility of private rights being established on public property.

2. Contracts designed to ensure the park department's control of hours and seasons of service, quality of service, deportment of attendants, correction of complaints, methods of supervision, payment of money, and various other matters of operation require pages and pages of provisions. As years of this sort of operation continue, the contracts will probably be lengthened in an attempt to cover all possible loopholes. It is well for the beginner to obtain contracts of this sort from other operators, or from other cities and other park departments as guides to his own contract draftings.

3. Specifications accompanying the request for bids should contain provisions permitting the park department to make investigations of the financial responsibility and business reliability of the concessioner and permitting the park department to use discretion in the exercise of judgment as to which of the bids received is the most favorable one to the park department. The reason for this is that the high bidder may not be capable of performing satisfactorily under the terms of the contract, this fact being positively demonstrable by reason of the experiences in past operations. This is a sort of ticklish business, but the park department should not be bound to accept the high

bidder when it is convinced that the concessioner cannot perform except very unsatisfactorily. After all, the primary purpose of this service is not profit but service to make the park experience more enjoyable. Profit is a motive, but not the primary one.

The biggest businesses in the park and recreation field involve the National Park Service and some of the state park operations, especially in providing hotel and summer-resort type of accommodations. The National Park Service has always contracted with private operating companies to build and operate hotels and tourist cabins. In order to permit the private investment to be amortized out of earnings the length of the term of lease has been extended over the years to as much as thirty years. The operation has had its vicissitudes as is well described by Professor John Ise in his "National Park Policy"* previously referred to. That discussion illustrates the problems arising from private investment on public property as well as some of the usual ones inherent in private operation of this sort of service. To obviate some of these problems the N. P. S. has sometimes resorted to operation by a government controlled nonprofit corporation acting in a monopolistic fashion. In a sense, this approaches self-operation.

State parks often followed the example of the National Park Service in providing lodges for overnight guests but usually made the investment themselves. In more recent years, the standard of this type of service has risen and in the case of Oklahoma, the state has virtually gone into the tourist business with convention type accommodations at the central hotel supplemented by a system of separate lodges. In this case, the capital investment is made by the state; the operation may be leased out in whole or in part. In other instances, proposals for elaborate tourist hotels on state park property have been submitted by private companies.

At reservoirs of the Army Engineers, the rules of operation may not permit the investment of any government capital for any revenue producing facilities. This often results in a crass temporary exploitation of public property and poor service to the public, especially in such operations as marinas, fishing docks, refreshment stands, etc.

Between the big businesses of national, state, and some of the larger municipal operations, and the very simple refreshment stand operation at the small local park, there is an

* See Particularly page 606, etc.

array of enterprises that are useful to park and recreation service and that are susceptible of either government or private operation. In all situations there are at least two very basic precautions that the park administrator must look out for. (a) He must at all times be able to control all phases of the operation in order to provide to the park user those services which will make the user's visit a happy experience – the real reason for the enterprise in the first place. (b) He must prevent private control, either real or implied, of any public property. The government must always be in unencumbered control and possession of its physical properties. Private investment on public property does not permit that unencumbered public control. There ought to be provisions for ultimate government ownership of any private capital investments that for one reason or another have been made on park lands or on any in-holdings of real estate within park boundaries.

What might appear to be exceptions to the foregoing, but which really are not exceptions, may be those quasi-public services which are provided by a "partnership" of government and private enterprise – museums, outdoor theaters, some zoological gardens, arboretums, sports stadiums, cultural and art centers. Many of these facilities are financed partly by government and partly by private capital. Often, the most satisfying arrangement is for government to hold title to the physical property (buildings and real estate) and private nonprofit organizations to maintain and operate.

Permits and Leases

Requests for the use of park property for various purposes (private, commercial, recreation) from individuals and organizations constitute a considerable volume of the official business of a park and recreation agency. Many of the permits are of a routine nature – picnic permits, permits for use of ball diamonds, etc. In these cases, rules and regulations have been established in accordance with general policies aimed at conveniencing the park user while at the same time, insuring safe and socially acceptable use of the facilities without undue damage to park property. Requests for other park uses are special cases requiring special consideration – religious services, and political meetings, public speaking generally, commercial ventures, and demonstrations, money raising schemes for "good causes," celebrations, etc.

Public Speaking – Indiscriminate public speaking (religious, political, current issues) can be a distinct nuisance to crowds assembled for purely recreational purposes. Many park and recreation departments have enacted ordinances forbidding the practice except by special permit. The denial of permits in some cases resulted in appeals to the courts which, generally speaking, have upheld the rights of citizens to freely assemble in public places and to speak their minds. This has put quite a dent in enforcement of ordinances prohibiting public speaking. A sort of hopeful compromise has been adopted in some instances, namely, designating certain locations at which public speaking on any subject will be permitted. Permits may still be required, but the purpose is only to serve as notice to the issuing agency so that if police protection seems advisable, it can be provided for. These locations are chosen so that the speaker will not find an already assembled audience to harangue; he will have to supply his own audience. However, to be a reasonable defense against the probable legal restriction, the location should not be so remote as to be entirely frustrating. In brief, the purpose is to permit public speaking without inconveniencing or annoying those seeking recreation in public parks.

Religious Services – Public park and recreation services are provided without religious impetus or motivation, and hence, church services are to be accorded the same treatment as general public speaking. Where the granting of permits does not interfere with recreation enjoyment, approval is in order. However, religious activities can take many subtle forms and the administrator is warned to look out for the possible establishing of precedents in other directions.

Political Meetings – These are to be treated like religious meetings. Here it must be kept in mind that when an elected official appears on the platform he is going to talk politics, and usually partisan politics. But you cannot completely stop them. Stern warnings may soften the most blatant aspects.

Commercial Ventures – These include the short time permit to sell Christmas trees, mobile refreshment carts at special functions, the testing out of a new piece of equipment, and a variety of other services. These situations should be scrutinized in some such way as this. Does the proposal do any damage to park property and, if so, is it readily repaired and will the permittee be willing to stand the cost? Is a fair rental charge possible? Will it inconvenience nearby private property owners? Will it unfairly compete with private business? Is it of such a character as will be consistent with the dignity of the department and consistent with the attractiveness of the area? Is it a legitimate service to the public? If the project passes these tests it may be approved. However, it is generally desirable to keep the number of these permits to a minimum.

Houseboats, Launching Ramps, Marinas, Water-Skiing, Boat Clubs – Park departments owning property on navigable streams, particularly rivers, may find themselves harassed by the presence of houseboats docked on the river bank. Like squatters, houseboat owners often are used to circumventing the law and bluffing authorities into believing that they know their rights better than park departments. They will claim they have a right to dock because their boat is on the river, only the gangplank going over to the shore. They insist upon having access to the land not only for themselves but for the delivery of goods and supplies which they need, that they are not in the nature of transients and can stay as long as they please. An appeal to suitable police authorities discloses the fact that generally speaking, police are not too well versed in the park department's rights to evict the houseboat owners from use of the adjacent land. Fact of the matter is that while houseboat owners or any other boaters can use the river to their heart's content without molestation and can tie up to any shore in an emergency, the owner of the adjacent land, even if the land itself lies between the established harbor line and the edge of the water, has control of who docks there and who uses the adjacent property. Consequently, the adjacent owner has the right to establish docking rules and regulations and establish fees for the use of such docks and the privilege of access to the adjacent land.

Marinas for boats of various purposes and of various sizes have been provided by many agencies of government in all its levels. The establishment of fees for the privilege of using the facilities is a legitimate operation. Like entering any other enterprise having to do with the sale of goods and services on public property, all the necessary precautions must be taken to see that the park department receives the money that is actually taken in over the counter and that it is otherwise protected by insurance against the usual hazards of doing business. It must be remembered that when a governmental agency gets into a business enterprise such as this, it loses certain immunities from liability it has when it is acting in a governmental capacity. In this case it is not acting in its governmental capacity, but in its proprietary capacity. Therefore, it is subject to all of the hazards of a private individual in the conduct of his business.

Inasmuch as lightweight boats of various sizes are now on the market, many owners find it convenient to store their boats on their own property some distance from the water and to transport the boat by trailer or otherwise to the scene of the launching. Numerous launching ramps have been provided by various governmental agencies for the convenient launching of these craft. Generally speaking, no charge is made for the privilege of launching, but inasmuch as cars are parked in adjacent parking lots, it is not unusual to invoke an automobile or trailer parking fee.

Water skiing being the popular sport that it is, certain precautions ought to be taken in governing the use of the waters on which this sport is carried on. The purpose of regulations is to segregate the activity of water skiing from the enjoyment of fishing and from the danger which water skiing might have to swimmers. It is not unusual to encounter a situation where the government of the waters does not rest with the owners of only a portion of the abutting land. While this produces complications, either the regulations or the opportunities of getting onto the water from the land can be manipulated so as to secure the necessary safety for the enjoyment of all the sports.

The Park Department may fully realize that the construction of private buildings on public land, even though the buildings may be used for recreation purposes, is a practice which leads to many difficulties. In this connection, boat clubs may present a special problem. The situation can arise in which all the possible practical access points to public waters are in the hands of the Park Department. If some forms of boating, which for proper enjoyment require club facilities, it is difficult to deny such facilities to be constructed on public property. While it may be true that the necessity for these facilities is decreasing as the mobility of people increases, still a Park Department may find itself in the position of being unreasonable if construction privileges are not granted. However, it should be recognized that public property is being used for private purposes and therefore, a legitimate lease arrangement ought to be entered into providing for the payment of an annual fee for the use of the land, the land to be occupied only at the discretion of the Park Department. The lease may be in force for a number of years and if the privilege is revoked within that period then definite liquidation costs ought to be established for each of the years, these costs being based upon the gradually depreciating value of the building which may be placed on park property. Sometimes in the past it has been argued that inasmuch as yacht clubs, privately owned but still to some extent open to the public, constitute a legitimate recreation use and therefore should not be subjected to an annual lease payment but ought to have the privilege of using the property for a nominal payment of a dollar a year. The fact remains that this is a special privilege given to a special few people which ought to pay a special price for that privilege.

Privately Owned Buildings on Public Property — Metropolitan and state parks and on some occasions city parks have been considered ideal sites for special use buildings by privately supported groups engaged in recreation work, either as a means to some other end or even as an end in itself. Such organizations include Boy Scouts, Campfire Girls, YMCA's, the projects of service clubs such as Optimists, Kiwanis, and others.

Influential people representing these worthy causes may successfully argue to the park department that they are engaged in recreation and ought to have the privilege of placing a small center of some sort on public property. Various reasons will be given why it is unobtrusive and good causes such as theirs should be properly supported by the public agencies. They may even suggest that the building will be open to others under their guidance.

No matter in what honeyed phrases these thoughts are expressed, the cold fact remains that a special, privately endowed group catering to a special class is seeking a special favor from a governmental agency pledged to serve all people on an equal basis and deriving its support broadly from all people within the district. If these requests are granted they should be on a monetary basis. Leases should be drawn requiring payment in a sum which is equal to that which would be charged by any private owner of similar property and also with the provisions for removal under equitable circumstances. If these buildings are of general service to the public, another possible solution is for the Park Department to construct such buildings itself and if used generally by all people in sufficient amount the service could be properly tax supported. If used only by a special few, a fee could be charged to cover the cost of operation.

The point is made here that there should be no privately owned buildings on public property and that if any such exists the owner should pay a fair value for the privilege that is conferred and the department should take all necessary precautionary steps to save itself from any liability whatsoever and to be free to recapture complete possession at any time under equitable circumstances.

Access to Boulevards and Parkways – Parkways are a part of many of the park systems of the country. One of the characteristics of parkways is that access to them is limited. This is not necessarily so of boulevards. Adjacent private property owners often request driveway access to their private property from the parkway. In almost all cases this is an objectionable situation, sometimes very mildly so and sometimes quite aggravated. The rights of the department in denying such requests must be investigated in each case for the laws and the situations to which the law may apply are not uniform. Very early in the history of Minneapolis parks one such request was denied which resulted in a lawsuit. The court decided that if the adjacent property owner had no other access to his property than from the parkway the private property owner was entitled to access. If, however, he had some other access possible to his property, the Park Department was within its rights in denying him access to the parkway. Where access is granted without the department being forced to do so because of the limit of the legal situation, the Park Department might find it desirable to grant such a permit for only a period of years so that the matter can be reviewed from time to time in the light of new circumstances. Also, it may be possible to have the private property owner relinquish some inherent rights he may have, such as absolving the Park Department from damage in case of change of boulevard grade or parkway grade in front of his house.

High Tension Line Permits – High tension power transmission lines need rights-of-way to insure adequate maintenance of the line and maintenance of the structures necessary to carry that line. Rights-of-way entering the city from quite a distance away, and sought after the city is pretty well built up, are difficult to find. Sometimes it is necessary to request a right-of-way of the park department over some of its properties. When this request appears it ought to be carefully examined to see if there is any other alternative route, or if none, the route across park property should be screened and the screening blended into the plan of the park. A lease fee or right-of-way price should be exacted and that price commensurate with prices paid to private property owners. Incidentally, if strenuous objection is often enough raised, the power companies through research might find some alternative method of power transmission and reduce the frequency of this objectionable feature especially in urban areas.

Social Welfare and Charitable Organization Requests – As a preliminary word of caution it should be noted that a public park and recreation agency is devoid of sentimental or emotional feeling in dealing with charitable and religious organizations. The promotion of these causes however worthy they may be in the ordinary sense, or the promotion of anything other than public recreation by the governmental agency sets the precedent of promoting some causes of questionable worth. Therefore, when requests for the use of park and recreation facilities are made by any of the agencies referred to, be it in a preferential capacity, or to raise money for a good cause, or to assist in promotion of their objectives – these requests must be accorded the same consideration as similar requests from other segments of the population. Some of these agencies will be providing recreation services as a means to their primary social welfare end. While close coordination of these services with the public service must be recognized and provided for, the use of public facilities should be on the same basis as for other organized groups and individuals.

One final word of caution in regard to permits for the use of or entrance upon park property: Have the permit in writing and the conditions therein imposed agreed to, as evidenced by the signature of the permittee; insure compliance by obtaining a cash deposit or a performance bond; insure relief from any and all liability arising from the issuance of the permit by requiring the permittee to secure and pay for insurance protecting the grantor of the permit against such eventuality.

Circuses and Carnivals

Circuses. In my boyhood in the city of Minneapolis, one of the great events of the summer season was the appearance of circuses. There was not just one circus, there were many of them: Ringling Brothers, Barnum and Bailey, Buffalo Bill's Wild West, Gentry's Dog and Pony Show and several others of lesser importance. The major circuses required large acreages of ground usually in the sparsely settled residential areas

of the city adjacent to railroad tracks and accessible by street-
car. Automobiles and trucks were not prevalent. One of the
great recreation experiences was to go to see the circus "come
in", that is, the unloading of the railroad cars, the erection of
the tents, all the work being done by manual labor with the aid
of some elephants. The circus was preceded by a parade
through a section of the town with the calliope always at the
end. These parades were colorful shows in themselves and
attracted considerable attention. Boys frequently had an opportunity of working for admission to the main tent show by
carrying water for the animals, especially the elephants.
Sneaking under the tent was a great sport, but it also had its
hazards.

I never imagined in those boyhood days that I would ever
be in a position of doing business with the exalted people of the
circus, but that became my lot in the early twenties. By that
time the number of circuses had dwindles by reason of consol-
idations and some had gone out of business entirely. The last
big combination was Ringling Brothers, Barnum and Bailey,
and now even they have ceased their tours throughout the country and have confined their activities to comparatively few
cities, including Madison Square Garden in New York. Even
though providing circus lots for circuses is not now a function
of park departments, the process is interesting enough and has
enough of the elements of licensing to illustrate many of the
principles involved in this sort of park transaction.

In the twenties there were still several circuses traveling
throughout the country. Suitable circus grounds, however,
had dwindled considerably so that a few park departments were
the only owners of sizable property favorable for circuses in
the large cities. By that time circus grounds on the edge of
the city were considered too far out and circuses were always
looking for properties near the downtown area. Soldier's
Field in Chicago was used for many years for a rather long
season of the shows. In Minneapolis we had a rather large
athletic field right on the edge of the so-called loop district
which contained a good-sized auto parking lot. Without using
the major portion of the field containing the best diamonds, we
used an area which provided for eight or ten of the ordinary
softball fields.

Whether or not to rent this ground for circuses became a
periodic issue with our Board. Our recreation division was
opposed to its use because it inconveniences 16 to 20 softball
teams for a period involved during the two days of circus plus

at least a week thereafter in the cleanup period. Sometimes in bad weather conditions, this period could extend for two or three weeks. The recreation division felt that the benefit to the city of the circuses was not sufficient to outweigh the disadvantages to the ball players and the spectators too.

The men on the Board, however, had been boys themselves once and argued that any American boy who did not have the opportunity of attending a circus was being deprived of one of his cardinal rights. There was, besides that, argument as to the amount of money which the circus brought into town while others argued about the amount which was taken out. Nevertheless, the rights of boyhood were every time the winner, and the recreation division took the hindmost. It is interesting as a sidelight to note how thoroughly ingrained our early experiences can be and how sacred become some of the traditional habits of childhood. The rights of children, the sanctity of education, of motherhood, truth and virtue all can be lumped into the emotional motives which frequently dominate our judgment. Maybe it should be so.

About six months before the circus came to town the advance man would come into the office unheralded and unannounced. He usually was accompanied by his feed man, that is, the one who provided feed for the animals. This man would usually act as a sort of unofficial contact for the circus when the advance man had departed. The job of the advance man was to arrange for all of the licenses that the various governmental agencies would require, to rent the grounds, to make contracts for all of the services and materials which the circus would need when it arrived. Through previous years' contracts, this was usually so well organized that the advance man could get all of his business transacted in probably 48 hours.

The park department was the owner of the lot. Representing them, it was my job to dicker with the advance man as to price. The first time I encountered this question I had no way of measuring what was reasonable and fair and I got very little help from the circus man. His job was to wind up his business in a hurry leaving me little time to make many inquiries of what had been the past experience. Besides, our Board met only twice a month and somehow or other I had to poll the members of the Board to get their reactions. They would have wanted to know the recommendations. Moreover, at this point I didn't even know whether the Board was willing to rent the lot or not. I stalled for time for a matter of hours which was granted and the circus man departed to return later.

After some scurrying around for information and after further discussion with the circus man, we finally arrived at a rental figure which I think was about $600, a figure which was submitted to the Board and accepted. Then we got down to details. They included decisions as to the following: money was to be paid by the so-called 24-hour man when he arrived in town prior to the showing of the circus. The use of the lot was to include say Sunday for the circus to be hauled in, showings Monday and Tuesday, and departing Tuesday night. A deposit is arranged for or would be arranged for by the 24-hour man to insure the proper cleaning up of the grounds when the circus had left. A bond was posted to insure the repair of any major damage to the grounds. At the insistence of the Board, a generous number of the tickets was to be provided for the use of Board members. This was a phase some of the Board members and I disliked very much and it is a practice which cannot be recommended. Incidentally, the distribution of these tickets is a nasty job because there are always some few who for good and sufficient reasons need more than their fair share of the tickets knowing that others are not going to use them at all. The agreement also includes the services which the circus will need in the way of providing water connections, police supervision, the use of automobile parking lots, and a description of the actual extent of the properties which they are to use.

It could be supposed that such an arrangement entered into in *one* year would be good for another year or for another circus. Such is not necessarily the case. Not all circuses are the same size or require the same amount of ground or can afford to pay the same ground rental, hence, the ground rental sometimes is based upon some sort of sliding scale having a relationship to the seating capacity which ranges from 4,000 or 5,000 to 15,000 or 16,000 in the case of the big circuses. The length of stay varies, too, and that makes a difference in the fee. The change in business conditions from one year to the next together with a measure of the net income from the previous year has an influence on the price in succeeding years.

The next circus man that comes to town is the so-called 24-hour man. As the name implies, his presence is 24 hours to 36 hours in advance of the circus. He picks up all of the business threads of the advance man, has copies of all contracts, and provides for the actual fulfillment of those contracts. Early in the game I recognized the desirability of insisting that the 24-hour man make his appearance in my office so that I would not have to spend half a day on the circus lot looking for him. I also found out that it is one thing to make such a requirement, but compliance might be something else. After all, I am the one looking for the money, not the 24-hour man.

In checking with the 24-hour man I made sure that he had actually contracted for the cleaning up of the grounds by some reputable company that would not only do a good job but would do it promptly. Moreover, his contract should provide for the entire work being done to our satisfaction and not have a dollar limit on it. I give him assurance that I will cooperate with the contractor to see that in no way is he held up by any actions of our department, that his compliance is complete, and that no more work will be required than is necessary and that he will not stall on the job.

It has been a source of real satisfaction to me to know that the men of the larger circuses are uniformly reliable. This may not be true of the smaller ones.

If the circus comes in and shows during unfavorable weather, for example, rain, the ensuing conditions can break the heart of a dedicated park man. Sawdust, shavings, paper, cans, are all ground into the soil. Wagon ruts and piles of debris abound. The pounding of many feet have removed all semblance of turf. Fortunately, most of the garbage has been removed, but otherwise the entire grounds can be in a terrible mess. At that point one can sympathize with the recreation division in not wanting the circus in town. If the conditions are particularly unfavorable the complete clean up job becomes an impossibility. In fact, it may be days before a clean up crew could do any effective work. Eventually, however, the worst mess is somehow taken care of. It is during this period that continual supervision of the contractor is necessary. So far as Ringling Brothers, Barnum and Bailey circus is concerned, I have never yet had any trouble in collecting any reasonable pay for damage to grounds and they always paid their contractor promptly for clean up work after it had been certified satisfactory by our Park Department.

Doing business with small circuses and carnivals is something altogether different. First of all, the reputation for reliability of small circuses is always in question. During the time we were doing business with them, many of them were on the ragged edge financially and careful investigation was necessary. Sometimes the payment for the rental of ground and for the clean up work was collected in advance and a suitable bond posted to pay any damage to grounds. Every possible precaution had to be taken not only for the payment of money, but to insure promptness of repair.

Very early in the history of these affairs our Board refused to do business directly with carnival companies and that leads to a discussion of permits which involve the operation of carnivals.

Carnivals. Merchants and professional people in some secondarily important business sections of Minneapolis banded together into businessmen's organizations. A few of these organizations set aside one day during the summertime in which all businesses along that street were closed and the entire adjacent residential areas were expected to have a day of fun and relaxation in some large park in their general vicinity. They called these affairs businessmen's picnics because picnicking was part of the recreation, the rest of it involving races, games, athletic contests, musical and vaudeville entertainments, the sale of merchandise at refreshment stands, probably some fireworks display in the evening, and carnival rides. Minneapolis' history in this respect may be of interest as an example of how these things can develop.

Many years ago these affairs were less pretentious and the businessmen acted as hosts to relatively small groups of neighbors and actually showed the customers of their communities a good time. They footed the bill. As time went on and the programs became more varied and more expense was involved and more people came, it became impractical to give away things, so the businessmen required some way in which to raise money.

Acting on the theory that these affairs were conducive to social recreation and that they promoted the "general welfare" as manifested by the great crowds that came, the Park Board granted the businessmen permission to erect a certain number of stands for the sale of ice cream, candy bars, and various kinds of refreshment for the people attending these affairs.

Carnival companies began to sense business opportunities and approached the businessmen's organizations with propositions to provide entertainment in the way of attractions of one sort or another, the association taking a percentage of the gross receipts after taxes. The Park Board viewed these matters with a fishy eye and refused permission, particularly on the grounds that some of these carnival attractions were mere gambling devices. In a few cases the businessmen had enough influence with the City Council to induce the Council to close off the streets adjacent to the park permitting the carnivals to operate on the street for a day or two. This was actually done for two or three years, creating quite a mess. It was an almost intolerable situation for residents facing these affairs. However, there were very few residents compared with the total number being made happy and their voices were drowned out entirely.

The Park Board concluded that this sort of an arrangement was certainly undignified for a municipality and decided to look the matter over in a realistic fashion. Meetings were held with businessmen's organizations and also with the American Legion Posts, for the latter held Fourth of July celebrations in much the same fashion, collecting money in this way in order to put on a good Fourth of July celebration, including the shooting off of fireworks at night. Everybody could understand that the previous method of operation was not in the best interest of either the businessmen, the community, or the city as a whole.

Detailed rules and regulations were finally drawn up by this informal committee working closely with the superintendent of parks and members of his staff. The result was that carnivals were actually permitted on park property provided the attractions were limited to rides of a specified number each giving something definite for the payment of money. No gambling devices or anything that approached gambling was permitted. Lewd sideshows were eliminated. Refreshment stands and the sale of novelties was also permitted. The location of all of these devices was to be in locations approved by the superintendent of parks, the hours at which the carnival attractions could be erected and taken down were specified, the length of time that they could remain there was specified, they should not be brought in before such and such a time, they should operate only at certain times regardless of when they came in. A statement of income and expense at the close of each celebration was to be submitted to the Park Department for review to see that no individuals profited by the affair. Any profit, over and above working capital required, was to be distributed to some charitable organization, usually a boys camp or some similar project, and these contributions were noted.

One would think with the adoption of specific rules and regulations for the operation of these celebrations that everything would work smoothly. In spite of the regulations, continual surveillance is necessary to see that compliance is obtained. There is always a desire to do something just a little beyond the provisions. Here is where a police division comes in mighty handy. No manager can afford to be too tolerant or lenient in the application of these rules and regulations because one deviation leads to another and he soon finds himself in trouble with many organizations to say nothing of the members of his own board. In all these affairs the carnival companies are the major ones to want an easing of the regulations to permit additional attractions, because after all, they probably are utilizing only a part of their organizations. The businessmen's associations will plead for additional attractions because "we cannot get such a carnival to come in unless we do, and if we do not get the carnival to come in we cannot finance the undertaking." The pleadings are almost heartbreaking. Sometimes they are influential enough to make modifications.

In reviewing this experience in retrospect, I often wonder what sort of a morass of tangled operations a Park Department would find itself in if it did not establish rules and regulations for the conduct of celebrations of this nature.

CHAPTER 12   EDUCATIONAL REQUIREMENTS*

Some of my associates in the administration of public parks and recreation departments might be startled by having their work called resource development and the tools of their trade dubbed natural resources. So was I when I first noted at Michigan State University that the curriculum of Park Management was a section of the Department of Resource Development in the College of Agriculture. I had never before thought of parks and recreation in the light of being a natural resource. Finding Park Management in the College of Agriculture is as old hat as finding Recreation in the Department of Health, Physical Education and Recreation – as is the case at Michigan State University. I do not particularly like the idea of putting two parts of the same discipline in two separate slots because I think public park and recreation service is one service and should be taught all as one piece. But I also know that this is a whole lot easier said than done because of our unfortunately tangled-up past, the traditions inherited from that past, the limited flexibility of our universities, and the dearth of competent teachers of certain qualifications including the possession of full-fledged, honest to goodness, degrees of Doctor of Philosophy which most universities now expect and often require. All in all, the resource development approach to the investigation of educational requirements in our beloved field may be enlightening, certainly refreshing, and maybe convincing.

Let us get used to the term "resource" in connection with public parks and recreation. The term is really appropriate when you consider Webster's definition as "a new or reserve source of supply or support," or, surprisingly to me, "a means of spending or utilizing one's leisure time." In the sense of being a reserve supply, authorities on the subject are inclined to look upon resources not alone as things, but as functions as well. Physical public recreation assets (parks of all classes) and the potential functioning of them (interpretive and organizational services) become natural resources susceptible to development for the benefit of mankind.

If resource is both physical object and function, any study of it must be concerned with both natural science (the physical and biological) and the social sciences having to do with human society and its elements. If the resource is to be utilized for

* Written in 1962.
See supplement in Appendix, p. 282.

the fullest and best ultimate use of mankind, the humanities
(cultural aspects) come into play. Recreation, largely involved
in the use of one's free time, achieves its zenith when free
time results in cultural use to become, as some would have it,
true leisure.* Surely, humanities must be included in our
basket of studies. For the actual process of resource development some know-how or technical skills are necessary.
Therefore, the basis for an education in the development of
the resource here called parks and recreation (the administration of public parks and recreation), must consist of selected studies in the natural and social sciences, the humanities, and sufficient technical skills to accomplish the development.

What specific sciences of the natural group and what sciences of the social group, which of the humanities and which
of the skills should be selected to form the ideal curriculum
capable of producing the best potential park and recreation administrator? Let it be said at the outset that if the profession
could agree on what kind of training is the best, its order for
such a curriculum could probably not be filled by any university. A university is not like a household appliance store
where you can pick out the appliance that fits your specifications. A university stocks only a few ready-made appliances
in the form of dentists, arrays of medics, engineers and lawyers, but it does have a lot of switches, screws, nuts and bolts
in the form of courses of study. You can select these, and in
conjunction with some homemade parts, you can produce a
workable appliance — the kind of education I and most of my
contemporaries received. We were horticulturists, landscape
architects, engineers, and recreation leaders. With better
guidance in the selection from a more complete line of studies
each of which may be better taught, the future administrator
can be assured of better training; but his course of study will
not be a standardized casting from a carefully designed, hand
molded master pattern. Each curriculum is going to be individually made from standard parts; only by accident will there
be two exactly alike, but they all may have much in common.

The reasons for this individuality stem not only from individual guidance as to the image sought but also from the individuality of university organizations and their practices. Of
the many courses of study that are offered very few are tailored to the special requirements of future administrators, the

---

* Of Time, Work and Leisure, De Grazia, Twentieth Century Fund.

courses are located in various departments; many individual courses cannot be studied without prerequisite courses which may have little significance here; the routine requirements of grade and credits both in number and applicability, the fact that a course may be offered only once in the whole school year, and the sometime requirement of military science, all are irritating complications that bewilder the uninitiated. This situation becomes a far cry from a simple fulfillment of an order for an idealized course of study in park and recreation administration taught as one discipline in one department guided by one counsellor from entrance to matriculation. We may *hope* for the classic notion of the best teaching techniques of the Greeks, i. e. , "the teacher on one end of the log and the student on the other", but all we can *really expect* is the inculcation of the spirit thereof. To concoct a reasonably good curriculum is a real task and to get one approved by the provost who is bound to cast a fishy eye on any new arrangement of studies out of the myriad possibilities that ingenious professors can think up is still another hurdle. Nevertheless, solid progress is being made, the results are better than heretofore and further advancement seems promising.

But back to our ingredients – in what proportion do we mix natural science, social science, the humanities, and the know-how? Heretofore, many of the meetings and training institutes of the professional societies have stressed skills – how to do this and that, what materials and equipment to use, how to grow things, and how to conduct recreation activities. These are the immediately practical things, the tools that help qualify the employee for advancement and permit the recent graduate to get a job and earn a living. These skills are even of usefulness to the administrator for they enable him to really help with the solution of operating problems and qualify him to *lead* his organization in the full meaning of that word. The skills are also ephemeral, being useful only in limited spheres of the administrative art and being rapidly obsolescent in this era of great expansion in the field of technology. Also before know-how can be operative at all in the development of a resource, the resource itself must be evaluated as to its worth to mankind in an environment so intricately institutionalized as is ours. Hence, the application of the basic sciences and the humanities soon emerge as the initial impetus for resource development and constitute the enduring considerations that continue to give meaning to the process itself. After the thinker has determined what to do, the doer comes on the scene and carries out the project under the direction of the thinker. There are more doers than thinkers and offhand, the doing is the apparant all. But the doers require less formal training than the thinkers, they command lower pay, and are more easily replaced. The thinkers are more valuable in administrative posts.

Granted that the study of the sciences and the humanities are the most enduring and the most valuable in preparing oneself for this particular resource development, we must look at them a little closer before we can mix them properly in a curriculum for park and recreation administration. Natural science is a whole bundle of sciences – the physical sciences include physics, geology, astronomy, chemistry; and the biological sciences include botany, zoology, physiology, pathology, genetics, and greater subdivision continues as the frontiers of learning are extended. Sometimes the teaching of any one of these studies may be tailored to fit some particular group, e. g., geology for civil engineers may differ from geology as taught to miners. Then again, is it necessary or desirable to master each one of the subdivisions of the natural sciences to know what the natural sciences are, or can one get a general overview in one series of courses which will satisfy our requirements? If the former procedure is followed a four or even a five year course will be all too short, so the latter must be resorted to at least in some instances. Since the same situation exists concerning the social sciences, (economics, sociology, politics, history, etc.) and the humanities (classical culture, ethics, belles-lettre) and even concerning the array of technical skills that may be offered, perhaps this is the appropriate moment to inquire just how thoroughly educated does the park and recreation administrator need to be?

I think it is reasonable to assume that education is a process that should continue so long as the mental faculties of an individual are able to assimilate learning. Certainly a complete education cannot be administered in a four year hypodermic dose. So our initial task is to make the student aware of the continuing nature of education. Then there must be awakened in him the enthusiasm for that learning beyond his four year course. The resolve to embark on that procedure must be made strong. The ability to study, to search out and assemble facts, to analyze those facts as a basis for coming to conclusions as bases for action, all within a framework of suitable ethics – these must be acquired through practice while in college for a continuum in education thereafter. Such are the essential and enduring values of a university education. Enduring values they may be, but the most practical for the graduate are the skills that make him immediately useful enough to make a living while he gradually brings to bear his greater depth of knowledge and reasoning ability which in the interim is being more securely fortified against his confrontation with destiny – the big break. Actually "the break" comes on so gradually it is not often classed as dramatic.

As to specific courses in the curriculum, (has it taken too long to get to the point?) – (1) *general* courses for overview of natural sciences, social science and the humanities; (2) specific science courses needed to lay the foundation of one or more of the specialized skills needed to get a job and make a living – recreation skills, civil engineering, landscape architecture, horticulture, maintenance of grounds and buildings, business administration including accounting, zoology, political science, law, land economics, land surveying, forestry and possibly others of like nature; (3) enough of some physical science (I like mathematics for this) to make the student wince and stretch his brain in analytical exercise; (4) electives of special interest to the student and pertinancy to park and recreation administration. These studied under the tutelage and guidance of competent and inspiring teachers, and St. George is equipped to enter the lists and with continued experience and education to ultimately slay the Dragon.

To cite specific study courses within the broad areas already outlined would serve no purpose except to propose examples. Universities are individual in their educational philosophies as well as in their course offerings. Students and administrators alike have preferences of emphasis on qualifications. One school may emphasize know-how more than the sciences, one group of sciences more than another, or the study of science in depth more than the general overview of a group of sciences. In the area of skills, some schools may choose to emphasize recreation leadership, another planning and design, another construction, and still another the art of administration. It is well that such is the case – it simply emphasizes that all education is not obtained in a four year college course, and also that there is no standardization in the art of administering a public park and recreation system. Even if there were such a thing as a standard administrator and a standard curriculum, the number of enrollees in it at any university would have to be in the hundreds to justify the setting up of a special curriculum. Each course of study, then, must be individual, but all can be compounded of the same classes of ingredients.

It is encouraging to note at least a rapprochement of the Park Management schools and the Recreation schools toward one discipline encompassing the comprehensive field of park and recreation administration. One of the previous criticisms has been that graduates of Recreation courses located in HPE&R departments have been weak in knowledge of the natural sciences (particularly the physical sciences) although reasonably strong in social sciences. The opposite is true of Park Management graduates who have spent their school lives in Departments of Agriculture. In both cases the humanities group has been only lightly touched, and really "brain stretching" courses have been all too few. Presently, some feeble, but encouraging steps are being taken to overcome these criticisms.

Teachers for the science courses are available. Teachers for some of the applied science skills are also available. Teachers with on-the-job field experiences in top echelon administrative posts are in scarce supply. These are needed to give substantive meaning to the sciences and the skills that are being taught and to give the final fillip of incentive to continuing the educational process beyond graduation. If one such teacher at each university was available to counsel and guide all students from freshmen to graduate students we would come as close to the "teacher at one end of the log and the student at the other" as could be hoped for. Of course, this is impossible and perhaps it exposes the student to too narrow an experience anyway. It is asking one teacher to be all wise. Nevertheless, some reasonable approach to this sort of guidance program should exist.

Practicing park administrators have a distinct responsibility in this whole program of developing future administrators. They should adjust their operations to efficiently utilize graduates who have secured special administrative training. No one expects the fresh-out-of-school graduate to assume a top, or near top administrative job except in a very small organization — say a town of 10,000 population. On the other hand, it is a waste of talent to keep a broadly educated man doing one particular class of work in which his skills are apparant and momentarily of considerable value. If a man is a good park designer, for example, it is not sufficient reason to keep him forever in the planning section without extending him the opportunity of practicing other jobs requiring the use of the knowledge acquired in preparation of more responsible positions. True it is that some responsibility for getting out of the planning calssification is his, but neither should promotions be limited to positions in that one classification. I think that large organizations should have a classification of "trainee" or "internee" which will permit temporary employment in any branch of the service for an overall view of department operation. I also believe that men endowed with a college education in park and recreation administration should be permitted to advance outside of their skill classification. Present administrators should make employment in their organizations fertile ground for the growth of college graduates into mature administrators. Moreover, employers need to be familiar with the quality of graduates that matriculate and with the courses of study they have experienced.

Forgive me if I have taken up too much space to say what I am about to say briefly.

I believe:

1. That a potential park and recreation administrator should have a good solid basic college education.
2. He should also have specialized knowledge and skills in at least one of the specialized divisions of a park and recreation organization as set forth in Chapter 7.
3. He should be imbued with the enthusiasm and zeal necessary to continue his high level education throughout his life.
4. The university has the responsibility of maintaining liaison with potential employers to keep abreast of current professional needs, practices and matters of mutual personnel concern.
5. Employing agencies need to recognize the full potential of recently graduated employees and provide varied opportunity for their full development.

It is for practitioner and student alike to recognize that one mark of an educated man is his ability to think clearly – to assemble all pertinent facts of a given problem, to analyze that data as a basis for reasoning, arriving at a decision, and thereafter to act. Technical skills are the most valuable educational resource early in the professional career, but as responsibilities increase and advances in the organization are made, an ever expanding knowledge of the natural and social sciences and of the humanities are more and more relied upon to wisely develop the natural park and recreation resources for the best use of mankind.

APPENDIX

Being speeches, articles, reports and notes pertinent to, and illustrative of, contents of preceding text.

Table of Contents

Bibliography . . . . p. 230
Olmsted's Principles - Waugh . . . . p. 232
On the Validity of Standards - Doell . . . . p. 233
Future of Minneapolis Parkways . . . . p. 237
Quotations from Charles Eliot . . . . p. 248
Quotations from Lewis Mumford . . . . p. 251
Urban Planning of Highways - Doell . . . . p. 253
Philosophy of Charles Paul Keyser - Keyser. . . . . p. 257
Supplement to Chapter 7 - Doell . . . . p. 262
Supplement to Chapter 8 - Doell . . . . p. 267
Supplement to Chapter 9 - Doell . . . . p. 271
Supplement to Chapter 10 - Doell . . . . p. 275
Supplement to Chapter 11 - Doell . . . . p. 278
Supplement to Chapter 12 - Doell . . . . p. 282
Land Policy Statement of Cook County - Cook
 County Forest Preserve District . . . . p. 284
Hennepin County Park Reserve District,
 Policy Statement . . . . p. 294
Park Board, the Director and Relationships . . . . . p. 305
Rules of the Board - A suggestion . . . . p. 307
Price Elements in Land Acquisition - Doell . . . . . p. 312
Rules for Community Celebrations - Minneapolis
 Board of Park Commissioners. . . . . p. 317
Miscellaneous Subjects - Doell . . . . p. 320

Bibliography

Butler, George D. Introduction to Community Recreation. McGraw-Hill Co., Inc., New York. 1959.

Butler, George D. Recreation Areas. The Ronald Press, New York. 1958.

California Public Outdoor Recreation Plan. Vol. I & Vol. II. State of California, Sacramento, Calif.

Clawson, Marion. The Crisis in Outdoor Recreation. Resources for the Future, Inc. American Forest Magazine. March & April, 1959.

Clawson, Marion and J. L. Knetsch. Economics of Outdoor Recreation. 1966. Baltimore, Johns Hopkins Press.

Craig, James B. Our National Forests – Lands of Many Uses. American Forests. July 1961.

Cross, Gilbert. The Costly Crush to Get Outdoors. Fortune. July 1962.

De Grazia. Of Time, Work and Leisure. Twentieth Century Fund, New York. 1962.

Doell, Chas. E. and G. B. Fitzgerald. Brief History of Parks and Recreation in the United States. Athletic Institute, Chicago.

Doell, Chas. E. and Paul J. Thompson. Public Park Policies. 1930.

Eliot, Charles. Landscape Architect. Houghton, Mifflin Co., Boston. 1902.

Gabrielson and Miles. Sports and Recreation Facilities. Prentice-Hall, Inc., Englewood Cliffs, N. J.

Hudson River Reports. Summary Report to Gov. Rockefeller, Feb. 1, 1966. Evaluation of Proposals and Alternatives – B. O. R., Aug. 1966.

Integration of Natural and Social Sciences in Developing Natural Resources. Dr. Raleigh Barlowe in Pamphlet Form, Michigan State Univ.

Ise, John. Our National Park Policy. Johns Hopkins Press, Baltimore. 1961.

Kamp. Park Land Acquisition and Open Space Preservation – Master Thesis – Texas Tech College.

Kelsey, Frederick W. The First County Park System. J. S. Ogilvie Pub. Co., 57 Rose St., New York City. 1905.

Land Policy – Forest Preserve District, Cook County, Illinois. By Cook County Forest Preserve. Revised Edition 1962.

Maricopa County, Arizona. P&R Dept. – Regional Park System Plan.

Meyer and Brightbill. Recreation Administration. Prentice-Hall, Inc., Englewood Cliffs, N. J. 1956.

Minneapolis Park System. Theodore Wirth. Minneapolis Park Board. 1945.

National Park Service. Supt. Doc., Washington. State Park Statistics – 1960-1961.

National Recreation Association. New York City. Recreation and Park Yearbook 1961.

National Recreation and Park Association. Washington, D. C. Recreation and Park Yearbook 1966.

Olmsted, Jr., Frederick Law and Theodora Kimball; Two Volumes. Forty Years of Landscape Architecture (Professional Papers of Frederick Law Olmsted). New York. 1928.

Outdoor Recreation for America. Outdoor Recreation Resources Review Commission. Also see Sectional Reports. Bureau of Outdoor Recreation, Washington, D. C.

Outdoor Recreation in Oregon. Oregon State Parks Report. June 1962.

Parsons, Mabel. Samuel Parsons and the Central Park of New York. G. P. Putnam's Sons, New York. 1926.

Shankland, Robert. Steve Mather of the National Parks. Alfred Knopf, New York. 1960.

Tilden, Freeman. Interpreting our Heritage. Univ. of North Carolina Press, Chapel Hill. 1957.

Tunnard and Pushkarev – Man-Made America. Yale Univ. Press.

Weir, Liebert H. Parks – A Manual. A. S. Barnes, New York.

Williams, Wayne R. Recreation Places. Reinhold Pub. Corp., New York. 1958.

Olmsted's Principles

Professor Frank A. Waugh of the Massachusetts Agricultural College (in Chapter 18, Vol. II of A History of Garden Art) summarizes the Olmstedian principles as follows:

"1. Preserve the natural scenery and if necessary restore and emphasize it.
 2. Avoid all formal design except in very limited areas without buildings.
 3. Keep open lawns and meadows in large central areas.
 4. Use native trees and shrubs, especially in heavy border plantings.
 5. Provide circulation by means of paths and roads laid in widesweeping curves.
 6. Place the principal road so that it will approximately circumscribe the whole area. "

On the Validity of Standards

By Charles E. Doell

(The occasion for the following discussion was this: The City Council of the City of Minneapolis had recently appointed a citizen's committee to advise the City Council on Capital Expenditure Programs. The Park Task Force of that Committee was beginning to learn about parks and recreation. To do so, meetings were arranged whereby the park officials were given the opportunity of expounding their operating philosophies. Historical material was first presented, followed by a recital of accepted standards by the Chief Park Planner at which point the interrogation began by questions from the Chairman who was a City Councilman representative on the Citizen's Committee.)

At the close of the foregoing presentation on standards, the Chairman called attention to the fact that all of the standards enumerated by the Planner had been established by some professional group. He inquired if any standards had been made by any groups not connected with park or public administration; whether any tax authorities or organizations of finance officers had made any such criteria.

Mr. Doell replied that to the best of his knowledge there were none.

The Chairman then implied that standards by professional groups might be in the nature of ideals attainable only at an expense which might be out of reason for the resources of the community. It might be likened to an individual employing an architect whose ideas for suitable and proper result were most generally far above the client's capacity to pay.

Doell readily agreed that in the final analysis the citizens were the ones to decide on what sort of standards they were willing to settle. The citizens were the ones to determine the character of their service, be that character good, bad, or indifferent. But every effort ought to be made by professionals to disclose what the minimum requirements for park and recreation systems were, and these, he insisted, were what were tabulated by the various groups of professionals. Going over the list of professional organizations it was noted that not all of them were actively engaged in municipal park and recreation administration. All, however, were interested in building and rebuilding cities to the best of present-day practices. In his opinion the analogy with golf course par was more applicable than the analogy of architect and client. But this resulted in no agreement, and so the matter was dropped.

(The written matter which follows the day's discussion which ended in "no agreement" was later submitted to the committee as further argument, as here follows.)

Something more should be said on the subject. The implication should not remain that the standards enumerated by the Planner are idealistic and attainable only by the most wealthy communities. This, then, is added to the oral discussion:

In establishing standards which communities should be expected to attain, the job of establishing them must necessarily devolve upon those who are especially versed in the study and the experience and the administration of the functions in question − namely, the professionals: Professional administrators, professional planners, professional social scientists, and similar ones. They have gleaned facts from experience − experience in operation, experience in character building, experience in municipal taxation, experience in dealing with the vagaries of public opinion. These men are versed in the history of the growth and decline of cities, their progressive expansion, the decay of neighborhoods, and the effect on the inhabitants. They, of all people, have the qualifications for establishing reasonably obtainable standards, not only for parks and recreation, but for other branches of municipal government.

Standards of design have been pronounced for practically all functions of municipal government: Water consumption per capita, capacity of storm and sanitary sewers per unit of service, capacity of streets and highways per unit of width, the safety factor to be used in building design and other building code requirements, public health standards, number of school pupils per teacher, fire fighting equipment and personnel relative to population and combustibility of existing buildings, police personnel per unit of population, etc. A city is judged by how closely it conforms to nationally accepted standards − standards that are established by students of, and specialists in, the functions in question. The judgment is made by local and prospective citizens, merchants, industrialists, investors and tourists.

In the particular case of the establishment of standards for the park and recreation facilities and services, various organizations have had access to a great deal of empirical information, which in itself has established many of those standards. For example: When it is pointed out that such and such a park has a radius of influence of one-quarter to one-half of a mile, experience has already shown in hundreds and hundreds of instances in cities throughout this country and Canada, that people rarely come farther than that distance to use the facilities contained therein. The resulting standard, therefore, is one established by people and not by the planning officials. They are simply voicing it as a fact.

The same thing may be said for certain standards of acreage of individual parks. If a park of five acres is supposed to handle a population of 5,000, experience has shown that it cannot handle 10,000. There just simply isn't room in the park to take care of the daily attendance in the manner which will give satisfaction or will permit a reasonable standard of maintenance within reasonable cost limits. Such an over-used area could well be a social detriment to the community in place of an asset. This, therefore, is the standard which is borne out by experience, established again by people, and simply voiced by the professionals.

Take even the standard of an acre of park for every hundred people in a city. Experience has shown that any material reduction from this standard is bound to leave large areas of the city unserved by park and recreation facilities to the detriment of the social welfare of those particular neighborhoods, and to increase the cost of other municipal services, such as policing, fire protection, welfare costs, and similar ones.

When community social centers are expected to serve a population of approximately 50,000 according to the standards established, it has been demonstrated time and time again, that unless that center is complete enough to serve 50,000 people in a community its erection and operation is unjustified from a purely economic standpoint. That is, the cost per attendant then becomes so high that government is not justified in underwriting the expense. It is more nearly in the category justified only by private support where people are willing to spend extra money for specialized service.

Standards for park and recreation facilities and service are not merely idealized pictures arbitrarily arrived at by professionals who have no regard for the ability to pay. These organizations are composed of men who have been sufficiently buffeted about by calloused politicians and hardshelled businessmen to know that their recommendations must rest upon

solid observation. In fact, because of the buffeting they have
had every one of them is very, very reluctant to actually voice
opinions as to standards, and have not had the courage to bring
them up to present-day expectancies. Nevertheless, experience, observation, and a logical reasoning from cause to
effect, has constrained them to express standards which can
reasonably be expected to be attained, or substantially attained
by any self-respecting city.

*Future of Minneapolis Parkways and Boulevards

The Main Question

Since it appears to members of the Board that some of the parkways and boulevards of Minneapolis may be turning into something more like general traffic thoroughfares than parkways or boulevards, the question arises as to the advisability of the Board's retaining jurisdiction over them.

Subsidiary Questions

In consideration of the main question, the following phases should be thoroughly investigated:

1. What are boulevards and parkways?
2. What is the duty of the Board in this respect, as defined by the charter?
3. What is the history of parkways?
4. What was the original intent of the parkway system of Minneapolis?
5. What are the specific thoroughfares here in question?
6. Have times changed so that the function of present parkways have changed? How does this apply to the parkways here in question?

What Are Boulevards and What Are Parkways?

A brief and simple definition which discloses the differentiation is found in Webster's College Dictionary:

"Boulevard — Originally, the flat top of a rampart; hence, a broad avenue or thoroughfare. "

"Parkway — A broad thoroughfare beautified with trees and turf. "

In present day usage among park men, the distinguishing feature of a parkway is that it is either a roadway through a park or a roadway with enough parklike aspects bordering it to simulate an elongated park. A boulevard is considered to be something much narrower and less parklike than a parkway, even though it has a narrow strip or strips of turf and a planting of trees. It is much closer to the aspect of a city street than a parkway. In Minneapolis, Minnehaha Parkway is unmistakably a parkway, while St. Anthony Boulevard, especially

---

* A report to the Board of Park Commissioners, Minneapolis, Minnesota, dated March 10, 1952 by Chas. E. Doell, Superintendent.

between Marshall Street and Fifth Street Northeast, is a boulevard.

Responsibility of the Board

The City Charter proclaims that it is the duty of the Board "to devise, adopt, and maintain parks and parkways in and adjacent to the City of Minneapolis. "

History of Parkways and Boulevards

Boulevards seem to have had their birth, if not their actual conception, in the seventeenth century in France. A number of the ancient walled and fortified cities, having increased in size beyond their original ramparts, found use for such encircling rights-of-way for the establishment of boulevards. Paris was such a walled city whose early fortifications gave way to boulevards.

Before considering the nature of these thoroughfares, at least two of their predecessors ought to be known. A game known as the "mail" was a form of croquet played in courts with a ball, mallet, and wicket. These courts were tree-lined and were usually along the old city ramparts or the river. In a foreshortened manner, their appearance was much like our present day tree-lined avenue or boulevard.

Then there was a form of promenade known as the "cours" brought into being by Marie de' Medici. To quote from an article in the Magazine of Art of February, 1951, by Christopher Tunard, entitled "The Leaf and the Stone" —

"Before her regency, there was no other way of taking the air save on foot and in gardens, but she introduced the habit of promenading 'en carosse' in the cool hours of the evening. To do this, she planted 'allees' of trees on the edge of the Seine, to the west of the Tuileries Gardens."

The form of the courts for playing "mail" and the green "allee" for the promenade constituted the precursors of the boulevard form.

The actual traffic artery lined with trees appeared in 1670 along Paris' old fortifications and, to quote our previously-mentioned author, was "a boulevard connecting the quarter of the Bastile with that of the Madeleine — 'to serve in all its length as a promenade' — to quote the official bulletin." If this is the beginning of boulevards (note how it fits into the definition in the dictionary), it must be recognized that the basis of the boulevard form was recreation, whether through a game or through a walk – this, in spite of the fact that the boulevard itself was to carry traffic, primarily vehicular in nature. There are numerous boulevards in Paris and most of them are in the nature of tree-lined thoroughfares. In the present day, they often extend through heavily commercialized districts.

The one great Parisian thoroughfare that might be accorded the name "parkway" is the world-famous Champs Elysees. If we consider that this starts from the Louvre at the Place de la Carrosel through the ancient garden of the Tuileries, past the Place de la Concorde and on up to the Arc de Triomphe at the Place de l'Etoile, a distance of approximately two miles, it has then traversed a park and gone for an additional mile as a broad, tree-lined avenue, with all the grandeur that was baroque France. It may have inspired the design of some sections of American parkways of a later day, but it was very likely not a real progenitor of American parkways.

The French boulevard was born in the days of formalized gardening art on the main continent of Europe. England borrowed only sparingly of this sort of garden art, and in the eighteenth and early nineteenth centuries rebelled against such formal arrangement of garden, and adopted the informal or landscape type of garden which then influenced the Continent as well as America. It was during this period that public parks were established, usually by the transference to the public of the private parks of nobility on the mainland of Europe and in England. While important public parks were established in England in the early half of the nineteenth century, the large municipal park was more generally established in America than elsewhere, and especially after the middle of the century. Especially was this true after the establishment of Central Park in New York just prior to the Civil War. The park drives that were established in Central Park might be termed true parkways. General traffic thoroughfares across the park from east to west were depressed and separated entirely from the parkways of the park itself. This was a unique arrangement.

Frederick Law Olmsted, Sr. and Calvert Vaux were the designers of Central Park. They had tremendous influence on the introduction of large parks in America, and themselves designed a great many of them. Other then famous landscape architects, including our own Professor H. W. S. Cleveland, were either close contemporaries of Olmsted or his students and disciples. All had the same basic philosophy as to what constituted a suitable large park and what, generally speaking, constituted a parkway system.

Practically all important park systems of the country established in the last half of the nineteenth century, and some
subsequently, provided for several parks of a hundred acres
or more, established in various sections of the city, and connected by a system of parkways and boulevards. Such a system
was envisioned for New York City, but never carried out –
probably because of the rapid urbanization of suitable areas.
This lack has been supplied in recent years with parkways on
both sides of Manhattan Island and by the famous system of
parkways in Westchester County, by the Merrit Parkway extending up into Connecticut, and by the system of parkways on
Long Island.

Boston was one of the first with a system of real parkways, under the direction of the Metropolitan Park Commission of Boston. It is interesting as a side light to know that
these parkways had their birth in made-work programs established as the result of the depression of 1893-94. Chicago has
such a park and parkway system, part of it designed by Olmsted, part by Jens Jensen, and part by Simons and Pettibone.
The conception of Minneapolis parkways and the park system
was provided by H. W. S. Cleveland, although, as you know,
his plan was not carried out in its completed form.

The purpose of these parkways was to provide a park-like
way of getting from one park to another, and to give a pleasing
access to these parks in various parts of the city. Some of
the parkways in Boston were established for providing an easy
way and a pleasant one for the people of the city to get to the
outlying park. The nature of these parkways may seem odd to
us now, in some instances. For example, in the book entitled
"Charles Eliot, Landscape Architect" (Charles Eliot was a
part of the firm of Olmsted, Olmsted, and Eliot in the eighties
and nineties), it is reported that the landscape consultants
advocated a broad boulevard with two roadways, including a
right-of-way for a trolley car, in order to get the mass of
people pleasantly from the downtown area to Middlesex Fells.
(See appendix, page 248.)

In 1886, Frederick Law Olmsted stopped in Minneapolis
enroute from the Pacific Coast to his home in the East. He
was asked to look over the prospects of a park and parkway
system in Minneapolis. H. W. S. Cleveland had already made
his report of such prospects in 1883, and Olmsted was just
asked to say what he cared to in regard thereto three years
later. Instead of saying much about the prospects of the City
of Minneapolis, Mr. Olmsted chose to outline the duties of the

members of the Board in respect to parkways and in respect
to parks.

After briefly tracing the development of cities and the then
present tendency of concentrating the business affairs of the
city in its center and providing for resident districts with
spacious homes somewhat apart from the business area, he
pointed to a third tendency in these words –

"Third, to make the means of communication between
the new semirural residence quarters of a city to be thus
established and its business quarters of such a character
that passage along them shall be a pleasing and refreshing
element of daily life. "

A little later on he says –

"What are called parkways, if judiciously designed,
are likely to become the stems of systems of streets which
will be the framework of the permanent residence quarters
of our cities in the future. The attractiveness of these
quarters, the degree in which those engaged in the business of the city will find in them relief from the fatigues
of their various occupations and take pride and pleasure
in the improvements that they may privately undertake in
association with them, will be an element in the prosperity of cities of great importance; of far greater importance, for example, than the situation and character of
their public buildings. "

One might go on and on in disclosing the character and
underlying purpose of boulevards and parkways, but so far as
I have been able to determine, there has always been present
in either or both of them an element of recreation as well as
an element of utility. Boulevards have found their roots in
(1) courts for games and in (2) promenades, as well as in
(3) the grand avenue. Parkways have been (1) the way through
parks, (2) the parklike connecting link between parks of sizeable area, (3) the means of carrying masses of people from
concentrations of population to outlying parks, and (4) the
means of the pleasant way between business and domicile.

In more recent years, in connection with county, metropolitan, and even sections of state systems, as well as between
a few important national parks, parkways have again been resorted to as the connecting links, and also as another kind of
pleasant highway on which the traffic is restricted to passenger
vehicles.

History and Original Intent of Minneapolis Parkway System

The final form of the parkway system of Minneapolis followed the same pattern as that of most American cities fifty to
seventy-five years ago, that is, the parkway is the connecting
link between the larger park areas of the city; and a special
parkway, Kenwood Parkway, extends from the central part of
the city to meet the Grand Rounds Parkway System at Lake of
the Isles. Such a system was inspired (but not wholly carried
out) in the first report of H. W. S. Cleveland in 1883, given
very significant impetus by the report of the Special Committee
on Park Enlargement headed by William Watts Folwell in 1891,
and for the most part completed during the superintendency of
Theodore Wirth, 1906 to 1935. The detailed history of the
parkway system is set forth in Theodore Wirth's history known
as "Minneapolis Park System — 1883-1944" beginning about on
page 113. A few quotations and references from the important
documents will suffice here.

From the Cleveland report —

"If desirable also, some of the principal drives may
be laid out as soon as the designs are sufficiently completed to indicate their courses, so as to afford opportunity for pleasure riding." And then further along —

"I have heretofore expressed to you my preference of
an extended system of boulevards or ornamental avenues,
rather than a series of detached open areas or public
squares. The latter are certainly desirable and always
form attractive features, but they are comparatively local
in their character, and fail to impart such dignity and
beauty as is conferred by a grand ornamental avenue comprising a continued succession of pretty gardens enlivened
by the constant passing of throngs of pedestrians and fine
equipages. But apart from the mere question of taste, I
would urge the introduction of broad avenues planted with
trees, as the best possible barriers against the spread of
conflagrations, in any town exposed to such winds as prevail in a prairie country." He then cites the fire experience of Chicago.

Then dwelling heavily upon the importance of obtaining
both banks of the Mississippi River and establishing drives on
either side, Cleveland describes a system of encircling drives
as the backbone of the park system. Then quoting him —

"With such extended pleasure drives so easily accessible and connecting with so many pretty parks of thirty

or forty acres in different portions of the city, it becomes questionable whether the necessity exists for driving parks of such dimensions as have elsewhere been thought necessary. "

It is apropos here to refer to Frederick Law Olmsted's letter dated 1886, previously quoted.

Then in 1891, a Special Committee on Park Enlargement was appointed with William Watts Folwell as Chairman and members Jesse E. Northrup and A. E. Allen. Sections of the report of March 14, 1891 are quoted –

"Attention is invited in the first place to the extension and completion of a great parkway, which shall practically encircle the solid parts of the city, opening to the people walks and drives of great length and forming the main framework of the park system. "

The report then describes such a system of parkways beginning at Loring Park (then Central Park), by way of Kenwood Parkway, Lake of the Isles, thence to Calhoun, thence to Lake Harriet, Minnehaha Parkway, to Minnehaha Park; then retracing steps to Kenwood Parkway, it describes the drive around the west side of Cedar Lake through the then Glenwood Park, and a new parkway to the north and across the north city limits to a new park in the northeastern corner of the city, thence south to join onto Stinson Boulevard, part of which was already included in the city park system, then through the University and along the river roads to Minnehaha Park. The report deplores the failure of predecessors to acquire the boulevard along Thirty-fourth Street from the river to Lake Calhoun, and then quoting from the report –

"The employment of streets of ordinary width as parkways to be maintained at the expense of the city at large is not a policy which your committee can commend. Such streets can be little else than traffic thoroughfares or residence places, and no reason can be given for exempting the residents upon them from such costs and charges as other citizens on other streets and avenues are obliged to bear. It is therefore respectfully recommended that proper legal steps be taken to relieve the Board of maintenance of Lyndale and Hennepin avenues as boulevards or parkways, and to relegate the same to the ordinary authorities of street maintenance. The avenues named can never, except in name, form parts of the park system, especially Hennepin Avenue since its abandonment to the Street Railway Company. "

However, in its recapitulation the report has as item No. 6 –

"The possible opening of one or more wide and noble avenues, within the present territory of the city. "

In his history, Mr. Wirth gives a little more detailed information about Hennepin and Lyndale avenues, part of which we quote –

"Lyndale and Hennepin avenue boulevards were maintained under park jurisdiction until December, 1905, but since the Board had not the authority to control traffic on those so-called boulevards because originally they were highways, they were abandoned as parkways, mainly because of the heavy cost of maintenance. The story of the partial improvement of these boulevards and of the Board's tribulations in trying to provide sufficient funds to maintain them during the approximate eighteen to twenty-one-year period they were under park jurisdiction is a convincing reason against jurisdiction of such parkways by the department without proper provisions to provide a special levy for their care. Parkways that serve the three-fold purpose of accommodating residential, commercial, and park traffic in one are always too heavy a charge against a general levy for park purposes. "

Immediately thereafter, Mr. Wirth goes on –

"In the 1919, 1920 and 1921 annual reports, the idea of providing desirable broad parkways as thoroughfares for Minneapolis was revived, when suggestions and plans were presented for four cross-town avenues or parkways – two for South Minneapolis (the so-called Thirty-fourth Street and Forty-second Street boulevards), and two for the North section of the city (the so-called Lowry Avenue and Broadway Street boulevards.)"

The apparant inconsistency in the Folwell and Wirth reports and writings, in which the abandonment of Hennepin and Lyndale avenues is advocated and applauded while the establishment of other apparently similar avenues as parkways is also advocated, can properly be explained thus – Hennepin and Lyndale avenues were neither links in the Grand Rounds Parkway System nor were they "grand avenues" in the same sense, as was, for example, the Champs Elysees of Paris or the boulevards of either Boston or Chicago. Being neither one nor the other, they have no place in the park system, and could therefore function only as traffic arteries or city streets.

Mr. Wirth also advocated the transfer of jurisdiction from the City Council to the Board of Park Commissioners of Thirty-third Avenue Northeast as the St. Anthony Boulevard between Marshall Street and Columbia Park. This is no more than a city street in width and was probably advocated because it was the only way in which the Grand Rounds Parkway system could be extended at that time. Mr. Wirth also advocated the extension northward of Stinson Boulevard from its terminus of Sixteenth Avenue Northeast northward to St. Anthony Boulevard. This, he reports, was partly because of the request of citizens along the route and the help and donations also from the Northwestern Terminal Company and others.

It is apparent that the parkway system of Minneapolis followed a traditional pattern in its original conception and in its final execution; that is, it provided a way by which the various parks or important parks of the system could be tied together. The scenic beauty as well as a certain element of grandeur motivated the desire for fulfillment. Also the matter of a Grand Rounds Parkway was intriguing. Whether it contained the elements of the old fortification boulevards of European cities, combined with the connecting parkway ideas of American systems, it is hard to determine at this late date, but no doubt it was felt that it was something unique, and containing as it did certain gems such as the river banks, Minnehaha Falls, a parkway along Minnehaha Creek, and the Lake District, it certainly would be of national prominence. Certainly, there was the element of recreation about it all. Some of the parkways contained bicycle paths, others bridle paths, all contained at first carriage-ways and in later years the automobile formed the basis of driving for pleasure.

Parkways Under Present Conditions

Has the development of metropolitan centers so changed in the past seventy-five years that the original concept of a parkway and boulevard system no longer holds?

Certainly, very enormous changes have taken place – in transportation, in communication, in the production of goods, in almost all phases and situations of our social life – but none in the fundamental nature of ourselves. Our wants, our instincts, and our impulses play against the background of an altered world, but in themselves remain unchanged.

Yesterday parks and parkways were established for the recreation of people. Today the same is true. Yesterday the large park was to provide a bit of the country in the heart of the city. Today, with greater mobility, people get to the country farther away and quicker (once they are past the city limits) but the congestion in cities has made the larger park of as great a value as ever. New Yorkers today see Central Park much more often than they do the countryside, Connecticut, outer Long Island, or the woods of New Jersey. Nearby metropolitan environs are no longer rural and we look to the county and metropolitan systems to preserve some of the natural aspect of the countryside.

Yesterday we used small squares and small parks for meeting places, ornamentation, and playgrounds. Today our neighborhood parks are more numerous, our regional parks more actively used, and we are resorting to even small play lots to furnish adequate recreation for all ages; for active recreation has received great stimulus in this mechanized civilization.

Yesterday we had parkways and boulevards for connecting important park holdings, for pleasure drives, for important and pleasant traffic ways from town to home or from center of population to the large park areas and for the dignified and imposing avenue. Parkways and boulevards were that element in the city plan that lent grandeur and culture to it and made its citizens proud to live there. Today, what?

Today I believe the parkway system of our American cities ought to perform the major part of their originally intended purpose. As Louis Mumford writes in his "Culture of Cities" (page 251) —

"This conception of a *continuous* environment of public greens and open spaces as an essential element in urban planning — and not an afterthought or a mere embellishment — was an important contribution to sound contemporary city design: in a more systematic and highly-developed form, it must still govern every rational conspectus of the new city. "

What so bothers us today about our parkways and boulevards is that they were designed for the leisurely horse-and-buggy days. Now, with the great volume of fast moving automobile traffic, the scale of our parkways and boulevards has been made small compared with the original concept of design. When this is coupled with continued pressure for more crosstown streets, stop-and-go signals, and in some cases the deterioration of buildings and properties along the parkways, a bewildered if not a frustrated outlook on the part of some park administrators has been created.   If the problem of shrinking budgets, relatively speaking, is added to the foregoing, discouragement is apt to result.

But all this does not alter the real worth of the original concept.   If we have been guilty of permitting our parkways to be debauched in the fashion aforementioned, or if we have been subjected to conditions beyond our control, our prime objective ought to be (1) to retain a scale in keeping with present day conditions, or, failing in this, (2) to find a suitable substitute before abandoning any parkway asset.   In other words, we should not simply sit idly by and see the complete deterioration of a parkway system come to pass any more than we should sit idly by and see our parks encroached upon by highways and other modern improvements without providing a substitute for the civic assets that are being lost.

Book Quotations and Comments

Quotations and Comments From the Book Entitled
"Charles Eliot, Landscape Architect"
Houghton, Mifflin Co., Boston 1902

On page 441, the following is quoted:

"The following article on the general subject of this chapter was published in the 'Engineering Magazine' for May, 1895, and was there attributed very properly to Frederick Law Olmsted; for it was only a concise restatement – with some new illustrations – of doctrines which Mr. Olmsted had been teaching all his life. It was really prepared, however, by Charles, his disciple and partner, a little more than a year after the letters of this chapter were written, Mr. Olmsted being unable at the time to write it himself. "

This next is entitled "Parks, Parkways, and Pleasure Grounds" –

"The aggregation of men in great cities practically necessitates the common or public ownership, or control of streets, sewers, water pipes, and pleasure grounds. Municipal pleasure grounds comprise all such public open spaces as are acquired and arranged for the purpose of providing favorable opportunities for healthful recreation in the open air. As there are many modes and means of open-air recreation, so there are many kinds of public pleasure grounds. The formal promenade or plaza is perhaps the simplest type. Broad gravel-ways well shaded by trees afford pleasant out-of-door halls where crowds may mingle in an easy social life, the value of which is better understood in Southern Europe and in Spanish America than in the United States. Agreeable and numerous open-air nurseries and playgrounds for small children present a more complex, but perhaps more necessary, type of public ground. Very few public open spaces suitably arranged for this special purpose are to be found in American cities, and yet it goes without saying that every crowded neighborhood ought to be provided with a place removed from the paved streets, in which mothers, babies, and small children may find opportunity to rest, and sleep, and play in the open air. Playgrounds for youths are needed, but these may be further removed from the crowded parts of towns. Public open-air gymnasia have proved valuable in Europe and in Boston. Public flower gardens are sometimes provided; but these are luxuries and ought to be opened at the public expense only after the more essential kinds of public grounds have been secured. Promenades, gardens, concert grounds, outdoor halls, nurseries, playgrounds, gymnasia, and gardens may, of course, be combined one with another, as opportunity offers. To properly fulfill their several functions, none of them need take out more than a small space from the income-producing area of a town.

"There remains another less obvious, but very valuable, source of refreshment for townspeople, which only considerable areas of open space can supply. The well-to-do people of all large towns seek in travel the recreation which comes from change of scene and contemplation of scenery. For those who cannot travel, free admission to the best scenery of their own neighborhood is desirable. It is, indeed, necessary if life is to be more than meat. Cities are now grown so great that hours are consumed in gaining the 'country' and, when the fields are reached, entrance is forbidden. Accordingly it becomes necessary to acquire for the free use and enjoyment of all, such neighboring fields, woods, pondsides, riverbanks, valleys, or hills as may present, or may be made to present, find scenery of one type or another. This providing of scenery calls for the separation of large bodies of land from the financially productive area of a town, country, or district; and conversely, such setting apart of large areas is justifiable only when 'scenery' is secured, or made obtainable thereby."

On page 445, under the subheading of "Park Sites and Boundaries", we find this —

"If the courses of brooks, streams, or rivers can be included in parks, or in strips of public land connecting park with park, or park with town, several advantages will be secured at one stroke. The natural surface-drainage channels will be retained under public control where they belong; they will be surely defended from pollution; their banks will offer agreeable public promenades; while the adjacent boundary roads, one on either hand, will furnish the contiguous building land with an attractive frontage. Where such stream-including strips are broad enough to permit the opening of a distinctively pleasure drive entirely separate from the boundary roads, the ground should be classed as a park. Where the boundary roads are the only roads, the whole strip is properly called a parkway; and this name is retained even when the space between the boundary roads is reduced to lowest terms and becomes nothing more than a shaded green ribbon, devoted perhaps to the separate use of the otherwise dangerous electric cars. In

other words, parkways, like parks, may be absolutely formal
or strikingly picturesque, according to circumstances. Both
will generally be formal when they occupy confined urban spaces
bounded by dominating buildings. Both will generally become
picturesque as soon as, or wherever, opportunity offers. "
        On page 456 –
    "The winter of 1893-94 was a season of great industrial
depression in Massachusetts, and an unusual number of men
were out of work. The legislature had this state of things in
mind when it placed $500,000 at the disposal of the Commis-
sion wherewith to buy land for, and to construct, parkways
which would make the new reservations more accessible to the
public. Doubtless the legislature thought that the Commission
could make the necessary plans in a few weeks, and set some
thousands of the unemployed at work. The Act was approved
April 21st, and on May 1st Charles (Eliot) began the study of a
first parkway, namely, one to connect the Fells with the centre
of the district. In a little over three weeks he prepared the
design which in all its essential features has since been executed. It soon became evident, however, that with all the delays necessitated by the indispensable surveys, taking-plans,
and negotiations with owners, it would be quite impossible to
begin actual construction that summer; and that the Commission needed time to consider the fair way of expending, in the
interest of the whole district, the moderate appropriation
placed at their disposal. It was the 30th of August before
Charles was prepared to suggest a preliminary plan for the
Blue Hills Parkway. This will be found in the second letter of
this group. Like the design for the Fells Parkway, it proposed
a central railway reservation with a roadway, a planting-strip,
and a sidewalk on each side of it. From the beginning, Charles
planned for electric cars on these parkways, that by them the
populace might reach the forest reservations cheaply but in a
pleasurable manner. The third letter of this series gives his
reasons for recommending the immediate acquisition of the
land for these two parkways, and the construction of as much
as possible of the Fells Parkway. It is plain in these three
letters that Charles was seeking the greatest good of the greatest number in expending the $500,000 for parkways. The
fourth and last of these parkway letters was a personal letter
to Mr. Charles Francis Adams, the chairman of the Commission, who had great difficulty in accepting parkways at all as
work to be done under the direction of the Park Commission.
Charles had at first sympathized very much with Mr. Adams;

but on further study and reflection, had come to the conclusion that the laying out of parkways to enable the people to reach agreeably their larger reservations was appropriate work for the Metropolitan Park Commission. "

From the "Culture of Cities"*
By Lewis Mumford — Harcourt Brace & Company
1938

On page 220, under the heading of "The Insensate Industrial Town" –

"By 1870, Olmsted had carried his thinking about parks beyond his original conception of the big landscape park, lying in the midst of the growing city. He saw that even better tracts of land might be destroyed on the outskirts and that by the time the urban mass had reached these outlying areas, they might be just as badly needed. Hence he outlined the conception of the complete *park system*. This system began with the individual square for local promenade and meeting, and the individual playground for active recreation. Such grounds were connected up by strips of roadway, greensward and rows of trees called 'parkways'; elongated versions of the strip common of New England – already embodied in the avenue of the Champs Elysees. Accordingly, by increasing passages of open space, it led into such neighboring wild landscapes – like that of the Palisades in New York or Middlesex Fells in Boston — as might and should be preserved. Olmsted's disciple, Charles Eliot, Jr., saw the further necessity of using the riverside and seacoast areas, no less than the pastoral or mountain landscapes so dear to the old, romantic planner; and had Eliot's timely warning been carried into political action by creating permanent park strips and footpaths along the beaches and promontories of Massachusetts and Maine, that splendid coast would not have been turned into the dissolute landscape slum so much of it has now become.

"This conception of a *continuous* environment of public greens and open spaces as an essential element in urban planning – and not an afterthought or a mere embellishment – was an important contribution to sound contemporary city design: in a more systematic and highly developed form, it must still govern every rational conspectus of the new city. Neither the medieval town nor the baroque town had such continuous areas; indeed, the notion of the country and the city as being continuously interrelated and interpenetrating was foreign to the earlier conception of urban organization.

"Unfortunately, the attempt to thrust park areas into a paleotechnic street-net met with countless obstructions. Though experience proved again and again that even under purely commercial terms these new open areas paid for themselves by raising the land values along adjacent properties, the commercial interests tended nevertheless jealously to oppose the removal from a speculative action of such large tracts of land. Meanwhile, the premature platting of streets and the speculation in building lots which went on in every growing center made it difficult to get hold of the necessary land. The failure to make the park system central to planning resulted in a certain belatedness in every program for parks and playgrounds: by the time the need had become pressing enough to demand action, the price tended to be prohibitive. Smaller towns here had an advantage over the bigger ones, though too frequently they failed to seize it.

"Still the landscape park and the park system were real social mutations in urban form: perhaps the only ones of importance outside the plan of the romantic suburb that the period could point to. In Europe, by happy sort of revenge, the old baroque fortifications which had done so much to cause congestion were torn down and replaced by parks: these formed the lovely rings and starlike green salients around a Bremen, a Lubeck, a Wien (Vienna), a Cracow, a Koln (Cologne). The immediate planting of big landscape parks helped break up the clotted urban massing of the great metropolis and softened the rigors of life for its inhabitants: and the best of these parks, such as Prospect Park in Brooklyn, held among the proudest works of art of this century. Eventually the idea and the example touched even the sordid milieu of the pure industrial towns, creating a guilty conscience, if not a fresh will to order. By 1890, the typical paleotect had begun to lose a little of his price and self-confidence in the insensate environment it helped create. "

Memorandum in Regard to the

Planning of Urban Highways

With Respect to the

Park and Recreation System

*Presented to the Minnesota
Highway Department 11/14/55
when highway planning in
urban areas accompanied by
Federal financing was just
beginning.*

by Chas. E. Doell, Supt. of Parks, Minneapolis, Minnesota

This memorandum is intended to suggest to highway planning officials some general principles and some specific points,
which the Minneapolis Park Department believes ought to be
taken into consideration in the planning of such highways. The
memorandum will take the form of stating some general principles pertaining to the Minneapolis Park and Recreation system; following that statement with both general and specific
suggestions pertaining to specific locations of the park system
which may be interfered with by highways.

We in the Park Department fully appreciate the complexity
of planning for new highway routes in urban areas. We recognize that a great many public and private agencies as well as
the actual standards of highway design must be taken into consideration. Consequently, this memorandum is not to be con-
strued as a dogmatic statement of general principles and specifics, but rather the statement of a position from which discussions with other interested agencies can proceed. We, like
other agencies involved in highway planning ought not to enter
into such a process with preconceived notions so thoroughly
fixed as to rule out compromise, for compromise in many
cases will be inevitable. However, justice and fairness can
always prevail. It is with that expectation and that hope that
this memorandum is presented early in the game so that its
fair consideration may not be an afterthought.

GENERAL PRINCIPLES

A. Although park and recreation areas of the city are relatively fixed in area and outline, it is realized that in the
final analysis they serve the people within the city. When
the social and economic habits and desires of the people
change with changing times it may be expected that the
outline of the park and recreation system may also change.
This is not an invitation to enter upon park property with
impunity. It is stated rather to negate the proposition that

park properties are inviolate. For various reasons some properties are inviolate, but *not all* of them. Alterations of the outlines of some of them may be justified and hence possible. This may be better understood from what follows.

B. The area of the park and recreation ground of Minneapolis cannot stand reduction. The area of the park system is slightly under that of the national standard of one acre to every hundred people. That standard is not going to be reduced in future considerations. Indeed, leading park and planning authorities are at present advocating a substantial increase in this standard. Aside from the obviously necessary scenic parks, neighborhood parks, play fields, and athletic areas, there is an ever increasing need and demand for the tot-lot areas in the residential districts, and much more open space in and adjacent to the central business district. Indeed, these open areas are quite essential to the preservation of all phases of activity within the central city of a metropolitan area. Consequently, there can be no reduction in the total acreage of the park system.

C. In consequence of the foregoing, if it becomes mutually agreed that encroachment of park property by new highways is in the best public interest, then any reduction in the area of the park must be compensated for in such a manner as to permit the establishment of an equal or greater park value of like nature elsewhere. This compensation may be in cash or in kind, so long as it is fair.

D. Appreciation of beauty is one of the fundamental instincts of man, and provides him with the inspiration so essential to the achievement of the nobler things of life. Through the last forty years of wars and economic upheaval, we have tended to forget that cities *can be beautiful*. We are on the threshold of an era that will have the leisure time and the money to spend for the beautiful. Since in the past the nature of parks and parkways have tended to produce an element of dignity, beauty, and even imposing grandeur, it is logical for us to suggest that those qualities be not ignored in the planning and design of new highways. We suggest that wherever possible the rights-of-way should be imposing enough to permit on occasion the interspersing of green areas to relieve the monotony of blacktop and concrete, traffic signs, and the feeling of constricted congestion. Width of right-of-way may help to provide that openness previously mentioned as being essential to the well being of the central city.

E. Neighborhood park and recreation facilities serve fairly well defined communities; so do schools, churches, libraries, and commercial areas. Indeed, the individual homes and the values thereof are frequently based on the proximity to the foregoing community facilities. Therefore, any new highway facility that tends to bisect, rather than skirt well defined neighborhoods, disrupts not only the property directly in the path of the highway, but all other neighborhood service facilities. The consequent disturbances and readjustments of these entire communities are cost factors which cannot be ignored in the installation of the new highway. Indeed, in some cases the actual cost of highway construction may be much less than the cost of redeveloping the community as a whole. In consequence of this a careful understanding of the boundaries of school districts, park usage, and similar neighborhood services ought to be well in mind.

F. In the standard concept of park systems of this country, parkways provided the essential and pleasant way of connecting the various scenic parks and recreation areas. Most of them in this country were laid out before the automobile era. Not a few cities have lost portions of their former grand parkways because of their present use as arterial streets and highways. Other cities have retained their parkway system inviolate, and others are beginning to regain that which was previously lost. In Minneapolis our Grand Rounds Parkway system has a national reputation. We believe that it is not necessary and it is undesirable that its essential character be changed by the introduction of either high speed passenger traffic or mixed traffic. For the most part parkways are not adaptable to high speed traffic without a complete change of character and alignment. Moreover we believe that high speed traffic ought to have pathways of its own, leaving the parkways for those who want a pleasant drive in a more leisurely manner, thereby fulfilling the first and the essential purpose of parkways. Consequently, not only do we believe that the establishment of highways ought to avoid the park system, but that wherever possible highways should be so located as to relieve the necessity of using nearby parkways in place of inadequate highways or arterial streets.

If necessity dictates minor exceptions to this general principle, we believe that parkway-highway intersections ought
to be protected by grade separations or semaphores as
the volume of traffic may dictate, and that the cost, maintenance, and operation of such structures ought to be an
exclusive cost to the State Highway Department.

Bits of Philosophy from Charles Paul Keyser

Retired Superintendent of Portland's Park Dept.

Excerpts from letter to Will O. Doolittle, January 5, 1962, and address to International Northwest Park Association at Portland, Oregon, July 19, 1951, which was transmitted with the Doolittle letter.

First let us put the record straight. I was born on Friday the 13th of December 1878, and grew to manhood along with "Injuns", mustangs and other hardy denizens of the arid sagebrush country in Northwestern Nevada. Then I spent ten strenuous years rawhiding around in the vocation of a civil engineer. Who would have ever thought I would spend 40 years thereafter, to limn a career in this Green Country, engaged in the gentle arts of the field of Public Recreation?

With all due respect to the kind words of my introduction and reference to "brains", I submit that anybody with brains employed in public affairs would be an oddity. I expect if a man have brains, and any common sense, he will employ them in something more remunerative than in the administration of public recreation. That does not say, by any manner of means, that compensations or rewards of merit will not be coming to the man in park and recreation service who has the disposition and cottons to his job. Lots of people would enjoy holding your position, and plenty of them could fill it. I should say that sheer brains is not a prime requisite; but what Solomon referred to as an understanding, together with initiative, vigilance, vision, and imagination, plus a well developed and maintained sense of humor, are all highly essential native qualities in an administrator who will leave his impress on the life of his community.

He must ever regard timing and showmanship without getting himself rated as a mountebank or specious promoter, or a father of extravagant or chimerical schemes. He will not care to account for himself as a reputed genius with the implications, but he must get used to having people expecting him to know all the answers in the many techniques that everybody's interests in the field of leisure will ramify into. He must acquire and beget savvy, which in the City Hall is known as police sense. Over his head he is not expected either by the elected or the electorate to be a super commissioner, or to go out of line on administrative policy. As an executive he cannot do much without the dependable and continual loyalty of his crew. He should use the deft touch of authority without seeming to ride or override anybody. On the inside-out he must "get around".

He must be at once eager and patient – should have the enthusiasm, and the fidelity, and the sporting instincts of a good dog. Economy must ever be his watchword. In Leisure nobody cares a whoop about efficiency. But he must forfend against raids and incursions and misuse of the public's property within his province, sedulously and even vehemently, like nobody's business. He should be a good figurer, but leave it to the cost accountants to *publish* and *declare* especially breakdowns and summaries with differences or remainders, the statistical dregs of sweet stories gone sour. Some think the world is made for fun and frolic, and so do we, and so does our not too exacting public.

Democratic government is necessarily politically selective, which means that it is a self-promoted organization primarily of and by politicians backed by a majority or a busy minority, ruling in the role of servants of the taxpaying public. In reality they manipulate for, or otherwise represent the active influences of the money-makers, the military, and the clergy, and withal contrive to engender a patriotism to provide cohesion and polity of, by and for the people.

Humanity is composed naturally of conflicting elements, fighting for peace and never satisfied. Down through the ages mankind has continued to dwell on earth, tribes to masses, surviving through a coordinating leadership in one form or another, with a control cast over the masses who either will neglect to think for themselves, or like to be beguiled by false prophets. This mass control, never complete, is the essence of government. In a democracy it resolves into more or less tranquil compromise, after so much shoving and dragging.

These individuals or groups, the politicians, who assume leadership ostensibly by consent of the governed, say what you will for them or against them, are the keepers of the national faith, the preservers of law and order, the getters of your public gifts. If they are an evil, they are a necessary evil and, as history shows in repeat, are not replaced for long by a more idealistic agency.

A politician to maintain his situation must go easy on both idealism and zeal to achieve. He is elected on a platform of issues and his main business must be issues. That would be all right if all issues to be met were clearly open or shut. A vocal minority will want its constitutional representative to take its partisan view. Another vocal minority will demand that a contrary stand be taken. Everybody will expect a piece of political pie, or a special improvement whether he plugged for it or not, and a reduction in his taxes. So the politician, who abhors counter-action, does nothing either way unless and until a more or less neutral or tranquil compromise may result. All of which is by way of leading up to the dictum that the preponderance of the body politic, that is, the rank and file of the citizenry, are passively progressive in their attitude toward civic betterment. We have mentioned the active interests. Mostly voters are normally passive. The politician knows that any measure can be successfully campaigned, and that nothing extraordinary will receive a favorable vote unless it is well campaigned.

Perhaps it would be well to spell out a few maxims pertaining to human living that might be called basic.

1.   Man is a creature of the surface of the earth shepherded principally by Dame Nature.

2.   While human life goes in cycles of tension and relaxation, variety will still be the flavor of living. That gives for fun and flowers.

3.   God made man acquisitive and self-seeking for survival, yet everybody has a God-given natural urge to justify his existence above and beyond his baser acquisitive appetites.

4.   We assume that the end or purpose of living is the true enjoyment of it, but we must recognize that the majority of the fickle public drift, and lack definite ideas of the sort of lives they may realize; and yet joy must have its own wellspring.

5.   Because the pleasure of anticipation by and large exceeds the measure of gladness in the satisfaction of fulfillment, the majority of pleasure-seekers will gladly put at least as much into the pursuit of happiness as they expect to get out of it.

6.   The people make the City or Community, and with a sense of proprietorship, like to take pride in belonging to it. They glory in its prosperity and enjoy its attractive or advantageous features.

7.   The destiny of a City is cast in the works of its influential citizens.

8.   There will ever be tides, and storms alternating with calms, and a general level of humanity that remains constant.

These are golden pieces-of-eight to refer our philosophy to, or to go to work with to fetch and carry a public recreation system in anybody's darling city. Call it darling and devote your talents to keep it so. You will be making it your own darling project. You won't do very much for your darling project without supporting appropriations, and appropriations will not be forthcoming unless they are conceived by somebody and demanded by individuals or groups that become aware of the need for them. That means more or less campaigning. Bear in mind that *any* political issue *can* be successfully campaigned. Acquisition and development, while a respectable undertaking, is relatively easy of accomplishment when properly approached. On the contrary, money for maintenance and operation is always and continually hard to get in adequate proportion. The people say use tax money for the more obviously pressing needs first. After you have raised the teachers' salaries, doll up the school grounds with what is left is a typical mandate of the sovereign electorate. With a show of logic they will be content with the thought that anybody can play anywhere. Bear in mind, also, that the same public will condone, even like, high first cost, but will never forgive makeshift or shoddy construction. And so we are apt to get ourselves magnificent edifices and gardens, and find ourselves dreaming, I say dreaming, of ways and means of keeping them from appearing shabby and neglected. Your public expects you to do things and do them well.

The question of interrelation of educational and recreational systems and combined use of facilities covers more of a scope than can be taken in on this spot in the program. I am all for it insofar as practicable, but until I see dude ranch outfits occupying dairy barns while the cows are out to pasture, I will be unwilling to concede that both services which are special and divergent can be shoehorned into or shooflied out of school properties beyond a limited degree. Neither service wants to be altogether emulsified or fractionated.

I also want to recognize in a line the profound influence that the gas tax, giving roads to go places, has had on urban recreation systems. Even so, there is plenty of freight for our barge.

Your park administrator will need the "fine Italian hand" in dishing out the news, and never let it wait long enough to go stale. His stuff is good news mostly, and the reporters and editors want it; at the same time he should contrive a control that will keep controversies such as the papers are keen for, from breaking into print for the wrong kind of stimulation of interest. He must expect to be pretty much or even altogether to blame when things break wrong. Credit belongs to the administration, not to the hired man – always.

Cities have their individual characteristics and their destinies in which climate, topography, strategic situation and other natural or commercial attributes factor. A city is also an agglomeration of wealth, and as a corollary is a nucleus of political influences. No concentration of population and wealth which becomes orderly in due course with its municipal government and municipal works in the modern day will be merely a place to grub and eat and sleep. It has to be a place to rear children; and it will be a place of social communion and culture. It must provide facility for leisure time activities.

My own philosophy, which seems to be here the case in point, is simple. I take the world and my city and all that therein is and has come to pass, as I find it, and although it be a good city as cities go, I do my best to make it go better, as an abiding place for its people. I seem to get along better if I regard my city, and most anybody else's for that matter, like Topsy who just growed and was a creature of circumstances and polyphase human influences rather than of wishful thinking. Patrick Henry said he knew of no way of judging the future but by the past. I submit that dictum will do for us day in and day out far better than by trying to keep the dust off of the long range plans that we all have collaborated with the idealists on, time and again. History in the making has its traditional way. One thing I am sure of: you cannot succeed ultimately on a policy of giving or getting something for nothing. What a man wants he will naturally either take or swap, but he will contemn charity without price, as such. Further: he will have no significant appreciation of any benefit, bauble, or boon that he does not toil or sacrifice or cheat for – in brief, win. Our sphere is not in the agonies and tensions. Rather it is in the foibles and pleasant places, and there we have our special part in making joy abound. But leisure, which in its nature is individual and free, must be also educative and constructive, and what is called soul-satisfying. Sheer time killing is stagnating.

Supplement to Chapter 7
Personnel Organization

One would like to start the discussion of personnel classification by discussing the form of political organization in
which the park and recreation department may find itself. The
textbook has escaped much of the detail of this discussion on
the grounds that a recent university graduate just entering into
a Civil Service position will have no effect upon the type of organization he finds himself in and will have small influence on
the form of that government for some years to come. He
should, however, recognize that there is no ideal which can be
pointed to as being far superior to any other. Some may be
better than others, but only pro tem. For it happens in American political life, especially so far as municipalities are concerned, perhaps less so on the state level, that reform follows
corruption and corruption ultimately follows reform. The full
cycle may be anywhere from a few years to a few decades, but
the cycle still is there. When reform takes place there is
usually a change in the governmental structure. In the interim, persons, their personalities and talents, are of more
importance to good government than the political structure.

This may be as good a place as any to make some observations about the body politic through the eyes of Charles Paul
Keyser as reproduced in the appendix of the text beginning on
p. 257. In doing so, let us be reminded that we are considering the opinions of only two men (Keyser and the author) whose
claim to knowledge of the subject is based wholly on personal
lifetime experiences, each in his own bailiwick and without
reference to scholarly appraisal. They do not claim to be
theorists, they are pragmistists and their word may have limited value.

Keyser says that democratic government is composed of
self-promoted politicians backed up by a "majority or busy
minority", and that they rule in the guise of "servants of the
taxpaying public". Actually, they respond to pressure groups
so long as they can make it look like something good for the
public welfare. He pictures the mass of the people as passive,

---

* The ensuing "Supplements" to Chapter 7 through 12 were first written as lecture notes
for discussion with classes of students beyond their first introduction to the study of park and
recreation administration. In consequence they may be left out of mere introductory courses.
Otherwise there is enough of significance in them to stimulate discussion and more serious
contemplation.

willing to be led (or fooled) by political leaders so long as a certain "tranquil compromise" of their individual and conflicting wants are not disturbed. The political leaders are careful not to disturb this "tranquility" and will sidestep decisions or conflicting demands until tranquility is once more achieved.

Reforms or new issues of any kind may unbalance the "tranquil compromise" but it takes real comapigning to revise that tranquility into a new state of tranquility. That campaigning is an essential part of the political process and politicians are expert at it. Even minority groups and minority issues can produce results, but hard campaigning is required to stir up the lethargy of the majority.

Reforms come about usually by the agitation of important citizen groups. Often within such groups a consensus has been reached that government ought to be more businesslike, and the reforms are made about this central theme. Economy and efficiency is always something the taxpayer is striving for. Without disagreeing with this objective, the author feels it is important to point out that from a practical standpoint, and without reference to any textbooks on the subject of municipal or state government, it is his opinion that there is a great difference, and an essential one, between business and government. The purpose of business is profit. Since competition is present, great efficiency of operation is all-important. Usually efficiency finds its capstone in a concentration of power at the top in one individual or as small a group as possible so that policy decisions can be made promptly and orders carried out immediately. Efficiency in business fosters autocracy in management.

On the other hand, while efficiency in the operation of governmental processes is desirable, essentially, that government must continue to be the reflection of people and their wants and desires, their need for protection of their minority rights as well as the rights of the majority, the adherence to the fundamental principles on which this country is based, the constitutional rights of individual people, (freedom from persecution, domination, the corruptive practices of boss rule), and indifference to the unjustified wants of individual and organized pressure groups. These are the primary objectives that citizens groups ought to look for in a governmental organization. A concentration of power in management may produce greater efficiency of execution but it is a dangerous threat to the public welfare. Abuse of that power may be costly in money and in the loss of constitutional protection. Checks and balances in governmental structure cost money, but they are worth it.

The tendency toward autocratic management in departmental operation of government also needs attention. It is fundamental that every individual has possessive and domineering characteristics, be the individual male or female, rich or poor, educated or uneducated. Each one wants to be superior to, or to dominate either delicately or forcefully, his colleagues and associates in business and in the social world. Even man and wife have that difficulty. This tendency, left to itself and unhampered in the operation of public business, inevitably leads to abuses. What would appear to be a virtue in a private business operation (this tendency toward autocracy), must be offset in public business by a certain degree of checks and balances.

An administrator in the park and recreation field, for example, whose ideas dominate all action, who surrounds himself with so-called "yes" men, who does not have the benefit of objective reasoning or the reasoning of others, who does not have to justify his plans and his actions to a superior authority, commission or other non-professional, is apt to run a very efficient department, but one which can easily ignore the rights of individuals and whole classes of citizens and, indeed, operate with bland unawareness of even the changing conditions brought about by chronological time changes. It must be kept in mind that no one man knows all, especially in this day of rapidly changing techniques, technical developments, modes of living, concentrations of population, the need for interchange of ideas with other disciplines, and a coordination of more disciplines into a more meaningful public service. In the face of these, the position of the lone operator is much more untenable than it ever was before.

Hence, the genius of the administrator is to lead his personnel into the habit of inquiry as to fundamental and changing objectives and to encourage free discussion among them and with him for the purpose of arriving at a balanced conclusion. For this purpose, he will need specialists in every direction and of every kind, demanding an ever higher standard of knowledge and performance. He must provide much of the correlative thinking required to mesh his operations with all other public services that deal with people.

The total function of park and recreation service can be broken down into a reasonable number of major divisional functions. The text has used a dozen or more which may or may not be all-inclusive. It assumes that this is the proper approach to personnel organization for permitting assignment of duties to the logical vocational and professional groupings. It is assumed that a combination of line and functional organization is inevitable and that staff operation is superior to individual management. The main objective or, more precisely, the main difficulty in this type of organization is the matter of communication – communication between divisions, between individuals on a horizontal level as well as communication of orders from the top to the bottom. The staff type organization permits this sort of communication between division heads at least, and also between sub-division heads. Other devices to cover the rest of the personnel cannot be ignored and must be especially provided for. But in sum total, communication, however it is obtained, is quite necessary to the smooth functioning of this type of organization.

Within each division the rank and file employees are grouped within vocational or professional classifications with sub-groupings into grades, each with salary ranges attached. A personal observation here seems apropos. Unlike physical park properties, which were previously discussed, personnel consists of people that have motivation, animation, and mobility. Only a part of this talent is hired and paid for by the park and recreation service. These people have talents of various kinds and have varying degrees of proficiency, all or part of which may be utilized in the eight hours daily work for which they are being paid. The personality and adaptability of the individuals involved are as varied as individuals may be. Although the talents of any one class of individuals may be similar, the impact of the individuality of each is reflected to a more or less extent in the overall proficiency of the job they are paid to do.

These characteristics, peculiar in each individual, are usually ignored in personnel classifications, but every manager of personnel knows they exist and influence the character and the quality of the work produced by each individual. Probably because of this situation as much as any other, the fitting in of individuals into classifications of personnel carries with it the urge to make special cases of the more proficient or the more adaptable. The seed of reclassification is thereby sown. History shows that when exceptions to the classification schedule become numerous, the painful process of a new classification study is made and reforms instituted.

This latter characteristic of individuality and personality adaptability should be taken into account by the administrator when devising his staff of division heads. A formal organization chart is one thing, but if it needs to be modified to get the right man, both from the standpoint of professional proficiency and personality adaptability, then changes should be made. After all, the effective life of an administrator is too short for him to wait for development to produce for him an efficient organization. He should try to bring that about himself.

Supplement to Chapter 8
Budgets

In the realm of government operations the path of budget requests from presentation to final approval is long, torturous, and seemingly continual. This may be one of several reasons why the subject of budgets is both fearsome and mysterious to many young executives.

The text attempts to take some of the mystery out of budget preparation, but probably has not stressed sufficiently certain practical aspects, e.g., is budget "padding" of estimates a desirable procedure; how does one avoid the "awful" possibility of arbitrary reductions of budget requests; what methods of justification of requests are most affective at hearings before boards of nonprofessionals, etc.

Fact is that, in summary, budget preparation, its justification through a maze of governmental procedures and budget control during actual departmental operations, is technical, time consuming, and often aggravating. Moreover, during the whole process, at one time or another, the administrator is called upon to exercise the highest degree of talent he possesses. And all simply to get the wherewithal to do the principle task of providing a suitable park and recreation service. If there is a thrill to obtaining land and buildings, in improving them for public service, and in providing the actual service, then one may consider the drudgery part of the job to be that of budget attention.

Let us follow the budget process in a typical municipal situation.

The fiscal year is assumed to be the same as the calendar year and so begins on the first of January. Adjustments in final budget figures are probably still being made at this stage so that a final printed operating budget may be ussued by, say, February first. During January and all succeeding months, money is expended presumably within the budget figures of the current year. Charges and distribution of costs are the concern of the Budget Director. He has worked out the correlation of budget with accounting procedures, so each month financial experiences are compared with budget allotments. During these months the Director is collecting information preparatory to the making of the request for funds for the next year.

The budget request for the next year usually is due July first of the current year. Hence preliminary budgeting begins soon after the final current year's budget is issued or roughly six months before operations begin. Do we "pad" this budget? The answer depends on departmental policy. The author's opinion is that the budget request should be solidly prepared to cover the costs of those operations which can be defended as suitable for the department. There is no over-estimating, no under-estimating. It is a true estimate. The request does not presume there is no use requesting funds for some things that are almost sure to meet with disfavor. Here is an opportunity to show what is desirable in the operation of a good department. On the other hand, over-estimating is like a falsehood: it is harder to defend than the truth and once discovered destroys confidence in any and all budgets that may be submitted and questions the validity of all statements made in defense of even an honest request.

Lesson number one, is that the budget request is an honest request reflecting the kind of department the administrator can justify as desirable. The items in it are carefully estimated, its compilation made understandable, and the detail readily available. Being sure of the estimates, and with confidence of the worth of the administrative operations implied in the figures, the executive can approach a budget hearing with reasonable assurance.

The first test of the worth of the budget request comes in getting approval of the board or superior departmental authority to submit the request to a formal legislative hearing. The latter hearing usually occurs about September first when all other departmental budget requests have been turned in and some sort of comprehensive compilation made of them. The departmental requests may be heard over a period of a month or more, but probably by October 15, decisions will have been made.

Legislative hearings are often dreaded by young executives; they are quite different in the techniques used than the hearing before the departmental board. In the latter case the main justification has to do with what is good for the department. In the legislative hearing, the park and recreation department is in competition with every other department of the municipality. The point of view to consider is not only what is good for the P. R. department, but what is good for the city, county, or state as a whole. It is not enough to beat the drum for the P. R. department. The request of the P. R. department should be woven into the desireable requirements for the kind of city operation that will enhance its worth for business enterprises and for enjoyable living.   It is at this stage of the procedure that the young executive feels frustrated, principally because he has not prepared himself with a knowledge of what is required for his particular city to best serve the interests of the whole municipal entity.

Lesson number two – broaden your knowledge of what constitutes a good city in your section of the country.   Learn the hopes and ambitions of other departments of the municipal government.   Join with them in coordinating services.   Work for a joint approach at budget hearings.   If the objectives are sound there will be popular support for the individual requests. Don't compete.   Join hands for cooperated effort.

The final legislative decisions very likely will affect little more than the total appropriation for the department.   Sometimes other limitations are imposed, but almost always the department is left with the task of adjusting the budget figures to fit an operation which must now be at variance with the original request.   This procedure is initially done by the administrator and his budget director and then it is once more presented to the P. R. departmental authority for final approval – hopefully before December 31.   A year has now passed. Only during brief intervals has the spotlight of administrative attention veered away from some phase of budget procedure.

For the usual municipal situation the foregoing procedure applies only to budgets for current operations.   Requests for capital funds financed by the sale of some form of municipal bond usually follows another path.   That path may involve a referendum, or it is possible that the chief governing body has authority to issue bonds within certain legal limits.   In the latter case, hearings on long range and immediate capital outlays follow some abbreviated procedure similar to that of current expense budgets.   Referendum procedures need not be discussed here.

Budget procedures in state and national situations have similar considerations as those of a municipality but with appropriate differences.   Budgets for current operations and capital expenditures are usually combined into one, are presented and justified at the same time.   The fiscal year often extends from July 1 to June 30.   The budget may be for two years rather than one.   The estimates must often be made a year and a half in advance, but the budget may be presented only once in two years instead of annually.

Much of the distasteful aspects of budget procedure can be eliminated by having complete confidence in the figures presented and solid reasons for the operational functions which are the bases of the budget figures. To obtain this sort of confidence certain suggestions seem appropriate.

1.   The accounting procedure should be so designed that functional costs are readily available.

2.   Functional costs being accurately tied in to the departmental financial accounts, can then form the basis for sound functional estimates.

3.   The compilation of the budget can then be made in accordance with the processes outlined in the text.

4.   A true tie-in with the regular financial accounts makes possible proper budget control during the year's operations.

5.   A thorough knowledge of the goals of operation and service that the department hopes to achieve influences the decision as to the items to be included in the budget.

6.   A continuing study of municipal affairs in general, the hopes and aspirations of other municipal colleagues, the attitude of business and the general public help to formulate justifications for the budget before formal legislative bodies.

Private businesses prepare annual budgets involving forecasts of expected sales and corresponding costs based upon the volume of expected sales. Government agencies engaged in the sale of merchandise and services as adjuncts to the main recreation purpose of the department are likewise expected to prepare operating budgets for these functions. The first such budget may not be nearly as close to performance as subsequent budgets based upon past experience. Budgeting of revenue producing functions coupled with cost analyses provides the basis of efficient operation of those activities.

The preparation of budgets of capital expenditures is a continuous operation principally for the planning and engineering staffs. The figures are estimates of cost of acquisition of land and of construction of facilities. Usually such plans envision the accomplishment to extend many years into the future. Cost estimates are, therefore, expected to undergo revision from year to year and are considered final only for the year in which the actual request for funds is made.

Supplement to Chapter 9
Policies – In General and On Relationships

Once upon a time, an elementary school teacher admonished her pupils to watch out for habits – choose the good ones and avoid the evil ones because "Habit is a cable. We weave a thread of it each day, until at last, it becomes so strong we cannot break it. "

The dictionary describes habit this way, "An aptitude or inclination for some action, acquired by frequent repetition, and showing itself in increased facility of performance or in decreased power of resistance. "

The text refers to the dictionary definition of policy as "a settled or definite course or method adopted and followed by a government, institution, body, or individual. " Presumably a policy results from pursuing a habit for some period of time.

The next step is a rule which is "a prescribed guide for conduct or action; an authoritative enactment; a regulation; a prescription; a precept. " The habit has here been pursued long enough for it to have acquired some authority.

Finally, there is the law, which is "the binding custom or practice of a community; rules or modes of conduct made obligatory by some sanction which is imposed and enforced for their violation by a controlling authority. " The "cable" is now complete.

Habit, Policy, Rule, Law – in that order do we increase the rigidity of the statement and hence decrease the flexibility of choice in adhering to it. Policies emanate from the best habits applicable to the business at hand. The more inflexible policies result in the adoption of rules of conduct; and the most inflexible rules become law. Choice in the decisions that can be made are greatest as to habit; there still is some latitude in reference to policy. Rules require adherence to avoid some possible unfortunate consequence, and that consequence is most severe when the law is broken.

We are concerned with policy in government, – good policy that is founded on good habit. Some policies may result in the promulgation of some rules of conduct or procedure. A few may find their way into law books. Policy is an arrested search for the ultimate best. It may be momentarily fixed but actually it is only at a way station preparatory to continuing its onward journey or going off in a new direction. It is not a free floating spirit or idea, however, because policy requires

the presence of purpose and a sense of direction – that purpose and guidance is to be provided, in our present case, by
the total PR administrative body. That is the subject to which
the text now draws attention.

Ethics and the public good underlie good policy – ethics
to guide decisions of the individual and the public good is the
mark of good departmental policy. Aside from policy decisions that have to do with operating or professional techniques,
following the path of goodness, indefinite as that term is, constitutes good policy.

Goodness is manifested in the concern of others, moti-
vates most of the relationships mentioned in the text. The administrator's concern for the superior authority in the former's attempt to place himself in the position of the elected
official, – in keeping him informed of events and essential
elements of PR service; in the administrator's attitude toward
his staff; in the department's sharing of public responsibilities
with other departments; the general attitude of helpfulness and
understanding with all agencies having similar or mutual public problems.

To the cynic this point of view and resultant attitude smacks
of a wholly unrealistic naivete. It is unrealistic only to the
cynic and the poorly prepared.

There are two points of view that are generally assumed
when approaching a confrontation, association, or conference
with others.

One assumes that the other is out for no good and he must
be on guard; he must doubt even the plausible because of the
assumption that the motive is bad. This attitude is sometimes
the result of unpreparedness, and hence the development of a
certain amount of fear of the unknown.

The second kind of attitude is based on friendliness. This
individual assumes that we are friends, have a common ground
on which we can agree, and from that point on we can frankly
discuss the issues, each attempting to see the point of view of
the other – even if the other is a shyster.

To hazard this second approach, one must have done his
homework well. He must be well prepared with facts and figures, and must be endowed with ability to clearly and convinc-
ingly state a position and to intelligently use persuasion without rancor. It should be easy to see that it takes much more
immediate preparation for a single encounter and a longer
period of practicing good habits of ethics and education to

assume the second attitude than the first. Shady or even pica-
yunish practices may have short term successes, but solid
progress is not made that way.

Keep the old copybook in mind, "Honesty is the best policy," and let honesty symbolize the virtues of good ethics,
hard work and solid know-how.

The text has not specifically discussed the pervading influence that the Bureau of Outdoor Recreation will have in the
future and hence the necessary prevalence of governmental
relationships in all governmental levels.

BOR is to devise an outdoor recreation plan for the nation;
it is to administer any act of Congress that appropriates money
for that purpose on a matching basis to the states. It is assumed that the states, in turn, will supplement Federal money
with some of their own for matching local funds for the acquisition and development of outdoor recreation resources. The
resultant relationships are destined to be numerous, and probably involved.

To be successful, this program must be approached with
open minds and sympathetic attitudes. It is a pioneer movement designed to stimulate the establishment of outdoor recreation facilities. No one has heretofore had such a responsibility and there is no definite pattern of procedure established. Mistakes are inevitable, but they can be minimized if
real cooperation of individuals and departments having PR responsibilities can be achieved. Cooperation is the key policy
word.

State governments are expected to establish BOR liaison
personnel and to make a state outdoor recreation plan. So far
the exact nature of that plan has not been prescribed. Consultation and cooperation between the State and BOR is here called
for. Probably, after several states have succeeded in the
preparation of acceptable plans, a definite pattern will result.
Patience and understanding are needed in this process.

In the preparation of a state plan, much more than a plan
of state parks will be needed. The recreation potential of other
state owned land – forests, wild life refuges, river reservoirs,
public access to lakes, the use policies of each – will have to
be assessed and made a part of the plan. The extent to which
the larger private enterprises, e.g. timber and paper companies, contribute to public outdoor recreation must also be
taken into account. To these factors add the numerous pro-
fessions and sciences that will be required to determine ecology, the historic points of interest, the future demands, the

economic values to be engendered, and the necessity of intelligent cooperation becomes a commanding one.

The relationships that have been all important on the local
level of PR administration will soon be compounded.   The
problems looming before us are not for the schemer, the shyster, the ill prepared educationally and morally to solve. Such
may operate to thwart progress, but progress must result
from people of a different kind.

Supplement to Chapter 10
Acquisition and Development Policies

Several of the subjects treated in the text have to do with techniques which may result in habitual use long enough to become departmental policies: the necessity of current master plan; suggestions for site selection; the maintenance of land records; possibly the selection of direct negotation or condemnation as the method of acquisition. In all cases, the subjects discussed are followed by appropriate summarizations for the purpose of emphasizing the points being made.

There are a few points in reference to financing capital outlays that may require special emphasis, (1) the sale of use rights to government owned property and (2) donations.

The sale of use rights includes a multitude of situations. Some of the more important are: permit to graze sheep and cattle; to harvest timber; to mine for road material, ore, or drill for oil and natural gas; to build buildings for rental such as hotels and motels; to permit flooding in connection with backwater from dams to be erected for water storage, electric power, navigation, etc.; to park automobiles and build parking garages; to lease land for private structures, ski lodges, ski lifts, and others. While there are special factors to consider in each of the above named situations there is one overriding policy to guide the decision in all cases. It is this. *The PR department, be it city, county, state, or federal, as an agency of the general public, should always have complete control of all of its properties and everything on it.*

If any private interest is in any temporary possession, the government agency ought to be in a position to promptly repossess at a pre-arranged price or under pre-arranged conditions either one or both of which situations having been agreed to at the time of the original entrance onto park property. There should be no opportunity for the private party to negotiate conditions in a situation which finds the public agency in a position of duress because of the need for prompt repossession.

An example or two may help to illustrate this point. A ten year lease is given a private party to build a facility on park property, the facility being for the purpose of rendering a service to park patrons. All terms as to price, etc., have been agreed to. One other provision is needed. The terms and conditions under which the lease may be terminated and full possession of the property returned to the public agency must be negotiated and not left to future settlement. If this is not done, the public agency, when it wishes possession after five years may find itself in the position of "paying through the nose" not only for the value of the facility, but for the value of a leasehold still having five years to run which cost nothing in the beginning. The facility could be a cheap refreshment stand or a multi-million dollar hotel or motel. The policy is the same.

If possession of the public property is for a long time (in excess of 50 years) or is to be permanent, the subject matter is one of sale and not permit. Here the merits of the sale is the issue and not the policy concerning permits and leases. The flooding of public land may be an illustration of the situation.

The matter of scrutinizing a proposed gift to a PR department before deciding whether or not to accept it, often strikes the young executive as being either an affront to the donor or just plain stupid. Especially is this so if the proposed donation is land, "Don't we always need land?" Usually this is so, but as has been emphasized in previous chapters, if the land is not in the right location, or is not of a suitable character or susceptible of being made suitable, the land is not worth accepting. It may be argued that the PR department might accept the land and then sell it or trade for something of tangible worth. Usually laws governing PR departments are so drawn that the department cannot operate a real estate business and the legal steps necessary to sell or trade land are difficult and hazardous enough to keep the occasions of sale to a minimum. If the donor is sincere, he will sell the land and donate the proceeds. *

It is not inappropriate to suggest to a proposed donor of say, an ornamental fountain, that the donation would not be complete without the installation costs being covered, or that donation of trees should be accompanied by the cost of planting.

The point is that the PR department should not accept everything that is offered. It should accept only those things that fit into its scheme of properties and services. And then the precautions outlined in the text are to be applied.

In regard to the preparation of plans for park improvement, engineering work in general, and the actual construction, policy

---

* To facilitate the conversion of offered assets which are not in useable form, a PR department may instigate the formation of a private Foundation whose sole purpose is to accept gifts of all kinds to be converted into useable form for the PR department.

decisions revolve about the question of how adequately and completely these functions are to be done by employees of the PR department and how much is to be done by contract with practioners outside the department. However, the most emphasis in this portion of the text, very appropriately concerns ethics — particularly as to conflict of interest and the matter of gifts from contractors and dealers.

Candidates for elective public office quite glibly put forth the trite expression, "A public office is a public trust." The politician can often say this without considering its significance, but the administrator must try to keep this thought in mind always. If he does not, his animal instincts will lead him to treat public property and his own position as personal appendages. Birds and animals stake out and defend their territories extra legally. The household dog will keep away all comers from his habitual haunts. A PR administrator gets so familiar with public property and so used to having his word have the force of law that unconsciously he thinks he owns the whole business. He needs to remind himself that he is only working here — that he is only the agent of the general public.

This attitude manifests itself when the "chief" expects preferential treatment at public events even if it inconveniences the public; when he habitually ignores rules and ordinances that the general public is expected to observe. Usually he does not *mean* to be officious, but familiarity with his domain has unconsciously made him feel that all this is for him about the same way the house dog treats the new mailman.

Familiarity breeds the "usual" and the "habitual" which becomes the acceptable, the policy. Why *not* favor a friend; why *not* accept a "gift" from him; why *not* have a business of my own on the side and why *not* throw a little business that way; why *not* give members of my family a little preference in hiring. If these motivate the decisions of the administrator the so-called "public trust" becomes more like a private fief. Continued a bit further, involvement in the law takes place and the law for public business is much harsher than in private business. Careers can be easily ruined that way. Too much stress cannot be given to the practice of objective honesty and the "public trust" phase of public business.

A reminder: Habit is a cable. We weave a thread of it each day until it becomes so strong we cannot break it.

Supplement to Chapter 11
Policies of Operation

Operating Manual

The principle policies of operation ought to be in the form of a manual of operations made available in whole or in part to all employees and members of legislative bodies. If any complete ones are in existence they are very few in number. It is no wonder then that a young executive in a new position of top PR administrator in a relatively small town should encounter confusion as to his duties and responsibilities. What is his procedure to be.

As the text points out, a search for the basic law authorizing the PR agency is first made. Minutes of the previous board or other legislative authority may reveal a pattern of decisions on various phases of operation. The rules governing board procedures may help. Conferences with superior officers or "old hands" may help to fill in. Aside from the law itself there may be found little tangible evidence of what the duties and responsibilities really are.

In the meantime, the telephone rings, complaints are received, the mail comes in, appointments are made, the office is looked over for suitable reorganization, a luncheon date, inspection of events and properties seem in order, and by the end of the day, "I'm tired." After a time of this repetitious procedure, the search for "what is my job" is left for a "rainy day" – or more probably, until a crisis appears which entails a precise knowledge of duties and responsibilities. An uncomfortable sort of truce may result without resolving the main issues. A few more such events arise and somebody's "head comes off." There is no way around it – a precise understanding of duties and responsibilities is necessary.

Forewarned, then, is forearmed. The compilation of a policy manual is *not* a "rainy day" chore. It is a *first order of business* matter; and the more thoroughly the young administrator knows it, the better. He certainly would not think of entering or conducting an athletic contest without having the rules established. Yet, not a few young executives are content to rely upon their own personal resources to get them out of a jam where rules have not been established. That is not the way to run a railroad, or a PR department.

The text should provide enough suggestions on the subject matter to include in a policy manual. From time to time as that manual is compiled sections may be submitted for approval by proper authority. Certainly no present day student of PR administration should leave his first administrative job without leaving a suitable policy manual.

Tax Support for P. R.

One of the basic questions propounded by taxpayers' organizations and civic bodies in general has to do with the amount of tax that is reasonable for a PR department in the various levels of government. Statistics purporting to show the experience of others are usually imprecise and anyway comparison with others provides poor justification for expenditures in a particular situation. Presently, comparisons with others is about all we have to go on, so the administrator is advised to become familiar with them. At the same time it must be admitted that the subject has not gained the attention of researchers that its importance deserves.

The text (pp. 207, etc.) suggests a sort of approach to this problem, but statistics are not satisfactory and hence even tentative results are scarcely worth recording. The approach is mentioned here only to stimulate more study and also to urge more precise methods of data gathering and reporting. The author feels that correlations between attendance (a measure of public approval), and public tax support (in addition to fees) will ultimately produce policy standards as to tax support, a sensible approach to fees and charges, and perhaps some evaluation of services being rendered. This research problem has merit and will cost considerable when it is undertaken. Possible results should expose lots better means of justification of expenditures than the emotional type of eloquence that is required today.

Permits and Leases

Requests for use of PR properties and services comprise a large percentage of legislative and administrative matters that have to be dealt with — particularly as to time consumed in deliberation. Rules and regulations can make the disposition of many of these requests a simple ministerial act. The text cites many of the more common situations with some general summaries for policy guidance, e. g. the last paragraph on p. 207 on concessioner — park department relationship. But there are a host of other situations, so many of which call for a special policy decision to cover a particular case.

Let the student once more refer to the nature of "habit" and its evolution into "policy. " Repeated decisions of a similar nature on similar matters will reveal a pattern, maybe a habit, which can be written up as a policy to guide future decisions. Looking for these in minutes of meetings, decisions of top administrators, etc. is a practice which the young executive should follow.

It is for purposes of illustrating some of the variety of problems that may be encountered in one series of transactions involving only one permit that the circus matter is described in the text, p. 213 etc. Traveling circuses are almost nonexistent today, but carnivals are still prevalent. They are tough to regulate so that they will operate in accordance with good business ethics and somewhat in the public interest. In such situations the rules of conduct shown on p. 219 etc. of the text will prove to be a good reference.

Religious Services and Public Speaking

Public parks are public properties and are open to the public. The law does not always recognize the recreation purpose of them as being of an exclusive nature. Many municipal PR departments had ordinances prohibiting public speaking without special permission which was not always granted. The purpose was to prevent a recreation gathered crowd from being annoyed by some itinerant speaker who may have thought he had a momentous message to deliver to a ready made crowd gathered for an altogether different purpose. Such prohibitions seemed reasonable until the law was brought into the matter, and it decided that such prohibition abridged the citizens right of free speech and free assembly on public property. We may not be sure that the decision would have been the same if some outlet on public property would have been provided by the PR department at reasonably located alternative – like the corner of London's Hyde Park.

In spite of this legal restriction of the powers of PR departments most religious organizations and all but the most obstreperous of the public speakers are willing to abide by reasonable restriction. The nature of such rules and regulations can often be arrived at by conferences with responsible religious leaders and organizations. But those who are extremely zealous (usually off-beat sects) and the rabble rouser are hard to deal with. In the one case, no earthly constraint applies to God's chosen messenger, so "get out of the way. " In the other case, "if I don't get permission, I'll do it anyway,

so make a martyr of me. " The text makes suggestions but
guarantees no more success than the U.S. has had in its dealings with Cuba.

Supplement to Chapter 12
Educational Requirements

The content of chapter 12 is not directed specifically to the student; but the student will find there some very important information. Take, for instance, the paragraph on p. 227, second sentence –

"Technical skills are the most valuable educational resource early in the professional career, but as responsibilities increase and advances in the organization are made, an ever expanding knowledge of the natural and social sciences and of the humanities are more and more relied upon to wisely develop the natural park and recreation resources for the best use of mankind. "

Putting this another way, "when the student takes his first job he must rely upon his knowledge of how to do things – grow things, build things, direct a recreation program. Some years later he finds that in order to advance, he must know how to work with people, how to work with the public, how a community, state, or a federal government serves its people, how each function fits into a pattern of government and a way of life, how to improve the culture of mankind. "

The first objective seems so immediately all important and the second so remote and intangible that all thought and effort might be placed on how to do things. Indeed, that is what was almost exclusively taught in the park and recreation management courses of a previous day. If they were not exclusively so oriented, at least the major emphasis was on skills. The student is even now prone to rely entirely on those skills for his job. Unfortunately, prospective employers as a whole are only now beginning to place real value on the potentials mentioned in the second part of the quoted statement. But the student must continue to have his eye on that same second part. And that brings up the thought expressed in the last paragraph on p. 224 –

"Certainly a complete education cannot be administered in a four year hypodermic dose. So our initial task is to make the student aware of the continuing nature of education. Then there must be awakened in him the enthusiasm for that learning beyond his four year course. The resolve to embark on that procedure must be made strong. "

In other words, the young "professional" cannot afford to lose sight of the necessity of knowing something about the world and the universe, about the people that inhabit it, the goals and processes of civilized communities and the part that PR service contributes to human welfare. His future advancement will depend not on skills alone, but upon how much he knows these things that he first thought were so remote and intangible.

To be able to think deeply and properly is one of the truly great assets a university hopes to give the student. It is briefly stated on page 227. ".... one mark of an educated man is his ability to think clearly — to assemble all pertinent facts of a given problem, to analyze that data as a basis for reasoning, arriving at a decision and thereafter to act." This ability may prove to be the most enduring result of the whole educational process. But one can hardly assemble all the pertinent facts or to analyze them without the very broad knowledge previously mentioned. As the problems become more generalized the more will general knowledge be needed. Hence, and once again the need for a continuing education comes to the fore.

Skills, knowledge of many sciences and the humanities, the ability to study and to think properly, are all resources that can be acquired with diligence both in college and a continuance of educational processes after leaving college. Attributes of personality quite often determine the difference between real success and mediocrity when educational achievements are apparently equal. How to acquire the full complement of excellent personality attributes is beyond this author's ken; however a hint or two may prove of value to the young PR administrator.

Confidence is quite necessary to convince others of the value of your proposals. A "bluffing" sort of confidence backfires and is bad. Solid confidence takes place when you know more about the subject matter than anyone else in the world and you possess a clear moral conscience. But this must not lead to arrogance, or intolerance. There must be a reserve of humbleness inside.

Confidence is necessary. Complete knowledge is necessary. A clear conscience is necessary. Forcefulness to the point of arrogance should be reserved for "gutter fighting" only. Quiet confidence born of excellent preparedness and a conscience not cluttered with a "past," plus a reserve supply of tolerance and humbleness equips one with powerful resources for daily contact with people.

Land Policy Statement of Cook County

FORWARD

The work of governmental bodies is given a sense of direction by the making and keeping of policies.

Policies, well made and well kept, are the foundation and guide to the administration of the Forest Preserve District. Through our policies we maintain the sense of direction from a literal interpretation of the basic statute or charter. We insure that our land acquisition program is well planned and properly executed; that our lands are held and not dissipated by allocation to various and sundry other purposes than for which acquired; that our development program is simple and confined to the purposes announced in the charter; that special privilege to individuals and organizations is denied and that all our citizens are treated equally; that popular opportunism is disregarded; that all possible effort is made to improve the quality and diversity of use by Cook County citizens through a broad educational program of notable success; that through policies well made and well kept we insure economy of operation and development; that the forest with its cultural, sociological and spiritual values is paramount.

To the work of acquisition of lands, the development, maintenance and operation in the Forest Preserve District must be added the very difficult and constant effort required in holding the lands of the District for the purpose for which they were purchased. The basic statute under which forest preserve districts are organized provides that boards of forest preserve commissioners have the power "to acquire – and hold lands containing one or more natural forests – or lands connecting such forests – for the purpose of protecting and preserving the flora, fauna and scenic beauties – and to restore, restock, protect and preserve the natural forests – along with their flora and fauna, as nearly as may be, in their natural state and condition, for the purpose of education, pleasure, and recreation of the public."

The Board of Forest Preserve Commissioners is under constant recurring pressure from well meaning individuals and organizations to use the lands for purposes distinct from the original intent. Typical of the requests have been those from organizations for areas for special buildings, from municipalities for the severance of forest preserve lands for their own civic buildings and activities, from school districts for the

separation of Forest Preserve lands for use as school purposes; from the federal government for the allocation of lands
upon which to establish research plants; from individuals and
organizations for the development of organized activities in
the way of specialized sports and spectator games – all of
which are beyond the Forest Preserve law, and are not within
the legal powers of the board of commissioners to provide.

In December 1926 there was appointed an Advisory Committee to the Board of Forest Preserve Commissioners. Since
then this group of citizens has given freely of its time and wide
experience in working with the Board of Forest Preserve Commissioners in selection of lands for acquisition, in appropriate
plans for development, and in the definition of policies which
have contributed immeasurably in maintaining the sense of
direction of the work of the District. Moreover, this committee has joined with the Board of Forest Preserve Commissioners in providing the very genuine and essential courage and
foresight required to purchase lands far ahead of their need,
guided by a plan of acquisition based upon intelligent population forecasts, sociological studies and sound land planning.

This committee is notable for the length and continuity of
service and for its insistence upon maintaining itself in a purely
advisory capacity. Through this cooperation the Board has
purchased only lands which fit into a sound general plan; it has
avoided the pitfalls of opportunism by not giving way to the
many and constant demands for special privileges, and particularly has maintained a policy of holding the land purchased,
preventing the dismembering of a well conceived acquisition
plan.

The Board of Forest Preserve Commissioners is aware
that to give way to well-meant demands for allocation of its
lands to municipalities and other organizations would be to
destroy the true purpose for which the District was founded.
The Board realizes that our forests are a great cultural resource immediately available to all people and that under well
kept policies these forests may be used and enjoyed in perpetuity by the people of the County of Cook.

John J. Duffy, President

The Board of Forest Preserve
Commissioners.

EXCERPTS FROM THE OFFICIAL PROCEEDINGS
of the
BOARD OF FOREST PRESERVE COMMISSIONERS

FROM THE PRESIDENT

April 8, 1946.

To the Members of the Board of
Forest Preserve Commissioners,
County Building, Chicago:

Ladies and Gentlemen:

It is apparent that the Forest Preserve District is going to be presented with various proposals for the use and purchase of Forest Preserve lands for purposes other than their original intent.

Knowing that many of the problems will be most difficult to judge, I have written the following letter to our Advisory Committee in the matter and request it to be printed and filed in the Proceedings.

Very truly yours,
CLAYTON F. SMITH,
President.

April 8, 1946.

Mr. Edward Eagle Brown, Chairman,
Advisory Committee to the Board of
Forest Preserve Commissioners,
38 S. Dearborn St., Chicago, Ill.

Dear Mr. Brown:

With the end of the war we are confronted with a tremendous expansion of suburban areas of the county, with proposed developments of school districts, sanitary districts, highway departments, and various and sundry municipal governments. Many of the problems involved require additional lands. The Forest Preserve District, as the largest public landholder in the county, is looked upon as a possible source of space. At the present time we have four informal proposals involving important acreage of the District.

This letter is a request to our Advisory Committee to review again the policies in the original report to the Board, and to give the Board its beliefs in the matter. As the requests for lands come before the Board of Forest Preserve Commissioners, I shall request my fellow-members of the Board to refer such matters to the Advisory Committee for review. I trust we may have the benefit of your time and advice.

Sincerely,
CLAYTON F. SMITH,
President.

Commissioner Traegar moved to concur in the recommendation of the President, and that all such matters be referred to the Advisory Committee. Which motion was duly seconded and carried.

No. 5236 — From Advisory Committee re acquisition of lands.

June 6, 1946.

Honorable President and Members of the
Board of Forest Preserve Commissioners of Cook County,
Cook County Building, Chicago 2, Illinois.

Ladies and Gentlemen:

In response to your request of April 8, 1946 for a review of the policy regarding disposal of Forest Preserve lands for other purposes, and for the beliefs of your Advisory Committee in the matter, we have the honor to present our analyses and recommendations.

The acquisition of land by the Forest Preserve District has been carried on for thirty years. This acquisition has required a great deal of foresight on the part of successive Boards of Forest Preserve Commissioners accompanied by a very considerably courage. In the development of the plan of acquisition the Commissioners have been assisted and supported by an Advisory Committee of citizens motivated entirely by a desire to be of public service.

The result is that the Forest Preserve District represents one of the most notable examples of land planning for citizen use in the entire United States. Moreover, the system of Forest Preserves annually becomes finer and of greater importance and service to the public.

A possible inevitable result of the extensive program of land acquisition by the Forest Preserve District, to complete and round out its comprehensive plan, is that some public bodies as well as private organizations may seek, or have sought, to obtain the exclusive use of a part of the property for a special purpose, either public or private. With the rapid expansion of population into the outlying portions of Cook County, both within and beyond present municipal limits, there will probably come to the Board of Commissioners an increasing number of such requests.

In the December, 1928 report of your Advisory Committee which was approved and adopted January 23, 1929, this subject was treated, in part, as follows:

"The Commissioners are importuned constantly to grant special privileges to organizations of all kinds by allotting to them a house or cabin, a special tract of forest preserve land for airplane hangers, a site for a livery stable, school building, hospital, dance hall, theatre, cemetery, private museum and many other structures and uses not actually a definite function of the preserves. The granting of such special privileges is in direct violation of the purposes of the preserves, and of the law. Although there are many worthy causes among those for which special arrangements are asked, none should be allowed on forest preserve property. There is plenty of land adjacent to the forest preserves for such uses and buildings so that those seeking benefit may have full use of the preserves without usurping public property for private buildings and uses. "

* * * * * *

"Airports, or landing fields for airplanes are wholly out of keeping with the purpose of the forest preserves. The use of any forest preserve property for such purpose is in direct violation of the law. "

Experience, since the adoption of that report, appears to call for a further statement and adoption of a clear policy with respect to any proposed severance of forest preserve tracts from the system which has been acquired by and for all the people of Cook County for the specific purpose of preserving forested lands, and with respect to the transfer of such tracts to another public body for a more restricted local use.

To the end that such transfers might not be made, the original statute was amended by withdrawing the power to sell lands acquired for Forest Preserve purposes. However, among a very considerable number of applications for such transfers, only a few have been submitted to by the Commissioners by not objecting to a condemnation suit brought by a municipality or other public body which has the statutory right of Eminent Domain. Such instances include:

Bloom Township Sanitary District, approximately 8. 6 acres for a site for a sewage treatment plant, in 1925;

Proviso Township High School District, approximately 18 acres for the expansion of the high school, in 1928 and in 1942;

Miles Center High School, and Park District, all of an isolated tract of land approximately 86 acres in area, for high school and park purposes, in 1924 and 1929;

Riverside Township High School District, approximately 3 acres for the expansion of the school, and in return for which approximately 2-1/2 acres were conveyed to the Forest Preserve District, in 1937;

State and County Highway Departments, which have acquired right-of-way easements, under the comprehensive plans for highway improvements.

The basic policy with respect to all uses of Forest Preserve lands should include reference to the underlying purpose of establishing the Forest Preserve system. This was and is to preserve for all time, and for all the people, the forests of the County and necessary lands connecting them. The statute includes the following pertinent language under which the Forest Preserve Commissioners are authorized:

"to acquire – and hold lands containing – natural forests – or lands connecting such forests for the purpose of protecting and preserving the flora, fauna and scenic beauties, and to restore, restock, protect and preserve the natural forests and said lands, together with their flora and fauna, as nearly as may be in their natural state and condition for the purpose of the education, pleasure and recreation of the public. "

Under this statutory authority, the Commissioners cannot consider themselves only temporary custodians of land and forests, or as an interim landholding agency from which other public or private bodies may draw at will.

Competent legal opinion has been given to the effect that if a parcel of Forest Preserve property were disposed of for other purposes the acreage of that parcel may not be deducted from the total legal acquisition limit of 39, 000 acres and another parcel of like area acquired in substitution. It is not inconceivable that the carefully drawn Forest Preserve District Act, which heretofore has met the test of legality in the courts, might be attacked successfully on the ground that the purposes of the act were being departed from in the event of the disposal of lands purchased under the specific power granted by the General Assembly.

It is also the fact that by far the majority of the property tax for servicing of land acquisition bonds is collected within the City of Chicago. The severance of one parcel in the interest of a relatively small suburban municipality is rarely if ever compatible with the general or total interest of all the people of the County. And it is rarely the case that it is impossible for the local problem to be solved in some alternate manner.

Should the Board of Forest Preserve Commissioners release lands indiscriminately to other public bodies, which did not have the requisite foresight and courage to plan for and acquire properties to serve their own needs, and by so doing furnish an easy solution to their problems, it would only serve to mutilate and scar what is a very fine thing.

Arguments to the effect that the Forest Preserve District holds lands which are not in intensive use, actually fail to recognize the intent and the purpose of the holdings as prescribed by the statute. The forests and meadows give spaciousness to the metropolitan scene where it is badly needed; they serve to dress the appearance of the entire region, to give dignity to and support the pride of the localities in which they lie, and to recreate and educate the entire citizenry, from young to old.

The valuation basis under which certain properties have heretofore been severed from the Forest Preserve and acquired by other public bodies has been, by custom, the amount per acre paid for the original land purchase, plus 10% plus the value of any improvements which have been made. This basis does not appear to be fair to the Forest Preserve fiscal accounts, and it has the definite effect of inviting municipalities and other public bodies to select Forest Preserve lands for their uses, and request their severance as an economy measure for their own purposes.

Should any future severance be insisted upon because of a public problem or should a situation arise which appears to be manifestly impossible to meet in any other manner, the Board of Forest Preserve Commissioners could request an exhaustive analysis and report of the matter by the Advisory Committee. Should such severance be found necessary, the exchange or disposition of the property should be on the basis of the then full, fair market value of the property as appraised by competent appraisers, plus the cost of any improvements.

This analysis of the legal background, of the plan of land acquisition and of the problems now being raised, brings your Advisory Committee to the carefully considered conclusion that no portion of the Forest Preserve holdings should be withdrawn from the possession of the District. However, should a public agency persist in its demands for the property the District should resist the condemnation to its utmost. Should it be found after an exhaustive survey and report, that certain small isolated tracts not now connected or impossible to connect with the main system of Forest Preserves might be relinquished without injury to the system, the above suggested policy with respect to valuation should obtain.

For the purpose of implementing this conclusion, your Advisory Committee recommends the adoption of a resolution based upon the accompanying draft.

Respectfully,

Advisory Committee to the Cook County
Forest Preserve Commissioners

E. E. BROWN, Chairman

To the Honorable, the President, and Members
of the Board of Forest Preserve Commissioners.

Ladies and Gentlemen:

Your Committee on Real Estate, to whom were referred sundry matters, having had the same under advisement, begs leave to report and recommend as follows:

SECTION 1

Your Committee has considered Communication No. 5236 from the Advisory Committee, containing a review of the policy regarding disposal of Forest Preserve lands for other purposes, which is published in its entirety, in the regular proceedings of the Board of Forest Preserve Commissioners, as of June 11, 1946. As a part of this report, the following Draft of Resolution appears. This resolution which follows herein, has been adopted by the Committee on Real Estate:

"Whereas in 1913, the Illinois General Assembly authorized the creation of County Forest Preserve Districts, and granted the Commissioners thereof, the specific power:

"To acquire and hold lands containing natural forests, or lands connecting such forests for the purpose of protecting and preserving the flora, fauna and scenic beauties, and to restore, restock, protect and preserve the natural forests and said lands, together with their flora and fauna, as nearly as may be, in their natural state and condition, for the purpose of the education, pleasure and recreation of the public, " and

Whereas, the Forest Preserve Commissioners of Cook County, have acquired to date, a system of forested lands and lands connecting them, totalling 36,000 acres, in accordance with a comprehensive plan for the acquisition of a total of 39,000 acres; and

Whereas, the rapidly increasing growth of population in the outlying portions of Cook County, has resulted in the occupation of large areas by residential, industrial and business uses closely surrounding the Forest Preserve holdings, which as a consequence are of constantly increasing value and importance serving the purposes for which they were acquired; and

Whereas, this same population growth has caused municipal, school, park and other officials to attempt to obtain Forest Preserve lands for their public purposes inasmuch as their plans have been inadequate, and in the belief that the Forest Preserve properties are available for their purposes;

Now Therefore Be It Resolved, that the Forest Preserve Commissioners in the discharge of their statutory duty, reaffirm and strengthen their long standing policy to the effect that Forest Preserve lands were acquired for one purpose only, that under the law no power is granted the District to divest itself of title to such lands, that the said properties are increasing constantly in value, for the purpose for which they were acquired, and that the continuous acquisition of the additional lands in the Comprehensive Plan will be jeopardized by any severance from the present holdings; and

Be It Further Resolved, that no severance of such lands shall be made for other municipal, school, park and similar public uses for which such public bodies have power to finance and acquire needed lands, and

Be It Further Resolved, that where the rare exception may arise under which a public agency persists in condemnation of Forest Preserve property, the Board of Forest Preserve Commissioners may ask for an exhaustive analysis and report on the matter by the Advisory Committee. In general, the Forest Preserve District shall resist rather than accede to such action, in Court, and shall place in evidence such exhaustive survey and report, together with the current appraised value of the full, fair market value of the land, the forest and of any improvements; and

Be It Further Resolved, that for essential highway needs, for essential sewer, water, or other public utility, underground, surface or overhead improvements required in the interest of all the public, the District may accede to such grants, in court, or otherwise, on the basis of the full, fair market value of the property required. "

Respectfully submitted,

JOHN F. TRAEGER,
Real Estate Committee.

Commissioner Ryan moved that the report of the Committee on Real Estate be adopted. Which motion was duly seconded, and decided in the affirmative by the following vote of Yeas and Nays:

Yeas: Commissioners Bobrytzke, Busse, Conkey, Elrod, Erickson, Fosco, Miller, Nixon, Ryan, Sneed, Traeger, President Smith – 12.

Nays: None.

2nd Revision
1/5/67

HENNEPIN COUNTY PARK RESERVE DISTRICT
POLICY STATEMENT

In 1965 more Hennepin County inhabitants lived outside the corporate limits of Minneapolis than lived inside the City. This is an important statistic especially psychologically. It is symbolic of a turning point in the gradual shift of county political dominance of Minneapolis to a more diffused base, shared by all cities and villages of the County. This trend has been operating inexorably, if only very gradually, for some years but now, and in the immediate future we shall witness a greatly accelerated pace of that interest in county-wide affairs. Changes in government services as well as governmental structure are bound to follow the broadening attitude of the people.

Parks and open space of all kinds greatly influence the physical planning of our county while recreation is a vital ingredient of county welfare. Indeed, as more than one philosopher has observed, the ultimate worth of our culture depends more on how we use our leisure time than upon any other factor, unless it be the factor that produces leisure itself.

With these observations and the present status of the work of this Commission in mind, it seems an appropriate time for the Hennepin County Park Reserve District to affirm its intended role in the welfare of Hennepin County and by the adoption of a series of Policy Statements indicate the goals of park and recreation service it hopes to achieve – all with the help of the citizens of the county and their elected officials in other governmental posts.

FORM OF ORGANIZATION FOR PARKS AND RECREATION

Many years of public discussion and political compromise preceded the 1955 legislation permitting this Commission to be established. More discussion and compromise resulted in authorization for a special bonding program and the inclusion of Minneapolis in the District. Further legislation is needed now; still more will be needed as the service of the Commission develops in consonance with the needs and will of the citizens.

As previously noted, proposals for alteration in the governmental structure of the county and its components will be made from time to time. In the process of political compromise, the interests of this Commission may be either a significant part or it may be only a pawn, extraneous to the central objective. Whatever the situation, let it be noted that the effectiveness of this Commission and the fortunes of park and recreation service depends greatly on the caliber of the Commission's personnel and the form of its political structure. Capable individuals, devoted to the central purposes of the Commission, are attracted to service on a commission that has power to plan, develop and govern its properties and to provide a service to the citizens with a minimum of restraint — e.g. the possible review of its financial affairs by the chief governing body of the county and the laws of the state.

Therefore, let it be the policy of this Commission that it advocate the continuance of, and continuous strengthening of, the form of governing structure which permits autonomous action in the affairs of providing park and recreation service and the governing of the properties necessary to provide that service.

THE GENERAL ROLE IN COUNTY AND METROPOLITAN AFFAIRS

The law is quite specific in its charge to the Commission that its primary duty is not the establishment of local parks but rather the acquisition, development and maintenance of large parks, wild life sanctuaries, forests and other reservations, etc.

In short, its job is to concern itself with what has now become known as "outdoor recreation."

On the other hand, the Commission has been given many other broad powers, even to the extent of accepting (if requested) control of park lands of municipal corporations within the county.

In view of the foregoing and of the generally accepted role of county and metropolitan parks in the nation's scheme of park services, extending from the neighborhood playground to the mammoth national parks, it may be assumed that this Commission is empowered to fulfill its mission of providing a complete, comprehensive recreation service intermediate between the municipal recreation service of the municipalities and the wholly "outdoor recreation" service of the State. Furthermore, the County Park Reserve District being the only

such service of county-wide scope, it must assume the pos-
ture of an "accrediting" agency as to the adequacy of service
provided by individual municipalities, urging each to attain
accepted standards.   In those cases where adequate local
measures still leave voids and pockets of substandard service,
the Commission should assume its responsibility either in filling those voids, or cooperating with others in filling them, all
for the overall good of the county.

Hennepin County being the most populous county in the
eight-county metropolitan area, it, together with Ramsey (the
next most populous) ought to take the lead in fostering the formation of a truly Twin City Metropolitan park and recreation
system.

*Therefore, let it be declared as a policy of this Commis-
sion that it assume responsibility for the adequacy of the
park and recreation service of the entire Hennepin County
by urging and aiding each of the political subdivisions to
fulfill its obligations in regard thereto, and by supplying
all other services needed to completely provide the people
of the county with the kind and amount of service intermediate between that of the large city and the state; also
that this Commission work for the ultimate establishment
of a Twin City area metropolitan park and recreation system.*

LAND POLICIES

A. How Much Land for Parks.

Up to the present the Commission has used a generally
accepted rule-of-thumb goal for County Park acreage of 10
acres per 1000 population.   For Hennepin County this would
require 15,000 acres as of 1985.   County-wide evidence can
be documented to show that this ratio is too low.   But each
county situation is an individual one, each requiring a much
more precise estimate, the intricate methods of measuring
which have only recently been tried.

The Commission has now either wholly acquired or has
under consideration, and available finances for, a total of almost 15,000 acres, all (except less than 100 acres) in large
tracts of 1000 to 4000 acres.   This is sufficient to fulfill the
rule-of-thumb requirements. Yet it is apparent that other and
similar tracts, principally closer to the urban fringe, (and in
the higher valued zones) will be needed to supply the full range

of future service. The acquisition of these additional tracts may be postponed so far as is practical until an investigation of the precise nature aforementioned can be made. Such a survey will also facilitate the planning for development of the tracts. More will be said hereinafter under the heading of Development.

As a policy, this Commission considers present holdings as being less than a well balanced system, especially inadequate in smaller holdings in or near the urban fringe and consequently advocates further investigations and subsequent acquisitions to round out a well balanced system.

B.   Classification of County Parks.

Parks are acquired and developed for the use of people for numerous recreation purposes under a variety of situations. For guides to planning, design, and uniformity of administration and responsibility of jurisdiction, park systems adopt classifications of parks. Municipal Parks include parks for neighborhoods, communities of several neighborhoods, large city parks, and parks of special use, all with zones of use within the corporate limits of the city. State Parks consist of the areas of superlative scenery and unique native characteristics usually called State Scenic Parks; these are where nature decreed without reference to population. They are often farthest away from people. State Recreation Areas (a second class) are of native character too, but of lesser quality because they are located with reference to population centers usually within 50 miles or so of such centers. Historic Sites and Parks constitute a third classification.

County Parks, filling the gap between municipal and state parks, are of the best native recreation resources of the county and are located within 25 or 30 miles of the center of population. The native character of each is to be preserved, but they are also to be enjoyed by people. They must not be wholly developed for active use. County Recreation Areas, separate from the large native reserves, need to be established with ample space for active use (picnicking, water sports, etc.) as well as to provide space for daytime use that smaller villages cannot provide. This division of park responsibility is similar to the division in state parks.

It is obvious that significant historic sites within the county must be located, and where practical, restored or otherwise marked.

If the Commission is to anticipate the ultimate in County Park function it must stand ready to accept responsibility as the public interest demands for such Special Uses as zoos, outdoor theatres, golf courses, ski runs, various museums, sports arenas, arboretums and horticultural conservatories, observatories and planetariums and parkways, all of which are of county-wide or metropolitan interest and require broad financial support, sometimes of private as well as government sources. Some of these form the distinctive features of a progressive metropolis, giving it individuality and prestige and dramatic character.

Therefore, this Commission adopts as a policy a classification of county parks as follows:

1. County Park Reserves – Containing 1000 or more acres of predominately native attractiveness devoted to daytime and overnight use only partially, and to nature appreciation principally.

2. County Recreation Parks – Containing approximately fifty to several hundred acres of naturally attractive land suitable for development of a wide variety of daytime uses and located so the majority of county citizens will live within five miles of a county park or a large municipal park.

3. County Historic Parks and Monuments – Areas of indefinite size marking historic sites of county significance.

4. County Parks of Special Use – Parks of various sizes for special public or quasi-public recreation purposes of a county-wide or metropolitan character established as the result of special surveys and investigation to determine extent of demand, feasibility of capital and operating financing, legality and public support.

C. Restoration of Lands.

The lands acquired for county Park purposes are selected because they have the qualities of potentially good park land, but in most instances are not immediately suitable for park uses. Much of the area may have been previously cleared for agriculture. Water areas may have been drained and farm homesites are present. In general the original native character of the land has been largely lost.

In the process of converting these lands into parks, it is essential that open space areas be restored to their original native condition wherein they may again contain abundant wildlife.

To speed up this restoration it shall be a Commission policy to direct the immediate handling of park reserve lands, upon their acquisition and control, towards the ultimate goal of restoration of the native landscape and elimination of unnecessary buildings, fences, and roads.

D. Development of Parks.

It shall be the policy of the Commission that park lands shall be developed in accordance with master plans of the system as a whole as well as for each individual park after said plans have been approved by the Commission. Opportunity for public review shall be part of the planning process.

As previously observed herein, parks are acquired and developed for the recreational use of people; hence the nature of the people and their wants need to be known before a park can be carefully planned for development. The process involves the determination of the number of people that will use a facility, how far they will travel to the park, what their social and economic status is, what they say they want to do, what they actually do, how much they may be guided to do if facilities were available, how often do they visit the park, how long do they stay, what time of day, day of week, seasons of the year do they come, and various other items of fact. The statistics can be translated into space that is required, the facilities in each space and some logical arrangement of spaces with reference to each other. Finally, a pleasing and efficient plan of development results. Where preservation of the native scene is vital, biological investigations of plant and animal ecology must be a primary factor in the development plan.

The adequate survey needed to accomplish the foregoing employs the service of a team of specialists in park and recreation management, landscape architects, sociologists, economists, foresters, statisticians, naturalists and engineers. It takes time and money, but it is the only sure way of getting satisfactory final results.

To coordinate the development of parks with the recreational needs of people the Commission resolves to have a comprehensive, socio-economic and ecological survey made and adopts as a policy that surveys of this nature be made from time to time in the future to keep pace with changing conditions.

Development plans for individual parks must be based on broad policies established for each classification of County parks.

THE COMMISSION ADOPTS THE FOLLOWING PRINCIPLES

AS POLICIES OF PARK DEVELOPMENT:

1. *County Park Reserves* – *Not more than 20% of County Park Reserves shall be developed for active use: picnicking, water activities, day-time and overnight camping, trails, and uses incidental thereto. The remaining 80% shall be retained in its natural state except where reforestation, drainage (or impounding) or other rehabilitation measures are taken to enhance the original native attractiveness. These native areas may be invaded by hiking and bridle trails, even bicycle trails (all carefully controlled) but not by motorized vehicles except that pleasure drives may be established in large park reserves. The developed or active use portion of the reserve may be in one or more locations.*

2. *The County Recreation Parks may be almost entirely developed for daytime but not overnight use, except that there must always be sufficient native area retained to impart the idea of spaciousness in the native out-of-doors. Whereas The County Park Reserves must always retain and preserve their native areas, County Recreation Parks are acquired, developed and managed exclusively for recreation purposes.*

3. *Historic Parks and Monuments: These are to be located by historians. Restoration and reconstruction of historic buildings are to be undertaken only (a) if authentic historical facts can be established, (b) if the project can be financed through wide public support, (c) the care and maintenance of a resulting museum can be privately financed, (d) if provisions can be made for public interpretation of the significance of the site.*

4. *County Parks of Special Use: Each of these parks is a special case by itself. All factors of public demand, public support, feasibility of initial and operating finances, the county-wide or metropolitan significance of the project, the inherent recreation and cultural aspects of the project are to be investigated before decisions for establishment are to be made.*

E. Future Acquisition of Land

All lands acquired to date have been the result of direct negotiation. Various provisions of occupancy have been made to accommodate as far as possible the wishes of the seller. Negotiations have been undertaken after appraisals have been made by competent real estate appraisors. It has been felt that the alternative process of condemnation is long, tedious, expensive, unaccommodating to individual circumstances and very probably leads to very strained relationships and impairs the public goodwill on which the success of the Commission's mission is based.

The titles have been in fee simple; no restrictive conditions except occupancy with definite time limits exist. While the Commission has had no objections to the acquisition of less than fee simple title (e. g. easements of various kinds) it has encountered no situation warranting that procedure. The Commission looks with favor upon county-wide zoning as a possible aid to orderly development and more efficient use of existing open space. In fact, regional planning is now appropriate.

Recent federal aid (through Housing and Urban Development) has resulted in some modifications of previous procedures but no serious handicpas have been encountered. Lands acquired through partial federal aid are, however, restricted to future use for the purpose originally intended – in this case – for county parks. Lands so acquired cannot be diverted or sold for other purposes without proper review and consent of the federal agency. However, even lands heretofore acquired in fee simple required court review before they could be disposed of, so the situation is little different.

The Commission adopts as land acquisition policy:

Lands shall be acquired by direct negotiation except in extreme cases to clear title or where negotiations have reached an impasse when eminent domain proceedings may be resorted to.

Appraisals by competent appraisers shall form the basis of negotiations; where federal aid is involved the federal procedures shall be followed.

The Commission endorses federal and state aid and that aid shall be enlisted wherever the Commission can qualify for it.

Any land offered as gift, devise or otherwise shall be accepted only if it fits into the overall park reserve system and if it is devoid of all limiting conditions of ownership save those that terminate at a fixed date or an event takes place that is sure to happen (e.g. the death of the occupant or donor).

POLICIES OF GENERAL USE

The use of the properties of the Hennepin County Park Reserve District is for the recreation of the people — but with some limitations and some directions particularly as to emphasis on some aspect of the total recreation picture. Ordinances and rules of conduct are promulgated from time to time and speak for themselves; but the underlying policies on which those ordinances are based are these:

Recreation uses must be of a wholesome character, conventional and not offensive to accepted mores and concepts of moral decency prevalent in the county at any given period of time.

The activities conducted on park property should be conducive to rejuvenation of mind and body in preparation of succeeding periods of productive activity, or of such inspirational nature as to enrich the hours of leisure in such ways as to promote the advancement of our culture which depends so much on the results of leisure time use.

More specifically, but still in general, the recreation service offered by the Commission is what has become currently known as "outdoor recreation" as distinguished from the organized and directed recreation programs usual with municipalities. Non-organized or low organized activities predominate: sightseeing, picnicking, swimming, boating, other water-based activities, nature appreciation, hiking, horseback riding, to name some of the principal examples. Entertainments and exhibitions consistent with the stated overall objectives have a place in the Commission's services, especially if special locations and facilities are provided and if there is countywide support for them. The native setting is an essential accent in all service — more greatly emphasized in the park reserve than in parks of other classifications but none-the-less present in all. Beauty in pattern and design of all elements complement the general purpose of the total service and must be conscientiously woven into all man-made construction.

The Commission relies upon taxation for its financial support. Some of its services are subject to user fees and charges but are not fully self-supporting. Nevertheless, in each park there must be some element of service free of special fee, e.g. trails, roadways for sightseeing.

CONCESSIONS

It has been traditional with municipal park and zoological park operation that a visit to the park should be enhanced by the possible purchase of refreshments, souvenirs, and sometimes rides on various entertainment devices, ponies, etc. Seldom have these services been offered in the purely scenic national and state parks. The Commission recognizes some enhancement to a park visit by the presence of these ancillary services, but deems that most, if not all, can be obtained quite readily outside the park confines and therefore, that no encouragement shall be accorded efforts, either by private entrepreneurs or by the Commission itself to engage in such business enterprises; that all businesses of any nature be conducted by Park personnel; and that in no case will private investment be permitted on park property.

It is the policy of this Commission that no encouragement be accorded to any attempt to conduct business enterprises of any nature on park property; the public shall not be exploited while enjoying such recreation as is provided in county parks. No private entrepreneur shall be permitted to make any investment on park property or to conduct a business thereon.

POLICY ON ENLARGEMENT OF DISTRICT

The Commission for some time has been thinking of the merit of extension of the District's boundary to include adjacent counties, and this question has recently been raised in other quarters. Here are some of the factors involved.

Political boundaries seldom coincide with logical design boundaries, e.g. rivers, streams, topography, ground cover, historical sites.

The people to be served are not inclined to choose places of recreation on the basis of political boundaries except as finances influence the selection.

The logical metropolitan total regional development is influenced by the location of large open spaces and those locations should be selected in cognizance of a metropolitan plan of development and growth. This procedure becomes difficult when the segments of the metropolis great open spaces in various nonuniform ways.

It is the policy of this Commission to cooperate in every way with forces seeking to enlarge the boundaries of the present district.

FOUNDATION FOR COUNTY PARKS

The park and recreation movement in past years has received many valuable gifts of land, endowments and other financial aids from generous civic minded benefactors. To encourage this practice and to aid possible grantors in converting assets which they may be inclined to donate to the public welfare but which may not be in a form usable by the District, the Commission looks with favor on the establishment of a nonprofit, tax exempt foundation for the furtherance of the County Park Service.

The Commission adopts as a policy the practice of promoting private donations to the work of the Commission and, to facilitate the practice, the establishment of a nonprofit, tax-exempt foundation to act as a recipient agency for the Commission.

The Parks Board, The Director, and Their Relationship*

One of the most critical acts of the Parks Board is the selection of its chief executive officer, the Director. It is through him that the Board ultimately expects to achieve its objectives.

The prospective Director should be equipped with a university education, consisting of a well-grounded knowledge of the basic sciences and humanities, with special training in at least one of the several facets of park administration – park management, horticulture, landscape architecture, recreation, engineering, public or business administration, or even law. He should have sufficient successful experience in the administration of park departments to demonstrate his executive and administrative ability and to manifest those personality traits which are conducive to the leadership qualities expected of him.

Such a properly equipped man should be given full responsibility and adequate authority to fully operate all phases of state park operation without interference from individual Board members. To accomplish this requires careful defining of the functions of the Board as well as those of the Director. Usually the division between the two is made by the Board retaining all the legislative and policy-making functions and assigning to the Director all executive and administrative functions. But a clearer understanding is necessary.

The special qualifications of the Parks Board members, as differentiated from the special qualifications of the Park Director, should be recognized. The former have been selected because of their special interest in providing for the people of the State a recreation service especially directed to the outdoors; their special knowledge of the mores and habits of the people; their sense of what constitutes high ethics and public morality in public service; their honorable standing in the community; their special experience in judging values of what is of the greatest common good; their financial responsibility to the public; and their reputations as civic leaders in general. What they are not expected to have is any appreciable degree of knowledge of park administration. That is to be supplied by the competent Director hired for that purpose.

---

* A suggestion to a State Parks Board.

Now, if the Director recognizes the special qualifications of the Board; and the Board recognizes the special qualifications of the Director; and mutual respect has been attained; a great step toward successful operation has been made.

Conception for the destiny for the Park Department rests with the Director; responsibility for success is his. He conceives and initiates for submission to the Board plans for acquisition, development, operation, and policy. The Board sits in judgment; they, like the general public, are to be convinced of the worth and the wisdom of the plans presented to them. The Board's ultimate judgment becomes final, and its actions over a period of time become the policy and the sense of the Parks Board itself. Such a combination of professionally inspired plans; together with their modification and ultimate adoption by a representative group of the best citizens of the State; followed thereafter by competent administration of those plans; is a combination that can't be beat.

To be a bit more specific seems now appropriate. Aside from some ministerial acts required by law, the Board will need to make decisions on the following matters, by the adoption of which the Director is automatically clothed with proper authority to carry out his functions: approval of the Director's personnel organization; the adoption of a classification of employees, complete with duties, qualifications, and salary ranges; adoption of the annual budget; adoptions of plans for acquisition of land and development of properties; approval of all contracts, leases, and licenses, except those in the purely operational field which can be delegated to the director; the adoption of a set of general policies; the approval of a manual of operations; and perhaps others. In each of these cases, specific recommendations have been submitted to the Board by the Director; and in each case, the Director's recommendations have been justified and clarified through questioning by the Board. Once they are adopted, the authority to execute is in the hands of the Director. All of his authority and instructions come from the Board as a whole and never from individual members.

With mutual respect and a clear understanding of division of authority based upon the above principles, the Parks Board and the Director, working in unison and cooperatively, will provide the best possible park administration for the State.

Rules of the Board – A Suggestion

MEETINGS

<u>Section 1.</u> Regular meetings of the Board shall be held at its office at 9:00 A.M. on the first Thursday of every month. If any such meeting falls on a holiday, the meeting shall take place within three days, the day to be fixed by the chairman, the hour and place being the same as for regular meetings.

<u>Sec. 2.</u> Special meetings may be called by the chairman whenever he deems it expedient, and shall be called whenever any two members of the Board shall so request in writing to the Secretary of the Board.

<u>Sec. 3.</u> The Board may adjourn from time to time and absentees notified thereof and, in case there is no quorum present on the day fixed for any regular, adjourned, or special meeting, the members present, or the Secretary, if no commissioners are present, may adjourn the meeting from time to time until a quorum is present or may adjourn said meeting sine die.

<u>Sec. 4.</u> A majority of the commissioners shall constitute a quorum for the transaction of business although a smaller number may adjourn from time to time.

<u>Sec. 5.</u> All meetings shall be open to the public.

<u>Sec. 6.</u> Each Board member shall be notified at least two days previous to any special meeting. Said notice shall be issued by the Secretary, and shall be in writing setting forth the time, place, and purpose of the meeting and shall be served personally or deposited in the post office at least two days previous to the time of the meeting. Other means of notification may be used (e.g., telephone, telegram, special delivery mail) but these may not substitute for the above provisions.

CONDUCT OF BUSINESS

<u>Sec. 7.</u> The order of business of the Board shall be as follows:
1. Roll Call
2. Approval of minutes of previous meeting
3. Petitions and Communications
4. Reports of Officers
5. Reports of Committees
6. Unfinished Business
7. New Business
8. Adjournment

Sec. 8. No business shall be transacted at any special meeting other than that named in the Call thereof except by consent
of four members. Any measure adopted by four members as
provided above shall have the same effect as if adopted at a
regular Board meeting. A call for a special meeting naming
the purpose thereof to be "for the transaction of general business" shall be deemed to cover any and all business that might
be transacted at a regular meeting.
Sec. 9. Meetings shall be called to order by the Chairman,
or in his absence by the Vice-Chairman. In the absence of
both, the Secretary shall call the meeting to order and those
present shall elect a chairman pro tem.
Sec. 10. The Board and its committees shall be governed by
the rules contained in Roberts' Rules of Order, revised, in all
cases to which the rules are applicable and in which they are
not inconsistent with the laws governing the Board or the rules
adopted by the Board.
Sec. 11. Every ordinance shall receive separate readings
previous to its passage which shall not be had at the same session unless in case of urgency when four members of the Board
may dispense with this rule.

ELECTION OF OFFICERS

Sec. 12. At the first meeting in each calendar year the Board
shall elect from its membership a Chairman and a Vice-Chairman who shall serve in said capacity for the calendar year.

As provided by law, the Board shall elect by secret ballot
a Park Superintendent as the chief administrative officer for a
period of not exceeding two years. The Superintendent, with
the consent of the Board, shall name the Secretary from among
the employees or may himself act as Secretary.

DUTIES OF OFFICERS

Sec. 13. The Chairman shall perform the duties devolving
upon him by law, shall preside at all meetings, shall preserve
order and decorum, enforce the rules and regulations of the
Board and as prescribed by law, he may invoke penalties for
nonattendance of Board members as the Board may decide
from time to time. He shall otherwise perform the duties
usually devolving upon a presiding officer. The Chairman
shall be an ex officio member of all standing committees.

The Chairman shall execute all bonds, deeds, contracts
or other instruments required to be executed on behalf of the
Board, the same to be attested by the Secretary.

Sec. 14. The Vice-Chairman shall act in the absence of the Chairman at any meeting when the Chairman is absent or disabled; and all the duties of the Chairman as a member of any committee or of any body of which the Chairman may be an ex officio member shall temporarily devolve on the Vice-Chairman.

Sec. 15. The Superintendent shall have supervision of the operations of the department as its chief executive officer and shall administer all the functions of the department subject only to the actions of the Board through its official proceedings. He shall give his entire time to Board affairs.

The Superintendent shall designate someone of his employees to be Secretary to the Board unless the Board requires that he act in that capacity.

He shall have charge of all personnel and shall organize them into appropriate divisions and have the general organization thereof approved by the Board.

He shall annually, submit to the Board a budget of income and expense upon the adoption of which he is given authority to make expenditures in accordance therewith so long as important deviations therefrom are reported to and confirmed by the Board and so long as the expenditures in any event do not exceed income.

He shall submit to the Board a monthly written report of administrative matters including a statement of current income and expense paralleling the items in the budget.

He shall submit annually an inventory of property of the Board for which he is responsible.

He shall perform all duties devolving upon him according to law and in accordance with routine county procedures.

Sec. 16. The Secretary shall perform duties required by law, keep the minutes of the Board under the supervision of the Superintendent, have charge of all records of the Board, keep the accounts, and have charge of office personnel and procedures, and shall, with the Chairman, sign all bonds, deeds, contracts, and other official documents.

Sec. 17. The standing committees of the Board shall all be appointed by the Chairman and shall each consist of three Board members and shall be as follows:

Budget, Finance & Claims
Policy, Personnel & Permits
Acquisitions
Development Planning

Sec. 18. The Standing Committee on Budget, Finance and Claims shall have general legislative supervision of the finances of the Board including supervision of budgets, budget control systems, financial policies and general accounting procedures.

This Committee shall review the list of claims for services and materials ordered by the Superintendent, recommending to the Board payment of same and in doing so shall advise the Superintendent of any procedures requiring future correction thereof and to that extent supervising policy pertaining to claims.

Sec. 19. Committee on Policy, Personnel and Permits shall formulate and recommend to the Board for Adoption formal policies in all branches of the Board's affairs and shall cause to be compiled a set of policies which, when adopted, will constitute a guide to future decisions of the Board. Policies in purely administrative matters will be prepared and administered by the Superintendent but they shall be consistent with the broad policies of the Board here referred to.

Matters of personnel, such as organization, salaries and wages, conditions of employment, are to be considered by this committee for recommendation to the Board. Actual supervision of personnel is an administrative matter under the direction of the Superintendent.

Recommendations for the process of issuing permits for the use of park property and rules and regulations to be adhered to concerning same shall be made by this committee to the Board for action.

Sec. 20. The Committee on Acquisition shall consider all matters pertaining to the acquisition of properties and shall make appropriate recommendations concerning same to the Board.

Sec. 21. The Committee on Development Planning shall review all plans for improvement of the Board's properties, and make appropriate recommendations concerning same to the Board.

Sec. 22. In general, the Committee organization is a convenient way for the Board to give more thought and time to Board matters by delegating some review and investigative functions to a portion of its members rather than reviewing all matters by the complete membership. The committees, therefore, are not operating bodies, but review and investigative bodies; committee actions are not instructions to the Superintendent but recommendations to the Board and/or suggestions to the

Superintendent. When their duties include "supervision" the word is used in a manner consistent with the foregoing. Any policy matters emanating from any of the committees other than the Policy Committee should be reviewed by the latter committee and result in a recommendation to the Board.

SPECIAL COMMITTEES

<u>Sec. 23.</u> The Chairman may appoint Special Committees for purposes not otherwise provided for in the duties of Standing Committees, and Special Committees of any size may at any time be appointed by the Board in such manner for such purposes as may be deemed necessary by the Board.

<u>Sec. 24.</u> An agenda shall be prepared by the Secretary some time before the day of the Board meeting and sent to Board members. Matters not on the agenda may be acted upon if four members consent thereto.

<u>Sec. 25.</u> No public hearing shall be held before the Board without affirmative vote of consent of all Board members present.

All public hearings shall be held before appropriate committees of the Board under the following conditions:

a) When directed by the Board
b) When requested by any member of the Committee to which the subject matter has been referred
c) When required by federal, state, or local law and in conformity therewith

<u>Sec. 26.</u> No officer, commissioner, or committee shall in any way bind the Board to do or not to do any certain thing, unless expressly authorized to do so; and no such action shall in any way be recognized by the Board, unless expressly ratified or approved.

<u>Sec. 27.</u> These rules and regulations, in part or in whole, may be suspended by four members present at any regular Board meeting, and may be amended or repealed at any regular meeting, subsequent to the meeting when the same is proposed, by a vote of a majority of the entire Board.

Price Elements of Land Acquisition[*]
(For Park and Recreation Purposes)
by Chas. E. Doell

What constitutes a fair price for land about to be acquired for park purposes?

This and other provocative questions are raised in the following discussion of the principle elements involved in the public acquisition of lands having recreational potential.

Once the decision has been made to acquire a piece of land for park or other recreation uses and adequate funds are available, it seems disarmingly simple to proceed with the purchase — an ordinary case of buying real estate. All that is required is to agree on the price. At that point complications set in.

The determination of price, sooner or later, enlists the aid of real estate appraisals. In direct negotiation it is the basis for the actual beginning of the negotiation; in condemnation proceedings it is the evidence of value given by an expert. Considering its importance it is proper to examine appraisals for their real meaning — their strengths, their weaknesses, and why they do not actually settle the matter of price.

Definitions can be brief or lengthy depending on what authority is quoted but in effect all mean that a real estate appraisal is the appraiser's estimate of a price that would be agreed to by a willing seller and a willing buyer, each thoroughly familiar with all pertinent attributes of the land in question and allowing a reasonable time for buyer and seller to locate each other.

Methods usually considered in making the appraisal include (1) a capitalization of the income from rental or use of the property, and (2) comparison with recent actual sales of similar property in the general vicinity of the property being appraised. Other methods may be used in some cases but the foregoing are the most usual. In all cases the highest and best use of the property in question is considered regardless of its present use.

Terms of values often encountered include replacement value, speculative value, sentimental value, separation value.

Owners of the property under consideration often feel they should be paid enough to permit them to relocate in as good a situation as they presently enjoy regardless of the appraisal.

* From "Parks and Recreation," January, 1968.

Such a claim is made only if the appraisal is below expectation. Juries in condemnation proceedings are often inclined
to consider this a legitimate claim; and cities often use similar arguments when parks are invaded by highways.

In theory, speculation value is not to be given any cre-
dence in either appraisals or as evidence of value in condemnation proceedings but frequently, if not as a general practice,
some value of this sort creeps into most appraisals.

Sentimental value is often rewarded in condemnation cases
by sympathetic commissioners and appeal juries.

Acquisitions which divide an owner's property into two or
more units or which reduce the acreage in such a way as to
limit or eliminate the remainder from being used as an operating unit are always considered in the valuation.

In some states (e.g. Minnesota) the highest and best use
of the property includes the use for which the land is being
acquired by the public agency. As far as the author has been
able to learn, no real estate appraisal takes this value into
consideration, but a knowledgeable lawyer will always bring
this out in condemnation cases. If land is being taken for a
park, its value for that purpose can well be far above its otherwise highest and best use (farm, residential development, industrial or commercial site) and this value has not been appraised. Land valued as a park (or other recreational resource)
is worth what a park authority thinks it is and is willing to pay.
Unfortunately, no valid economic value has so far been placed
upon that factor. Economists have used various means of
appraising the value of parks in various kinds of situations but
this one element of value has continued to elude them. This
value may be termed social value to distinguish it from economic value. Without including social values in the valuations
no true appraisal is possible. All this leads to unfortunate
misunderstanding.

Note that the appraisal assumes a <u>willing</u> buyer and a
<u>willing</u> seller. In park acquisition cases the seller is more
often unwilling than willing. If his unwillinghess is not frivi-
lous, but is justified because of his peculiar circumstances,
his claim to a higher price to compensate for his hardship may
be justified, even as compared to a seller of similar property
who, because of <u>his</u> peculiar circumstances, is happy to sell.
Although the validity of the appraisal is upset by the presence
of an unwilling seller, too often it is assumed that it <u>does</u>
apply because the unwillingness is unjustified. It may <u>not</u> be.

In direct negotiations between a park district and private owners, one or more appraisals may be obtained as a basis for the beginning of negotiations. Offers and counter offers may result in a price agreement considerably above the appraisal but still below what the park district considers the property to be worth for park purposes. Purchases made at prices above the appriasal may attribute questionable motives to the district commissioners because of the general belief that the appraised value is a true indication of what the maximum price should be. This administrative dilemma requires some finesse if one is to escape without adverse publicity.

In addition to the foregoing, another problem occurs when federal aid through BOR, HUD, or other agency is involved. It is very probable that the federal agency will not participate in the financing of any part of a negotiated price higher than the highest of several appraisals. In other words, the federal agencies either do not recognize that social values are a part of actual value when the purpose of the acquisition is for recreation, or it refuses to help to pay for that value. On the other hand, HUD which has had long experience with urban redevelopment, recognizes costs of displacement of property owners, over and above the appraised values.

The only alternative that local park authorities have to modify or escape the above limitations is to use their power of eminent domain. This alternative obviates public criticism but eliminates much of the flexibility of dealing with individual situations. Retaining public good will during the condemnation proceedings is far more difficult than it is in direct negotiations where adjustments can be made for time of occupation, life tenure, extending time of payment over years for tax advantage to sellers and numerous other possible settlements. Moreover, condemnation does not result in escaping the effect of the social value factor because in one guise or another, evidence of this value will be introduced and will usually be given consideration.

Condemnation has some very useful purposes besides being a positive, inexorable way of obtaining title. It is useful in clearing an otherwise cloudy title to the land, in the bringing together of heirs and claimants who could not voluntarily agree on price, on obtaining clear title from a recalcitrant, stubborn landowner, and it is a very useful tool to bring owners to a reasonable price conclusion in direct negotiation cases. Condemnation proceedings are slow and expensive to both parties. Threat of proceedings facilitates price negotiations.

Inasmuch as condemnation often results in strained relationships and is resented by owners whose property is being
taken, the power of eminent domain may be denied the acquiring agency because of the political power of the landowners.

Land acquisition for park and recreation purposes is not
free from the effect of the law of supply and demand. Once
land is designated to be acquired for park and recreation purposes, a new and additional value (other than its otherwise
highest and best use) has been placed upon every parcel within
the future park's boundaries. A new class of buyer, a new
use, has come to the market place. Every landowner instinc-
tively knows that the new buyer is prepared to pay more for
the land than its present or otherwise potential use warrants.
Call this new element demand, or social value behind the demand, or call this situation a hopeful sign of the presence of a
"sucker" buyer, or an intelligent realization of a higher and
better use, the hard fact remains that the demand price has
risen. The gap between what a fair appraisal is, and what the
park district considers the land to be worth as a park, has
widened.

Experience has shown that the acquiring agency can settle
for a lower negotiated price for the first parcel of a large
number, than for the last parcel. Why not? The first is one
of many; the last is one of only one. Scarcity has increased
the relative value of the last. A smart property owner, holding out to the last, is likely to get close to what the park district believes the land to be worth as a park – and this can be
far above its appraised value as those appraisals are made
today. Perhaps a nice question to raise is this: The Constitution says that no one shall be deprived of his property without due process of law and just compensation. If just compensation is the value of the highest and best use of his property,
should not all owners be entitled to the value of their land
valued as park land? How does the present day appraisal fit
such cases?

In Summary. Land acquisition for park and recreation
purposes is not a simple process. One should not "send a boy
to mill;" only the highly knowledgeable, honest, and reasonable
man should be intrusted with negotiations.

Real estate appraisals have real value but are not the most
reliable of land value measurements in park land acquisition.

The indeterminate factor is the social value of land used
for park and recreation purposes. It may be conceded that
social value for all recreation land resources is not uniform.

It may vary with situations and circumstances.   In no such
situation or circumstance has it been measured in dollars and
cents.   Some say it cannot and should not be so measured.   If
it <u>could</u> be, and <u>were</u> measured it would help solve the case of
the California Redwoods, the Grand Canyon controversy, highways versus parks, as well as the problems posed in this article.

Rules Governing the Holding of Community Celebrations and Fourth of July Celebrations on Park Property*

1. All features of the celebrations are to be confined to park property. No adjacent streets are to be closed off or celebration features conducted thereon. Where necessary to protect pedestrians and to eliminate traffic hazards, temporary snow fencing is to be erected bordering the park.
2. There shall be provided by the celebration committee a reasonable amount of free entertainment such as band concerts, vaudeville entertainment on the bandstand, games, races, and athletic contests. In the conduct of games, races, and athletic contests, the Recreation Department of this Board will continue to cooperate as they have in the past. Playground instructors and officials will be provided to actually conduct them. Please contact the Recreation Division at FE. 2-1116, Ext. 276 or 288, if this service is needed.

   To raise money, celebration committees may be permitted to make charges for the following and for no other: Sale of refreshments, sale of novelties exclusive of those which may be found to be objectionable, pony rides, photograph booths, dances, and *nine rides* approved by the Superintendent, such as merry-go-round, ferris wheel, miniature electric autos in a confined space, and variations of these. They are to be properly safeguarded with snow fence.

   The Board shall be saved free and harmless from any public liability or property damage caused either to itself or third parties which result from the operation thereof. To accomplish this, a bond of indemnity in good and sufficient amount to be determined and approved at the time that the application for permit is considered, shall be furnished for the relief of the Board from public liability or property damage to third parties, and in order to indemnify the Board for damage resulting to its property by reason of moving in and out of such large equipment, the extent of the damage depending upon the weather conditions, a bond or cash deposit in the sum of $100.00 shall be required to be posted with the Secretary of the Board

* Minneapolis Park Board

before the day of the celebration to take care of any damages to property that may result.

Charges for the dancing on the tennis courts shall be made for an entire evening's dancing. The practice of charging for individual dances is to be discontinued. No preparation shall be used on the tennis courts to make them smooth for dancing except "Spangles", made by the 20-Mule Team Borax Company, or an approved equal.

Celebration committees shall have the right to sublet any or all of the foregoing to concessionaires, but the responsibility for the proper conduct thereof, charges to be made, etc., are to be retained by the celebration committees. Charging for any of the above features are to be confined entirely to the day of the celebration, except that any rides that are set up ready for operation the day before the celebration or on such days that the Board of Park Commissioners may specifically designate. All features of the celebration are to be entirely removed from park property the day following the celebration.

3. The celebration committees shall submit with the application for a permit a financial statement of the celebration held the previous year, such a statement to indicate the gross income and expense in reasonable detail, and a statement of the use made of the net proceeds for the previous year's celebration.

4. Free fireworks displays shall be permitted and the shooting of the fireworks shall be commenced not later than 9:30 p.m. (Central Standard Time) and shall be continuous thereafter, and shall be entirely completed not later than 10:00 p.m. (Central Standard Time). Celebration committees shall see that public liability insurance is carried to protect the public against loss by damage resulting from the fireworks display, and the Board shall be indemnified against any loss from the same cause. Only experts and duly qualified persons shall be permitted to fire the fireworks.

5. Any celebration contemplated at Columbia Park shall be held entirely within the park area on Picnic Grounds No. 1 and No. 2

6. No beer is to be permitted on park property, either for sale or for consumption by individuals.

7. No auctions are to be held on park property. The Superintendent is directed to stop any picnic that attempts to hold an auction on park property.

8. No work or activity in connection with such picnics or celebrations shall be carried on in any parks between the hours of midnight and 7:00 a. m. and no equipment should be parked on the streets adjacent to the park and in front of private residences before 7:00 a. m. in the morning.

9. All temporary electrical installations and the operation of the same for furnishing lighting and power to tents, stands, concessions and amusement rides shall have the approval of the Electrical Inspector of the Building Inspector's Department.

10. Beverages will be dispensed in paper cups only.

Thoughts on Several Subjects

left with a Seminar Class at Mich. State Univ., March 1962.
By Chas. E. Doell.

The discussion at each of the seminar sessions was with few exceptions permitted to take its own course without much guidance. Sometimes we went a little afield of our subject matter. Sometimes we followed unimportant avenues. A few times we missed some of the most fundamental points. But by and large a good job was done in the original investigations, in the appraisals of the individual making the investigation, and on reports of each of the sessions. Certainly we have had the benefit of expressing ourselves and of being criticized. We hope that the analytical abilities have been strengthened, even though no conclusions have been reached.

For most of you, these analytical studies have been conducted without the benefit of much, if any, actual experience in the Administrative field. It has occurred to me that the observations of one who has had long years of experience in Park Administration might help to illuminate the various subjects we discussed. I don't ask you to accept these observations without question or do I expect you to always agree with the analysis. I submit them in the hope that they may be helpful and so I give them to you by way of saying good-by to a stimulating group of young men.

Sleeping Bear Proposal for Michigan by National Park Service — (Dealing with the Public). The way you men criticized the National Park Service for their ineptness in dealing with the local public who had personal interests in this project, was bordering on the unmerciful. The public relations job of the National Park Service did seem poor, and the remarks of some of the top officials as reported by the newspaper, displayed poor taste. I got the impression that each of you thought you could do a lot better job if you were in the top position. However, when your stated methods reduced to such generalized terms as "use more tact" and "win the people to your side," the actual remedies became nebulous. You seemed to express very little sympathy for the representatives of the National Park Service appearing before a hostile audience. Your thought was that if the situation had been in *your* hands, the public would not have become hostile. The public would have been preconditioned.

It is reasonable for me to predict that each one of you sooner or later will find yourself in that unenviable position —

in spite of all you may do to prevent such a situation from developing. It so happens that almost all national parks have become controversial issues when their pending establishment has been up for consideration. I am not sure that there is anything inherent in the nature of national parks to make such a situation inevitable. What I can say with some degree of confidence is that the establishment of parks, the improvement of them, the relocation of them, all have potential controversies as elements. Wise and adroit, indeed, is the Park Administrator who can avoid all such controversies or being confronted with them, can treat hostile audiences with enough finesse and tact to dispel their animosities.

The Detroit Area. The purpose of discussing the park situation in the Detroit Area was to indicate the complexity of the Park and Recreation Service in a large metropolitan area. In this case, we must deal with the governments of the city of Detroit, of numerous satellite suburban towns, of Wayne County, of the Huron-Clinton Metropolitan Park District involving five counties, and the State of Michigan because of its significant holdings in this general area. The problem is to provide a public park and recreation service uniformly to all geographical areas in the Metropolitan District and in all the functional characteristics of that service from the Neighborhood Park to the State Recreation Area. This complex problem is one that is confronted by all large metropolitan areas, sometimes with the additional complexity of involvement in more than one state.

The problem of supplying park service as well as several other governmental functions in the whole metropolitan complex is a distinct challenge to the ability and understanding of all the professionals involved. There is also present a formidable challenge to the various political subdivisions for each to not only shoulder their respective responsibilities, but to coordinate and complement their work with that of their neighbors. Generally speaking, no adequate solutions have been found. The way to efficient and effective metropolitan governmental services has not appeared. That is why a study of this situation at Detroit is so illustrative and so provocative.

Such frustrating situations as this will sometimes confront you men when you are in practical Park Administration. What do you do? You cannot ignore problems like this without shirking some of your responsibilities as an educated man, as a

responsible park administrator, as a civic leader. Your intelligent analysis and your thoughts must be applied to every
problem in your own and in related fields, if you are to render
the kind of service that your education demands. Remember
that you are not the only one who has made an investment in
your education. The State has supplied a good share of that
expense and you have an obligation to extend yourself in solving public problems. You must talk, write, and patiently act.
You will be joined by others. In time, solutions to the most
difficult problems will emerge. You must do your part; you
can't sit idly by.

Fees and Charges. On the matter of entrance fees, I believe we must continue to rely upon the public welfare provisions of our Constitution to justify the existence of parks in
all levels of government. I think we must recognize they are
there for the recreation of the people, because it is in the
public interest to do so. Consequently, the Government ought
to provide in all its levels at least a minimal service and to
provide such additional services as the public is willing to pay
for and which cannot be provided for individually, effectively,
and decently by private enterprise. I see no excuse for entrance fees on the local level and I deplore the practice, however justified, of exacting entrance fees for nonresidents.
Alleviation of the latter practice I think ought to be sought in a
more sensible metropolitan government.

The charges for special services which cost more per unit
than the minimum amounts provided by the Government, is
properly chargeable to the user. This applies to all levels of
government.

The application of an entrance fee for state park or for
county parks unless that fee is for the entrance to a section of
the park wholly developed for various active recreation uses,
is unjustifiable. It is only an expediency and too often reflects
weakness on the part of the administration in convincing the
public and their representatives of the worth of state parks.

On the national level, if in the future it becomes necessary to limit attendance (I believe other solutions will make
this unnecessary), a high entrance fee may be justified. I see
no necessity for high entrance fees for revenue purposes. I
see some sense to an entrance gate, for passing out guidance
literature, the giving of information by the attendant, and other
more or less personal services. A small fee could be imposed to pay for such service. I see no objection to paying a
fee to view certain projects of a historical nature, historical

sites, monuments and archaeology curiosities, where the attendant cost is high and where personal service is much greater than that required in a park of general scenery.

As to concessions, I lean slightly toward Government operation; government ownership of all structure and equipment, direct government control of all services. I concede this is harder on the Administrator, that frequently it requires special Civil Service rules and regulations, very careful audit control, and has a number of other administration headaches. The main advantages are that there is no possibility of private vested rights, either actual or implied by private operator, there is positive control of service, and hence a flexibility of operations to meet changing conditions hourly, daily, or seasonally, and there is no possibility of unethical relationships between the administrator and private operators. I also concede that local tradition, the inflexibility of handicapping rules and regulations in a specific instance would cause me to favor private concession in some instances.

I think the lack of capital outlay is an inadequate excuse for private operation. I think that private investment on public property is a dangerous thing. Private operations on publicly owned property, however, can be condoned.

The granting of concessions on the basis of best income even when bids are made upon specifications which apparently cover all points, I think only accidentally results in good service, but I also know that often that is the only way that a legislative body will act. The controlled monopoly idea, I think is much better, but monopoly is a nasty word and hard to sell.

The Toronto Area. It is of interest to all of us that the organization of the Metropolitan Toronto is not considered a true amalgamation of all metropolitan governmental services and hence is not the final step in metropolitan organization. It is but a step forward and its future is still doubtful. In brief, that organization of Metropolitan Toronto involves the assumption by the metropolitan government of all governmental functions which are of a metropolitan nature, leaving to the individual cities and townships within the metropolitan area those functions of government which are of local significance. Obviously, there are some functions which are common to both, and this has led to what has been named the "aspect" form of administration; that is, decisions are reached between the metropolitan government and the local governments as to which "aspect" of a certain function are to be the responsibility of each.

In so far as parks are concerned, it was decided that Metropolitan Toronto will establish and operate those parks which are above the local neighborhood and community playfield type and that local governments will provide for the neighborhood facilities. Some compromise was made in the case of the city of Toronto because of tradition and prestige.

Other facets of the metropolitan government including what might be termed watershed or conservancy districts, in a small way involve the province of Ontario. The whole complicated but neatly interwoven and interlocked system of financial supplementation of one branch of government by the other in supporting parks was described. In spite of the slightly lower goals for park acreage in the Canadian city as compared to the standard goal of the United States, one gets the impression that this interlocking device, in spite of its inadequacies and complications, fits together more neatly than does any similar situation in the various metropolises of the United States.

The Toronto situation, differing as it does from the run of the mill experiences of the United States cities, is something to watch in the future and to appraise its achievements.

"Interpretation," February 26, 1962. Mr. X developed the topic of Interpretation from a broader meaning than is usually attributed to the expression when it is called "Park Interpretation." Park Interpretation is often associated with the Park Ranger Service of the National Park Service, or the naturalist on conducted tours through the woods, or the nature museums etc. Mr. X applied interpretation to all of park service: reports of accomplishments, description of services offered, sales pamphlets and brochures, silent markers and canned broadcast guides, museums and finally the personal service of the naturalist historian or other specialist.

This great array of assets at hand suggested to some that it should be actively used for a purpose – and immediately we found deep water.

Good man that he is, Mr. X seemed to be bent on promoting a few "causes" near the end of his presentation using interpretation to do the promoting. When questioned on this, someone remarked, "Why not use parks to promote the public welfare? If we don't do so, why do we interpret at all?" We tried to relate parks to the general welfare, but somehow we seemed to support rather than to discredit Mr. X's thesis. I am afraid the question kind of sneaked up on me, and I was neither prepared nor was it the place for a rather lengthy discussion on this subject matter. Consequently, I am giving you my thoughts on the subject now, with the feeling that you probably won't be convinced because this subject is in an area of philosophy which is difficult to rationalize. In this case, the best way to learn is to get burnt.

It has always been my thesis that a park and recreation service is an amoral and irreligious function. A public recreation service is an end in itself. When we attempt to use that service as a force for good, or to promote a cause, or to be an active accessory in the promotion we are heading for trouble. Off hand this may not square with the idea of recreation service promoting the general welfare but let us discuss that after examining a few examples.

Example (1) Summer evenings in our town can be pretty warm during Sunday evening church services. The community Methodist Church asks the Park Board for permission to hold its Sunday evening services under the trees in a neighborhood park. It's a good cause so why shouldn't the request be granted.

One branch of the Baptist Church in our town believes in revival meetings. They have a large Bible Institute and dormitories across the street from a rather large cosmopolitan type park just on the edge of the central business section and in the apartment house district. The park is heavily attended at all times by apartment house dwellers looking for some open space in which to just walk, or sit, or watch the ducks on the pond, the tennis players, soft-ball players, and the shuffleboard players. Once or twice a week in the summer, the Baptists would like to have a revival meeting or, as they call it, a community hymn sing. Some may consider this a good cause but to those who are engaged in recreation pursuits, such a thing is a distinct nuisance.

The Salvation Army would like to do something like the Baptists do on Sunday afternoon, but during the Thanksgiving Day and Christmas periods. They would like to set up their charity kettles in a place like this. Of course, the Volunteers of America would like to do the same thing.

And then there is the itinerant Preacher, − the racketeer who strolls through the country with his brand of the Holy Gospel as a sword against the powers of evil. His primary purpose is a fast buck from gullible people. If he is denied the privilege of taking up a collection from the public, at least he can promote his temporarily rented Gospel Temple.

Professor John Ise in his "Our National Park Policy" shows that this religious inclination extends to even the National Parks. Let me quote: "there have always been a few devout souls who wanted to combine the glory of the park with religious observance of some sort who have believed that the national parks were just the places for religious devotion; but most park men have not warmed to the idea.   For years there had been agitation for the building of a 'Shrine of the Ages' near the south rim of Grand Canyon 180 feet or 250 feet from it according to the man doing the surveying. " This project actually received some official support. Continuing, Ise says, "This would seem to be a rather cheap and unseemly business. The cost has been vaguely reported at a million dollars.   It is reported that other religions are considering the erection of similar religious shrines in other parks. "

Note how a simple request for a Sunday evening service in a park can expand to a point that it threatens the free unencumbered recreation use of facilities and programs too.

Example (2) Again, in our town there is an athletic stadium seating about 20,000 people.   Appropriation for erection was obtained on the ground that it could be operated out of funds obtained for its rental.   One of the important regularly scheduled affairs included the ten day civic celebration held each summer, several of its events taking place at this location.   The Catholic Welfare Organization sponsored a professional football game but expected to pay the normal fee.

Then there appeared a private recreation organization which was attempting to maintain a private community center building, and wanted to hold some affair which would produce revenue to help maintain their enterprise.   Inasmuch as they were in public recreation service, they felt that not only should they receive preferential rates for the rental but should actually get it free.   They were doing the same thing that the Park Board was doing "so why shouldn't the Park Board assist them ?"

Other organizations such as the Red Cross, The American Legion, The Veterans of Foreign Wars, local colleges, the high schools, all were in the wings each with their special plea.   If there was a break in the "no preferential" treatment, everyone of these other good causes would have to be treated likewise.   Each and every one could make a very strong case about their efforts to promote the public good.   All of them would be worse off without this central facility, but that situation is lost sight of, when each organization pleads its own case.

Example (3) Jewish Synagogues have their supporting organizations much like the churches have their Ladies Aid

Societies.   The Jewish people like to hold picnics on Sundays and several of the ladies will bring extra cakes and other food stuffs which at the end of the picnic are sold. Sometimes "Mr. Abrams" has brought something from his secondhand store and it can be either raffled or auctioned off. In fact, some merchant member may bring a number of articles, – appliances, furniture and what not, – which it is nice to dispose of in a like manner which will bring a little money into the Synagogue. It's a good cause. Is there anything wrong with it?

Would you like a bingo party on Wednesday night by the Catholic organization, the raffling off of an automobile by the Lions Club to promote some of their charities; or by the Northside Business Men to improve the economic stability of their community?

Example (4) A summer tent camp for crippled children or one for tubercular patients is bound to touch a sympathetic chord and they have been known to have been granted space in some of our native type parks. In fact, there may even be some resident camps for underprivileged children. Did you ever try to separate underprivileged from other children? If you permit tent camping, how about a training camp for the Golden Gloves boxers? Or a summer camp for Boy Scouts? In fact, why not permit the erection of headquarters buildings for a number of these character building agencies. Such things have been done, only to find out in time that either real or assumed vested rights of a part of a public park have been usurped by special segments of the public. The problem then, is to call halt and reverse the procedure which too often approaches the impossible.

Separating what is good from what is not good, is a big task in itself. Using a park and recreation department to help out in good causes or to act against bad causes, requires a Solomon's judgment. Even the matter of promotion of cultural things has to be carefully scrutinized. Mr. X suggested, for instance, that within some park it might be possible to set up some foreign family living in the fashion of their native land, in order to further international good will as well as to get us familiar with foreign customs. If any of you have had the experience of an Indian Village in your parks, which is carrying out the same theme, you'll never want another. One cannot discriminate in which cultures we care to give assistance. This does not mean that "exhibits" as parts of an overall exhibition (e. g. a zoo) are necessarily prohibited.

All of this illustrates that a public recreation service must be considered good in itself – something which will promote the public welfare sufficiently to justify its existence under the Constitution of the United States. How do we rationalize that in the face of the above examples?

A public park and recreation service promotes the public welfare by promoting the well-being of its citizens through the process of recreation. Recreation, as we know, can be something good or something bad. Public governmental recreation service has sought to restrict its promotion to those recreation pursuits which are wholesome, conventional, and which are generally acceptable to the mass of the people. This still leaves a great area of selection and we do have some additional restraints through our laws. Beyond those restraints, (legal and public acceptance) the public recreation service must remain indifferent to moral and religious issues. It is amoral and irreligious. A lot of park administrators and a lot of park departments have discovered this only after they have had their fingers burnt – sometimes quite badly.

INDEX

ACKNOWLEDGEMENTS
Michigan State University, iii
Texas Technological College, iii
Prof. Louis F. Twardzik, iii
Prof. Leslie M. Reid, iii
Dr. Raleigh Barlowe, iii
Prof. Elo J. Urbanovsky, iii
Minneapolis Park Commission, iv
Howard J. Moore, iv

ACQUISITIONS
Chapter 10 on Policies of, 163
Site Selection Notes, 163
Processes of, 179
Price elements involved, 312

ADMINISTRATOR, MANAGER,
SUPERINTENDENT, DIRECTOR or
CHIEF EXECUTIVE
Chief Executive, 120
Relationship with Legislative
Body, 305, 152
Administrator and Executive Staff,
156, 194

APPENDIX
Bibliography, 230, Olmsted's Principles -
Waugh, 232, On the Validity of Standards-
Doell, 233, Future of Minneapolis Park-
ways, 237, Quotations from Charles Eliot,
248, Quotations from Lewis Mumford, 251,
Urban Planning of Highways - Doell, 253,
Philosophy of Charles Paul Keyser - Keyser,
257, Supplement to Chapter 7 - Personnel
Organization, Doell, 262, Supplement to
Chapter 8 - Budgets - Doell, 267, Supple-
ment to Chapter 9 - Policies - In General
and on Relationships - Doell, 271, Supple-
ment to Chapter 10 - Acquisition and
Development Policies - Doell, 275, Supple-
ment to Chapter 11 - Policies of Operation -
Doell, 278, Supplement to Chapter 12 -
Educational Requirements - Doell, 282,
Land Policy Statement of Cook County -
Cook County Forest Preserve District, 284,
Hennepin County Park Reserve District,
Policy Statement, 294, Park Board, The
Director and Relationships, 305, Rules of
the Board - A Suggestion, 307, Price
Elements in Land Acquisition - Doell, 312,
Rules for Community Celebrations -
Minneapolis Board of Park Commissioners,
317, Miscellaneous Subjects - Doell, 320

ARMY ENGINEERS
Land under control of, 15

BARLOWE, DR. RALEIGH
Acknowledgement, iii

BIBLIOGRAPHY, 230

BOARDS, COMMISSIONS, LEGISLATIVE
AUTHORITIES
Relationship with chief executive,
305, 152
Matters properly before it, 152
Effect of Board action on policies, 193
Purpose of Board Record (Minutes), 193
Rules for conduct of affairs, 307

BOSTON COMMON
Established 1634, 10

BOSTON METROPOLITAN PARK
DISTRICT
A typical system, 47
Comments by Charles Eliot, 248

BRYANT, WILLIAM CULLEN
Early advocate of Central Park, 10

BUDGETS
Preliminary to budgeting, 86
Chapter 8 on, 137
Sample budget, 144-147
Policies on, 195
Supplement to Chapter 8, 267

BUREAU OF OUTDOOR RECREATION
Federal Aid by, 8
ORRRC report, 15
Operations of, 73, 72
Land Prices, 314

CENTRAL PARK, NEW YORK
Its establishment, etc., 11
Its threatened loss of original identity,
14
Some features in its design, 28
Purpose of Olmsted, 53

CIRCUSES and CARNIVALS
Discussion, 213

CITIES and SUBURBS
  The park and recreation systems of, 17
  The urban situation, 82
  Minneapolis as a case in point, 84
  Detroit and environs, 321
  Toronto area, 323

CIVILIAN CONSERVATION CORPS
  Its work in re parks and recreation, 69

CLASSIFICATION and STANDARDS
  General Acreage Standards, 16
  Of City Systems, 18
  Reasons for, 18, 19, 36
  Complications in applications to City
    Systems, 21
  Simple application to city parks, 24
  The Dallas system of, 25, 27
  Standards applied to city; theoretical, 30
  Standards applied to city; actual, 32
  Standards applied to suburbs, 37
  Standards applied to state and Federal
    holdings, 76-78
  Classification and Zoning, 80
  Areas Required, 82
  Validity of Standards, 232
  Land Policy, Hennepin County, Minn.,
    296
  Classification of Parks, Hennepin County,
    297

CLEVELAND, H.W.S.
  Minneapolis, Parkways, 242, 240

CLEVELAND METRO. SYSTEM
  Discussion of, 49

COMMUNITY CHEST AGENCIES
  Policy in re, 160

COMMUNITY CELEBRATIONS
  Rules governing, 317

CONCESSIONS
  Who operates, 204
  Hennepin County policy on, 303
  Comments on, 323

CONFLICT OF INTEREST
  Policy in re, 183

CONSTITUTION of UNITED STATES
  The General Welfare provisions, 1

CONSTRUCTION - CONTRACTS
  Policy in re, 182

COOK COUNTY FOREST PRESERVE
  DISTRICT
  Discussion of, 50

CORPS OF ENGINEERS
  Its Functions and Operations, 71

DALLAS, TEXAS
  System of Classification and Standards,
    25, 27

DEDICATION
  To Harold S. Wagner, Frontispiece

DEVELOPMENT of LAND for PARKS
  Chapter 10 - Policies of Development,
    163
  Plans and Basic Data, 180
  Construction, 182
  Letting of Contracts, 183

DOWNING, A.J.
  Early advocate of Central Park, 10
  Associated with Olmsted, Sr., 11

EAST BAY REGIONAL PARK DISTRICT
  Referred to, 53

EDUCATION
  A stray thought, 85
  Requirements - Chapter 12, 221
  Supplement to Chapter 12, 282

ELIOT, CHARLES
  Boston Metro. system, 47
  Parkways, 240, 248

ESSEX COUNTY PARK SYSTEM
  Discussion of, 47

ENGINEER - ENGINEERING
  In re personnel organization, 133, 114

FEES and CHARGES
  Policies on, 198
  Who operates revenue producing
    businesses, 204
  Comments on, 322

FINANCES, FINANCING - See also
  "FEES and CHARGES" and "BUDGETS"
  Financing capital outlays, 167
  Financing by various devices, 173
  Foundation for County Parks, 304

FISH and WILDLIFE SERVICE
    With reference to a Recreation Movement,
        13
    Land acreage under control of, 15
    Function and operation of, 72

FORESTS
    Division of Forestry - Fed. Agr. Dept. , 13
    Acreage under control of, 15
    Forest Service, 70

GIFTS
    Policy in re, 184

GOSDIN, PROF. MARK
    Acknowledgement to, iii

HARDING, PRESIDENT
    Comments on Welfare Clause
        of the Constitution, 1

HOUSING and URBAN DEVELOPMENT,
    FEDERAL DEPARTMENT OF
    Federal Aid through HUD, 8
    Operations of, 74, 72
    Price elements in land acquisitions, 314

HURON-CLINTON METROPOLITAN SYSTEM
    Discussion, 52

IRVING, WASHINGTON
    Early advocate of Central Park, 10

ILLINOIS PARK SYSTEMS
    Discussion of, 48

ISE, JOHN
    Our National Park Policy, 64

KEYSER, CHARLES PAUL
    Philosophy of, 257
    Reference in re politics, 262

LAKE MEAD
    As an early National Recreation Area, 13

LANE, FRANKLIN K.
    As Secretary of the Interior, 64

LARGE CITY PARKS
    Purpose according to Olmsted, 53
    Planning for, 101, 93

LEISURE
    Recreation and Leisure, 4

LOS ANGELES COUNTY SYSTEM
    Discussion of, 52

MACKINAC ISLAND STATE PARK
    Early state park, 13

MAINTENANCE
    In re personnel organization, 115, 126

MANAGEMENT
    As an art, 2

MARIPOSA STATE PARK -
    LATER PART OF YOSEMITE
    Early part of State Park movement, 13

MARYLAND NATIONAL CAPITAL PARK
    and PLANNING COMMISSION
    Discussion of, 52

MATHER, STEPHEN
    As First Director National Park
        Service, 64

METROPOLITAN and COUNTY PARKS
    Planning for, 101, 94
    Boston Metro. System, 47
    Cleveland Metro. System, 49
    Cook County, 50
    East Bay, 53
    Essex County, 47
    Huron-Clinton, 52
    Los Angeles County, 52
    Maryland Capital Park and Planning
        Com., 52
    Milwaukee County, 51
    Union County, 48
    Westchester County, 49

MILWAUKEE COUNTY SYSTEM
    Discussion of, 51

MOORE, HOWARD J.
    Acknowledgement, iv

MUMFORD, LOUIS
    On parkways, 246, 251

NATIONAL PARK SERVICE
    Experiments with Bureau of Reclama-
        tion in re National Recreation
        areas, 13
    Land under control of, 15
    In re planning National Parks, 97
    On Sleeping Bear, Mich. proposal, 320

NATIONAL RECREATION ASSOCIATION
    Year Book of 1961 listing recreation
        departments, 13
    Standards of City Park facilities, 39

NATIONWIDE PLAN
    Nationwide Plan, 79

NEIGHBORHOOD PARKS and
    COMMUNITY PLAYFIELDS
    Preparing plans for, 100, 101, 93

OHIO PARK SYSTEMS
    Cleveland and Akron, 49

OLMSTED, FREDERICK LAW, SR.
    Design of Central Park, 11
    Olmsted type parks, 14
    Set the pattern for large city parks, 28
    Purpose of large city parks or regional
        parks, 53
    Principles according to Waugh, 232
    Comments at Minneapolis, 240

PARKS
    What is a Park, 7
    A System of Parks and Recreation, 8
    Correlation of Park Systems, 8
    Brief History, 9
    City park systems oldest of American
        public recreation services, 13
    Recreation Resources of, 17
    Classification and Standards - City
        Parks, 19 etc.,

PARKS, COUNTY
    Reference to Milwaukee County System, 14
    Reference to Los Angeles County System,
        14
    Preliminary matters, 46
    Some typical systems, 47
    Boston Metropolitan System, 47
    Essex County, 48
    Union County, 48
    Cleveland Metropolitan, 49
    Westchester County, N.Y., 49
    Cook County Forest Preserve District, 50
    Milwaukee County, 51
    Maryland National Park and Planning
        Commissioners, 52
    Detroit, Wayne County and the Huron-
        Clinton Metropolitan System, 52
    Comments on Typical Systems, 53
    Area Required, 54
    Classification and Use Zoning, 55

PARKS, NATIONAL
    Began with Yellowstone Park, 13
    Recreation Areas, 13, 14
    Development and Purpose, 61
    Before 1916, 62
    National Park Service, 63

PARKS, STATE
    Early State Park Movement, 13
    Development and Purpose, 61

PARK and RECREATION ADMINISTRA-
    TION
    Nature of Park and Recreation
        Administration, 1
    Purpose of a Park and Recreation
        Service, 3
    Correlation of Park and Recreation
        Systems, 8

PARK and RECREATION FACILITIES
    A system of Park and Recreation
        facilities, 8
    Correlation of Park and Recreation
        Systems, 8
    Standards and Classification for cities,
        General Acreage Standards, 16
    Acreage and other standards for
        cities, 18, etc.
    Acreage and other standards for
        counties, 54, 55

PARKS, SPECIAL USE
    Parkways and Boulevards, 56

PARKWAYS
    Their function, 29
    Definitions and historical development,
        56
    Future of Minneapolis Parkways, 237

PERMITS and LEASES
    Policy on, 207
    Circuses and Carnivals, 213
    Carnivals, 218

PERSONNEL
    Preliminary to personnel organization,
        86
    Chapter 7 on, 106-107
    Essential Functions, 108
    Assignment of Functions, 109
    Operation of Staff and Personnel, 124
        120-123
    Chief Executive, 120
    The Board or Superior Authority, 122

PERSONNEL, continued
   Departmental Operations, 126
   Operations - Maintenance, 126
   Operations - Recreation, 130
   Operations - Engineering, 133
   Operations - Public Relations, 134
   Chief Executive, 120
   Chief Executive and Legislative Body, 152
   Administrator and Executive Staff, 194, 156
   Supplement to Chapter 7 on personnel, 262

PLANS and PLANNING
   Park Systems and the City Plan, 18
   Preliminary to planning, budgeting, and
      organization, 86
   Making the Plan, 87, 90, 99, 102, 103
   Basic Resource Material, 88
   Park Plans and Departmental Policy, 90
   Investigative Reports, 92
   Investigative Reports Summary, 98
   Operation after construction, 104
   Summaries, 105
   Relationship with Planning Commissions,
      158
   Parks and Highways, 253

PLAYLOTS
   In the Dallas classification, 25

POLICE
   In re personnel organization, 118

POLICIES
   Classification and standards in re policies,
      20, Policies in General - Chapter 9, 148,
      Policies in Relationships, 151, Policies in
      Relationships - Chief Executive, 152,
      Policies in Relationships - Chief Executive
      and staff, 156, Policies in Relationships -
      Planning Commissions, 158, Policies in
      Relationships - Schools, 158, Policies in
      Relationships - Community Chests, 160,
      Policies in Relationships - Other Govern-
      mental Agencies, 161, 160, Policies in
      Relationships - State and Federal Agencies,
      161, Policies in Relationships - Press and
      Public, 162, Policies in Acquisition and
      Development - Chapter 10, 163, On Site
      Selection, 163, On financing capital out-
      lays, 167, Financing by various devices,
      173, In re processes of acquisition, 179,
      In re land records, 180, In re land develop-
      ment, 180, Plans for Development - Basic
      Data, 180, Construction, 182, Letting of
      contracts, 183, Operation - Chapter 11,
      Policies on, 191, Effect of Board action on,
      192, Administrator and Executive Staff, 194,

POLICIES, continued
   Wages and Salaries, 194, Operating
      Budget, 195, Plans for New Projects,
      195, Matters not otherwise covered,
      195, Common problems on, 197,
      Neighborliness and cooperation, 197,
      Attendance at Professional Meetings,
      197, Fees and Charges, 198, Amount
      of Tax Support, 202, Who operates
      revenue producing businesses?, 204,
      Permits and leases, 207, Circuses and
      Carnivals, 213, Carnivals, 218,
      Supplement to Chapter 9, 271, Supple-
      ment to Chapter 10, 275, Supplement
      to Chapter 11, 278, Cook County Land
      Policy, 284, Policy Statement -
      Hennepin County, Minn., 294, On
      Interpretation and Use of Park Property,
      324

PREFACE
   To Second Edition, i
   To First Edition, iii

PRESS and PUBLIC
   Policy in re, 162

PROFESSIONAL MEETINGS
   Policy in re, 197

PUBLIC RELATIONS
   In re personnel organization, 134

RECLAMATION SERVICE
   Experiment with National Park Service
      in re National Recreation Areas, 13

RECREATION - see also PARK and
   RECREATION ADMINISTRATION
   What is recreation, 3
   Limitation on meaning of, 4
   Recreation and Leisure, 4
   Word "Recreation" in Today's
      Parlance, 5
   The "Tools" of, 6
   Early history of Recreation movement,
      12
   Transition factors of Recreation Service
      Local to Federal, 59
   In re personnel organization, 130, 116

RECREATION RESOURCES - See also
   RECREATION FACILITIES
   The Country's Physical Recreation
      Resources - Cities and Suburbs,
      17, 15
   Metropolitan and County, 46

RECREATION RESOURCES, continued
    State and Federal, 59
    Summary, 79
    General View of, 15
    Similarity of State and Federal, 59
    Transition Factors - Local to Federal, 59

REID, PROF. LESLIE M.
    Acknowledgement, iii

SCHOOLS
    Policy in re, 158

SECRETARY or COMPTROLLER
    In re personnel organization, 113

STANDARDS - See CLASSIFICATION and
    STANDARDS

STATE PARKS - See RECREATION
    RESOURCES - STATE and FEDERAL
    Planning for, 96

TABLE OF CONTENTS
    Table of Contents, v
    Appendix Table of Contents, 229

TEXAS TECHNOLOGICAL COLLEGE
    Acknowledgement, iii

TWARDZIK, PROF. LOUIS F.
    Acknowledgement, iii

UNION COUNTY SYSTEM
    Discussion of, 48

URBANOVSKY, PROF. ELO J.
    Acknowledgement, iii

VAUX, CALVERT
    With Olmsted, designer of Central
        Park, 11
    With Olmsted, set pattern for large
        city parks, 28

WAUGH, FRANK
    Olmsted's Principles, 232

WESTCHESTER COUNTY (N.Y.)
    PARK SYSTEM
    Discussion of, 49

ZONING (USE)
    Zoning and classifications, 80